IMAGES
of America

CANTON

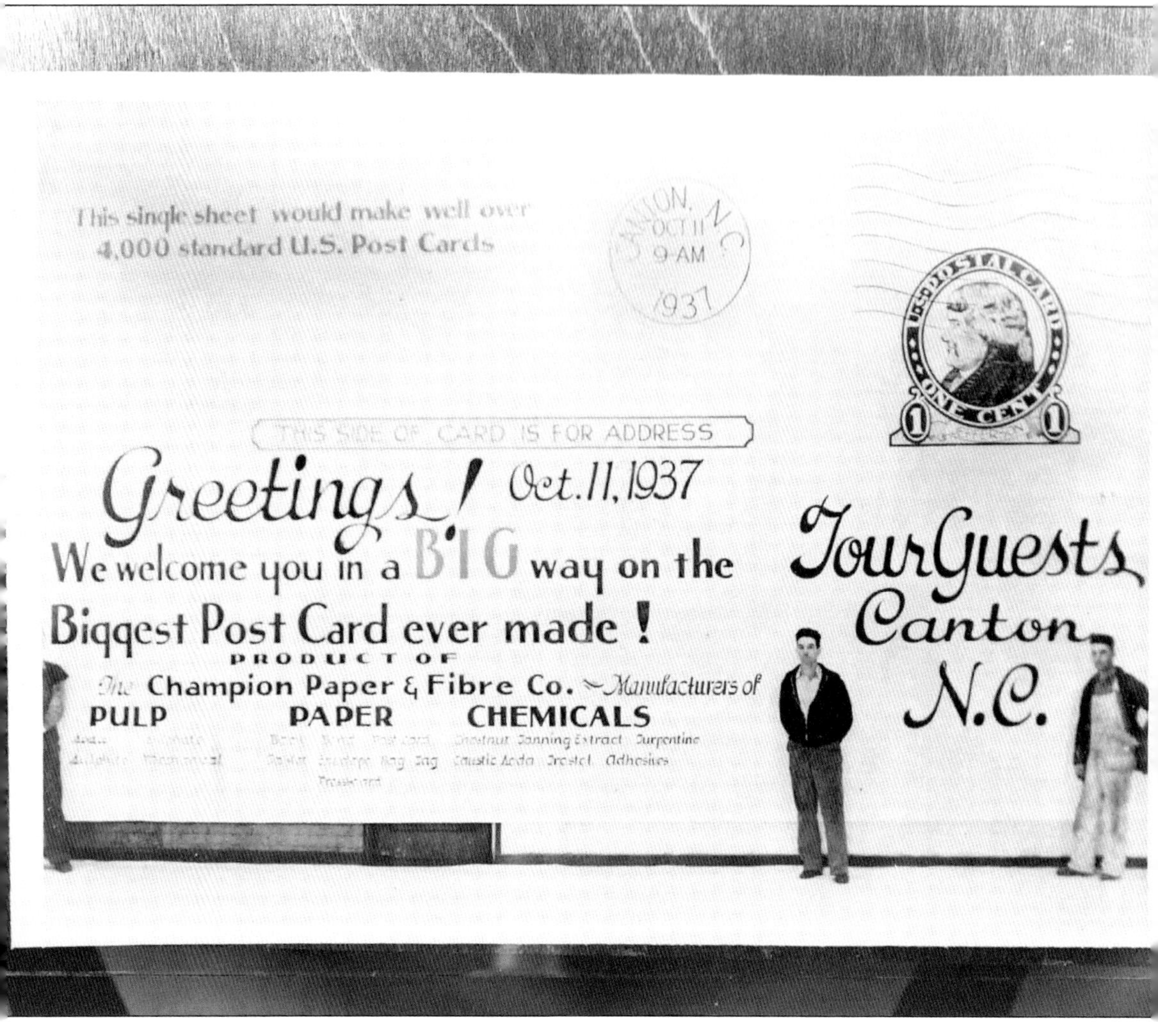

World's Largest Postcard. Champion was proud of its enormous output as one of the largest paper mills in the world. This gigantic postcard was displayed on the facade of the Canton Drug Store as a welcome sign for the visiting North Carolina Governor's Council. It was made with Champion paper and postmarked October 11, 1937. Said to be the largest postcard ever made, the single sheet was the size of more than 4,000 standard postcards. (Courtesy of the Canton Historical Museum.)

On the Cover: This 1954 aerial photograph of Canton shows the industrial heart of the town—the Champion paper mill—as well as the Pigeon River (lower center), the old North Canton School (just above the mill's tall smokestack), and the Newfound Mountains in the hazy distance. (Courtesy of the Canton Historical Museum.)

IMAGES
of America

CANTON

Michael Beadle

ARCADIA
PUBLISHING

ISBN 978-0-7385-9926-7

Published by Arcadia Publishing
Charleston, South Carolina

Printed in the United States of America

Library of Congress Control Number: 2012954718

For all general information, please contact Arcadia Publishing:
Telephone 843-853-2070
Fax 843-853-0044
E-mail sales@arcadiapublishing.com
For customer service and orders:
Toll-Free 1-888-313-2665

Visit us on the Internet at www.arcadiapublishing.com

*To Carole Corwin for her constant encouragement and inspiration,
and to Cindy Grady for instilling in me the value of hard work*

Contents

ACKNOWLEDGMENTS

This book would not have been possible without the technical support, diligence, and photographic expertise of Roland Osborne, a Canton resident, retired Champion employee, and excellent photographer. Canton owes a great debt to Roland's tireless work in scanning, editing, printing, and saving thousands of the town's historical photographs, many of which are reproduced in this book. Thanks also go to Wayne Carson, the director of the Canton Historical Museum, for being so gracious in sharing an abundance of photographs, time, and historical information for this project.

Many thanks go to many other gracious people, including Edie Burnette, Anita Churm, Bonnie Stamey, Cathy Walsh, Zelda Ponder, Ernie Stines, Rev. Mike Jordan, Rev. Terry Penland, Rev. Esta Jarrett, Tammy Ingle, Gerry Kelly, Marsha Miller, Ryan Jacobson, Jane Whitted, June Jolley, and so many others, for supplying the photographs, documents, and oral histories that went into this book.

Finally, thanks go to my Arcadia acquisitions editor, Katie McAlpin; my wife, Nicole; and family members and good friends like Peter Yurko for their support and encouragement as I worked on this project.

Introduction

Long before white settlers came to Haywood County and established the town of Canton, the area was home to Native Americans. According to the Cherokee myths, just south of Canton the great hunter Katani and his wife, the great corn maiden Selu, lived in the mountainous forest that is today known as Shining Rock Wilderness Area. The land was rich in wildlife, with fertile soil for farming.

Archaeologists who have studied the Garden Creek site just south of Canton near Bethel estimate that prehistoric human activity took place here as far back as 10,000 years ago. The 12-acre site features two villages that contain three mounds near the Pigeon River. Bone tools, turtle shell rattles, hammerstones, beaded necklaces, river cane mats, clay smoking pipes, shells, and copper have been found in the digs that have taken place there since 1800.

In September 1776, a Colonial army of about 2,500 men marched through the Canton area as part of a preemptive strike against Cherokee towns thought to be in league with the British during the Revolutionary War. Led by Gen. Griffith Rutherford, the army assembled at Old Fort and marched over the Blue Ridge Mountains along river valleys, crossing the Pigeon River and into western North Carolina's Cherokee towns where it burned settlements, trampled crops, and confiscated livestock. It would become known as the Rutherford Trace.

Some of the soldiers of that Colonial force later returned to the area to settle and build farms and families. Settlers of German, English, and Scots-Irish ancestry moved into western North Carolina by the late 1700s and early 1800s. Present-day Canton was once referred to as Pigeon River, named after the passenger pigeons that commonly populated the area and were later hunted into extinction. Travelers heading west had to cross the Pigeon River at narrow, shallow segments, so the area would also be known as Ford of Pigeon. By the mid-1800s, a stagecoach service provided limited transportation for passengers, mail, and materials into the area.

Railroad tracks would not be laid to Canton until 1881. With increased access into the mountains by train, more settlers came, and the village of a few houses grew rapidly to include streets with general stores and enterprising merchants. The town flirted with a few names such as Vinson (after a postal clerk) and Buford (after a railroad executive) before settling on the name Canton after an iron-truss bridge in town built with metal from Canton, Ohio. With a name formally approved in 1895, the town of Canton launched into an era of furious building over the next 20 years.

The single most important change to Canton came when Ohio industrialist Peter G. Thomson decided to build a pulp mill in the heart of town in 1906. The massive industry, which cost $2 million to build, would begin operating on January 1, 1908. Construction had been delayed by a shortage of labor, a national economic crisis, and heavy rains that swamped the site. However, within the next few decades, the Champion Fibre Company would become one of the largest, most productive paper mills of its kind in the world, churning out paper, pulp, chestnut extract, and caustics. More than a century later, it continues, though under a different name and under different ownership.

Canton's history is deeply rooted in its industrial foundation. In addition to supplying thousands of local jobs for several generations, the paper and pulp mill brought a diverse population of skilled workers to the area, a higher-paying wage than many other local mountain communities, and a rich blend of culture from the mill's international reputation. Reuben B. Robertson, an attorney from Cincinnati, Ohio, hired to oversee the construction of the Champion mill in Canton, became plant manager and eventually president of Champion. Under Robertson's paternalistic policies, mill workers enjoyed health benefits, access to a company store and a local credit union, a thriving YMCA, and steady employment even during the Great Depression and world wars. Known as "Mr. Champion," Robertson was the guiding force and familiar face of the company that dominated Canton's social, economic, and cultural fabric for more than half a century. The town's popular, long-running Labor Day festival is a testament to the civic pride and hard work that endures in Canton.

Nestled near the Great Smoky Mountains National Park, the Blue Ridge Parkway, Pisgah National Forest, and the Appalachian Trail, Canton is a short distance from some of the most scenic mountain attractions in the eastern United States. North of Canton, the Rough Creek Watershed, which once served as the town's reservoir for drinking water, has been saved by the town as an 870-acre preserve with pristine waterways and 10 miles of hiking trails.

Though its reputation is primarily born from the chemical process of converting trees to paper products and its lingering "smell of money," Canton is a place where people are the greatest resource. Over the last century, it has produced military generals, soldiers awarded the Medal of Honor, Hall of Fame softball pitchers, high school state championship teams, legendary musicians, lauded doctors and ministers, a North Carolina governor, and an award-winning novelist and poet laureate. This book celebrates Canton, its people, its churches and schools, its commerce and culture, and its stories that continue into the 21st century.

One

Early Canton

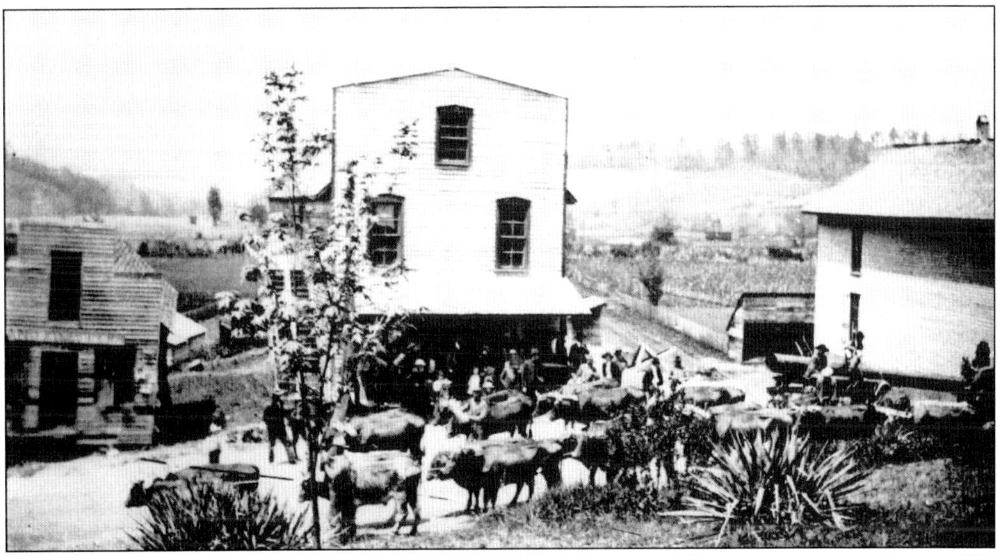

Main Street. One of the earliest images of the village that would become Canton, this c. 1895 photograph features a team of oxen that is probably headed to a logging camp south of town. The two-story general merchandise store in the center was owned and operated by Charles T. Wells, who moved to town in 1881 and founded what would become Wells Funeral Home. (Courtesy of the Canton Historical Museum.)

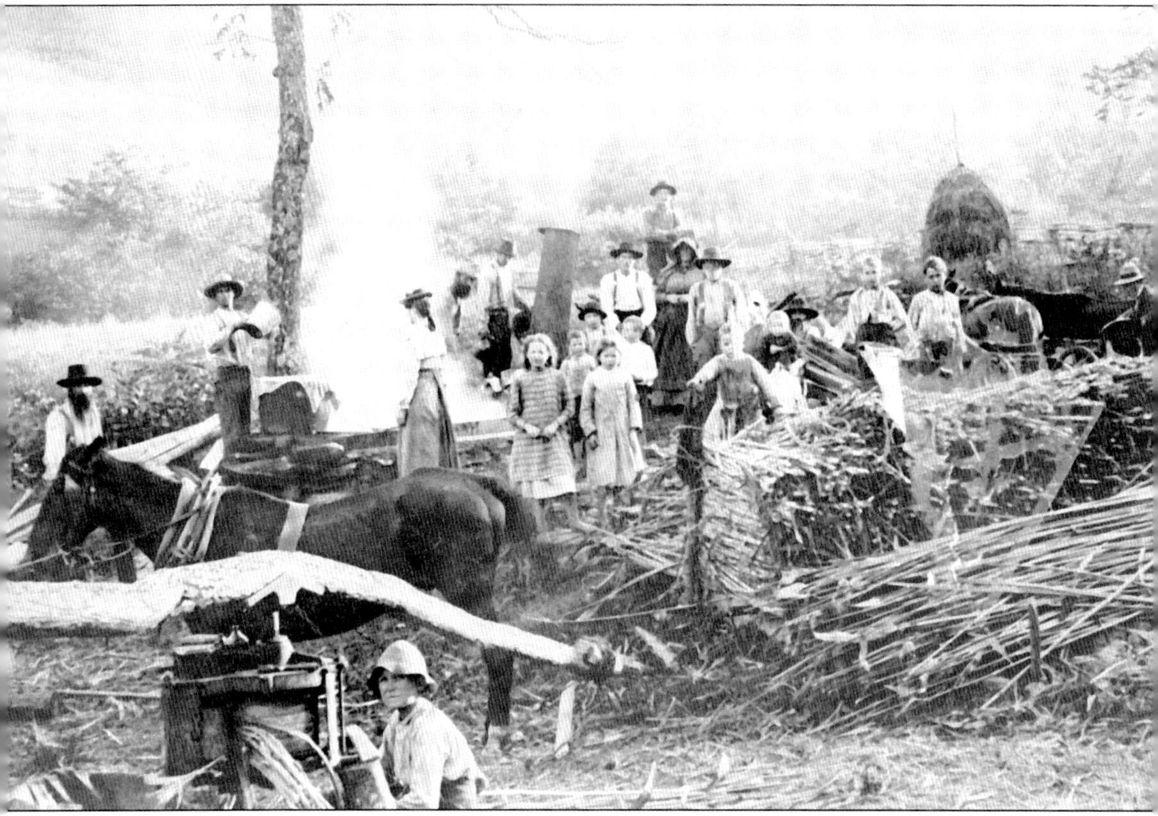

SWEET MEMORIES. Harvesting or processing crops often involved an entire family or multiple families from a community, who shared labor, exchanged tools, and traded produce. This shared responsibility of the workload helped foster strong friendships and kept families stocked with food and supplies for the harsh winters. In this 1890s photograph taken by S.A. McCanless of Asheville, at least 21 people are involved in making molasses in the Newfound community, east of Canton. Stalks of sorghum cane were cut and squeezed through a roller mill turned by a mule or a horse. Cane juice was collected in a pan and cooked over a fire until the juice boiled out, leaving syrupy molasses. Machines such as the sputtering, hit-and-miss engine were later used to speed up the arduous, smoke-filled operation. (Courtesy of the Canton Historical Museum.)

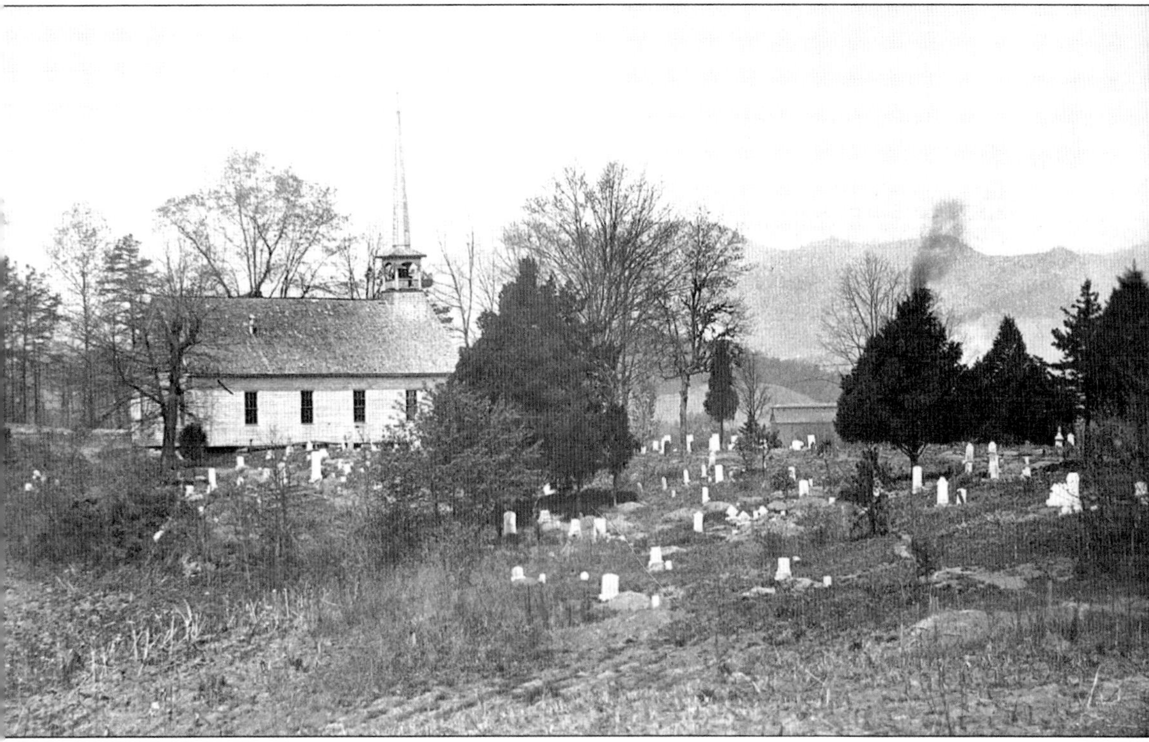

LOCUST OLD FIELDS. One of the oldest cemeteries in Haywood County, this site, along present-day Academy and Locust Streets, was once home to Locust Old Fields Baptist Church, founded in 1803. The church in this photograph was the third structure built on this site before the congregation moved down the street to become First Baptist Church of Canton in approximately 1915. The "old fields" name is often a reference given to areas where Native Americans had cleared and used land before white settlers came. After the church congregation moved, the Town of Canton took over the cemetery. An arched entrance sign, built of river rock and concrete, was erected around 1920. At the start of the Civil War, Confederate soldiers mustered up at Locust Old Fields and encamped here in the fall of 1863 and again in the winter of 1864–1865. Many veterans and notable Canton residents are buried in this cemetery, including Henry Abel (1759–1822), a Revolutionary War soldier born in Virginia. Abel and his wife, Margaret Chambers, were among the charter members of Locust Old Fields Baptist Church. (Courtesy of the Canton Historical Museum.)

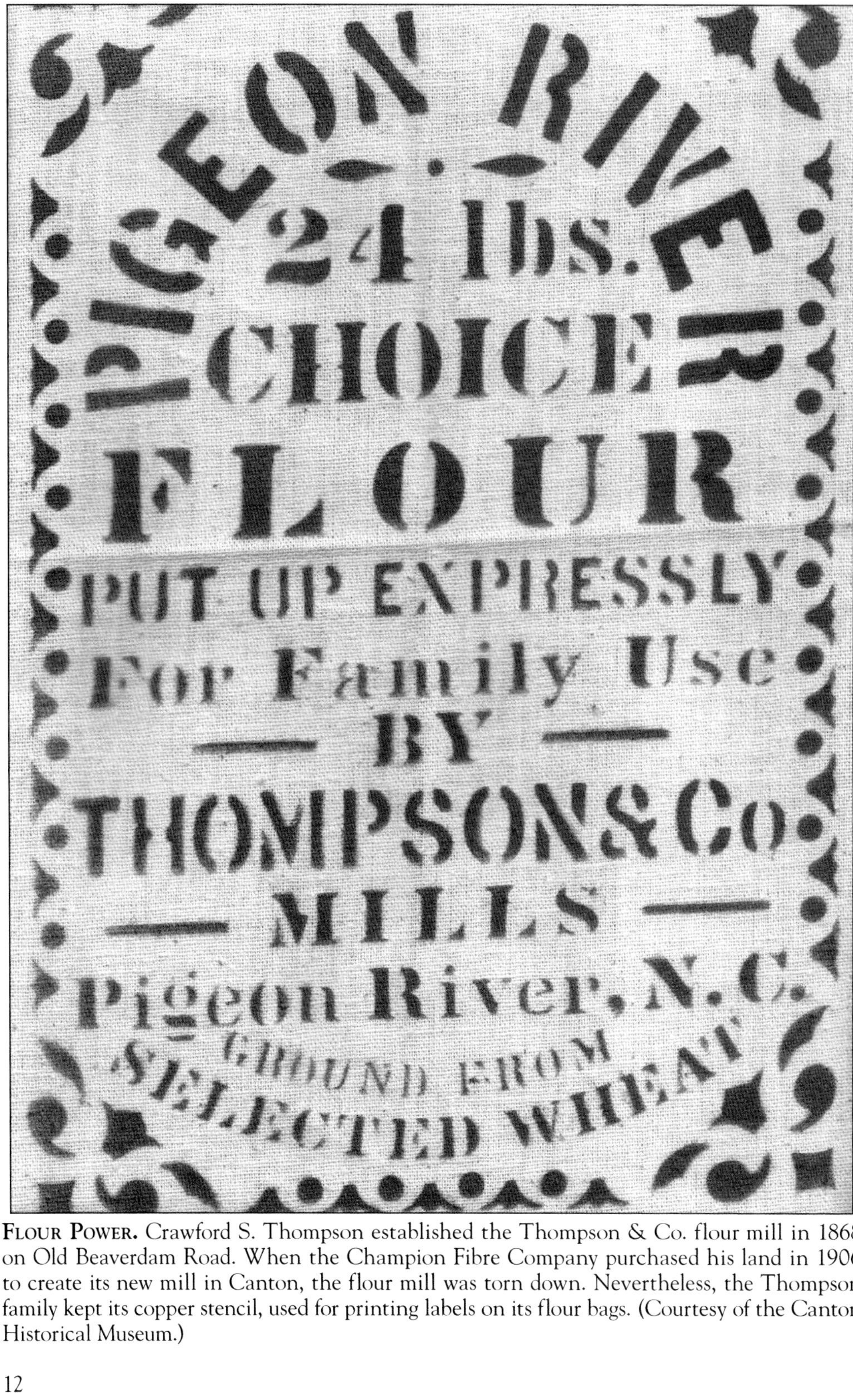

Flour Power. Crawford S. Thompson established the Thompson & Co. flour mill in 1868 on Old Beaverdam Road. When the Champion Fibre Company purchased his land in 1906 to create its new mill in Canton, the flour mill was torn down. Nevertheless, the Thompson family kept its copper stencil, used for printing labels on its flour bags. (Courtesy of the Canton Historical Museum.)

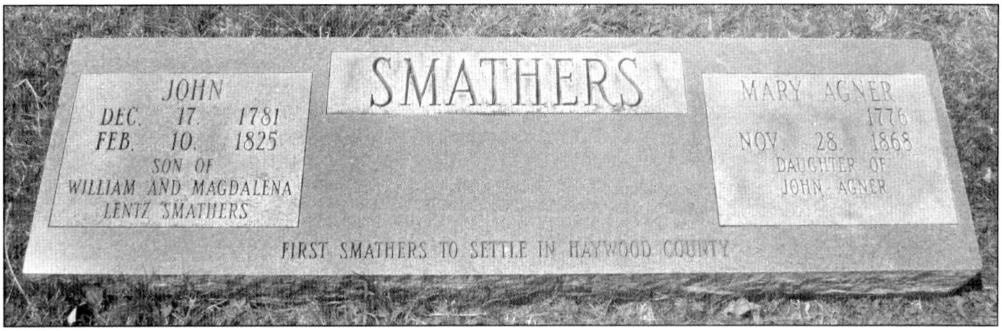

SMATHERS GRAVE. The Smathers were one of the earliest families to settle in the Canton area. Since they were of German descent, the community was known as Deutsch Cove, meaning "German Cove," but the name was later softened to Dutch Cove. As one family story goes, John Smathers and Henry Smathers were watching their children play one day and became troubled that they might grow up fighting each other living so close together. To prevent future animosity, they decided to flip a coin to see which family would stay and which would move away. John and his family remained in Dutch Cove, while Henry and his family moved west. John married Mary Agner and had five children. The couple lies buried in Locust Field Cemetery. (Courtesy of Nicole Wilhelm.)

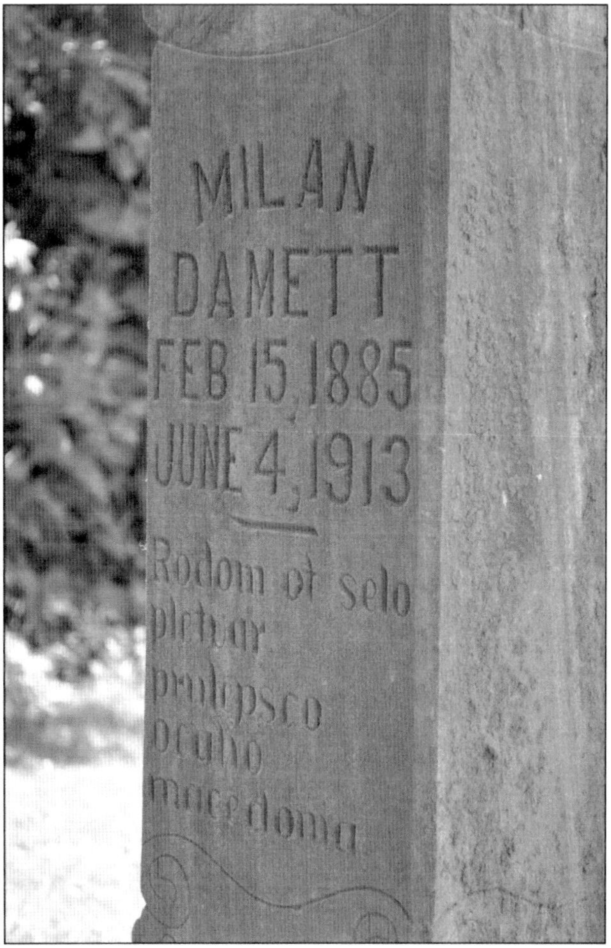

FOREIGN AID. During the construction of the Champion paper mill in Canton, contractor Frank Gilbreth hired approximately 100 Bulgarians, whom locals referred to as "Rooshians" because of their foreign language. This tombstone, located in Locust Field Cemetery, marks the grave of Milan Damett from Pletvar, Macedonia. He was most likely part of the workforce that built the mill. (Courtesy of Nicole Wilhelm.)

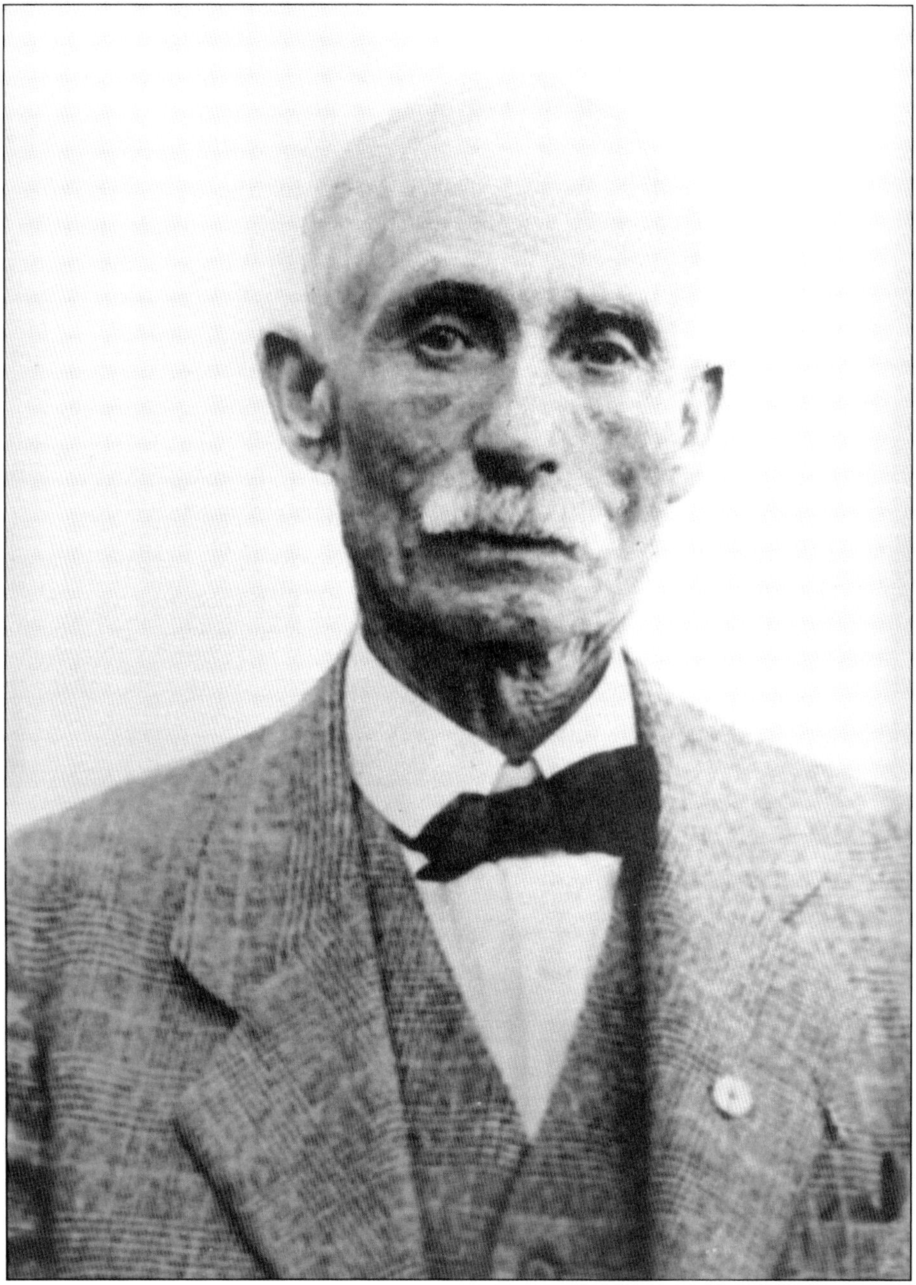

INVENTOR. Calvin Filmore Christopher (1859–1940) may not have received much notoriety during his lifetime, but his inventions live on as a testament to his ingenuity and insatiable curiosity. He is credited with about 100 patents, including an automatic switch for streetcar rails, a collapsible rim for automobile tires, and grocery store scales that could show the grocer the price of an item by the pound. Another invention of his was a cradle that continued to rock for 30 minutes after it was set in motion. A tall, slender, well-dressed man, Christopher was born in Pittsburgh. His father moved the family to the Bethel area, near Canton, after the Civil War. One of Christopher's most lucrative inventions was a ditch-digging machine that was sold to the French government and used in World War I. (Courtesy of the Canton Historical Museum.)

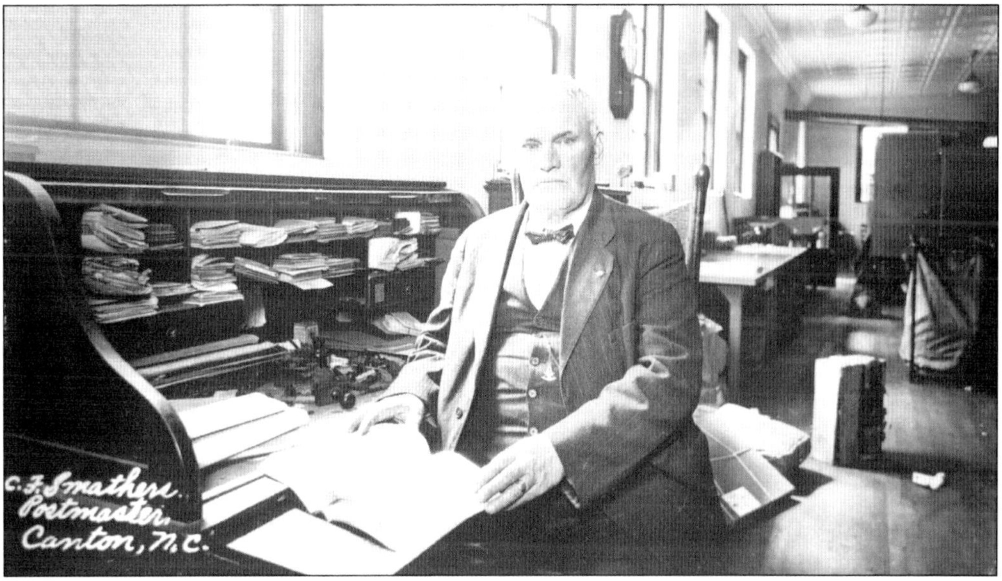

Post Office. The Pigeon River community established its first post office in 1837. By the early 1900s, Canton's post office was located at 26 Park Street in a three-story commercial building, where this photograph of Canton postmaster Charles F. Smathers was likely taken. In 1939, the Depression-era Works Progress Administration (WPA) spent $70,000 on Champion-donated land to erect a new, one-story post office building at 32 Park Street. The building is now used as offices for Evergreen Packaging. Canton's present-day post office was built in 1983. (Courtesy of the Canton Historical Museum.)

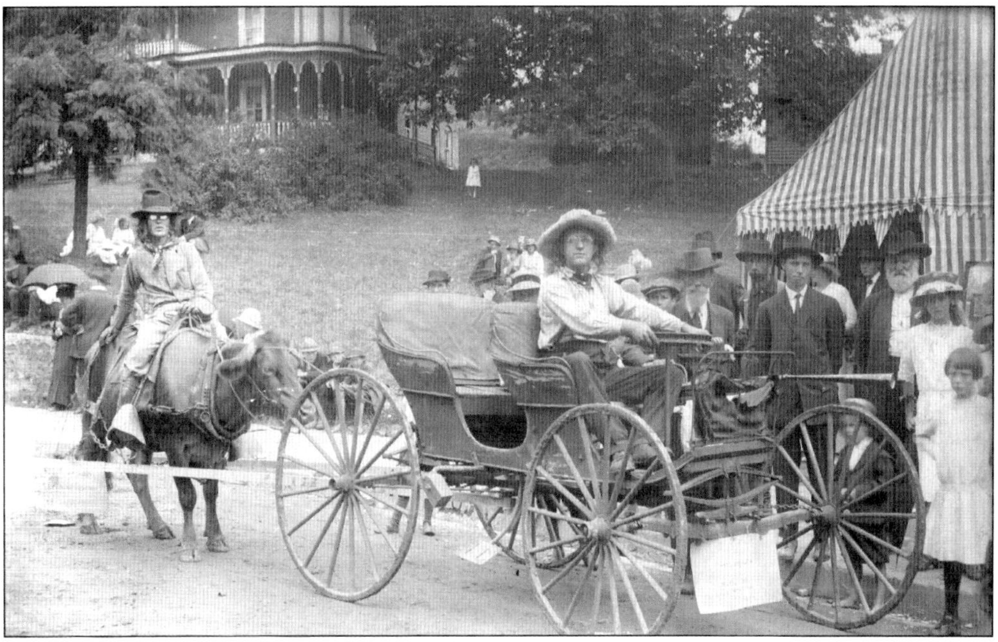

Hampton House. This procession through Canton took place around 1905 and ran past the Hampton House, in the upper left corner of this photograph. W.J. Hampton came to Canton in 1873 from the Leicester community in Buncombe County, opened a general store along Main Street, and became a leading businessman. (Courtesy of the Canton Historical Museum.)

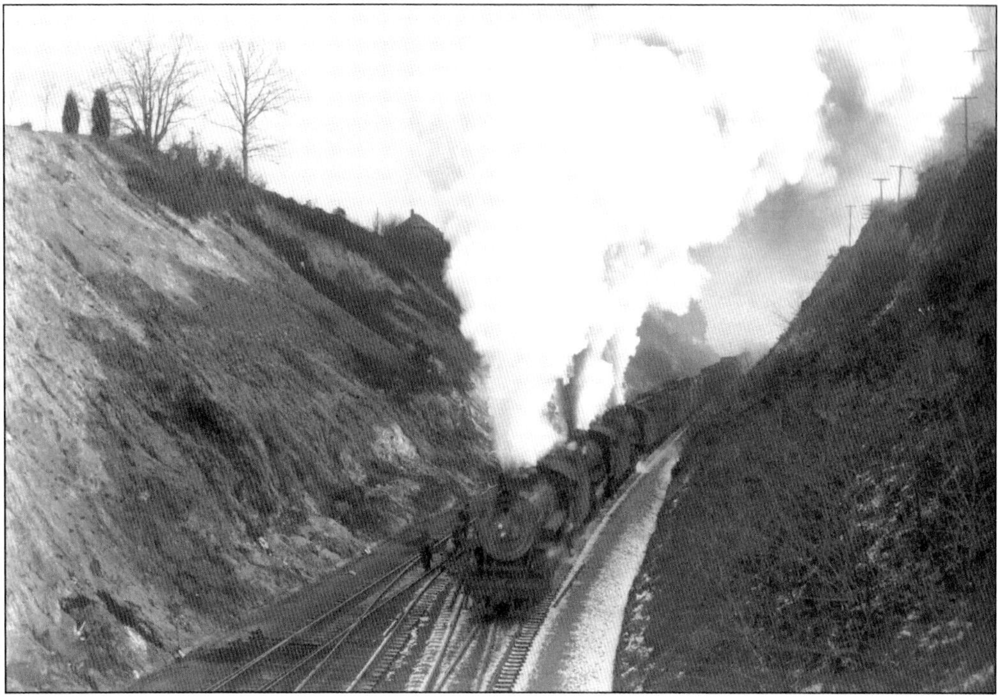

Picking Up Steam. Transportation into the rugged mountains of western North Carolina began with footpaths, horses, and wagons. By 1830, a stagecoach came once a week from Asheville to Waynesville. In 1881, the Western North Carolina Railroad reached the Pigeon River community, bringing passengers, lumber, and merchandise. In this photograph from the early 1880s, a triple-header steam engine chugs towards Canton. (Courtesy of the Pack Memorial Library, North Carolina Collection.)

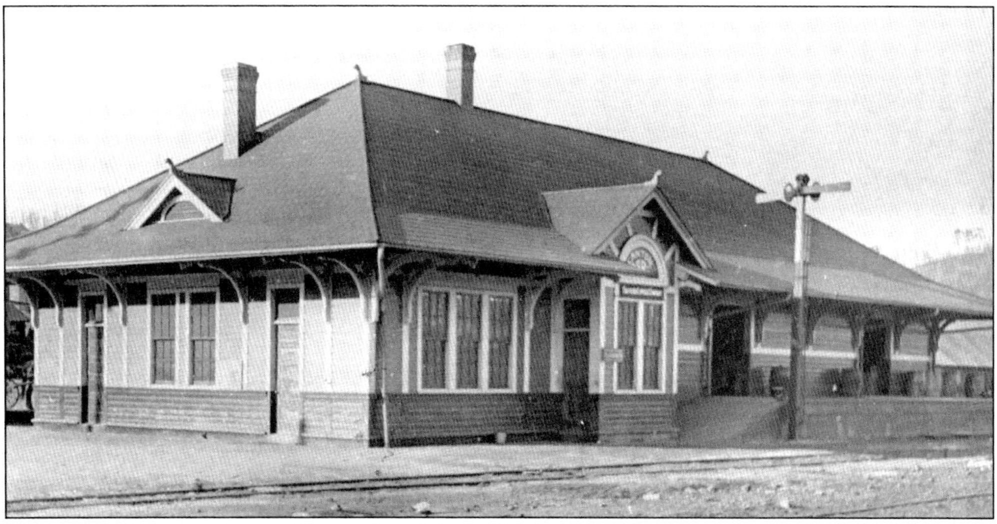

Southern Railway Depot. This railroad depot, built around 1910 and demolished about 60 years later, was a larger, brick structure that replaced the original depot, which was erected just after railroad tracks were laid to Canton. Southern Railway took control of the rail lines in Canton in 1894. Train service and the paper mill transformed this mountain hamlet of 230 residents in 1900 to a bustling town of 1,393 people by 1910. (Courtesy of the Canton Historical Museum.)

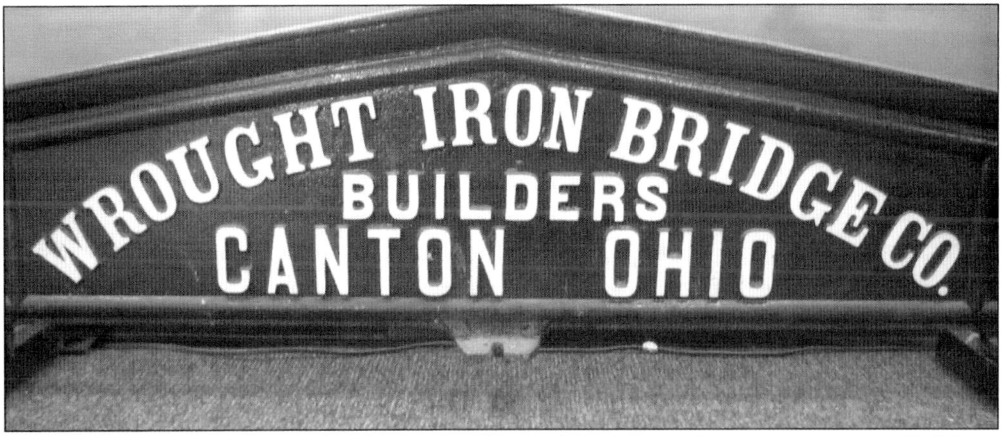

Canton Bridge Sign. In the late 1800s, residents of the Pigeon River community called their village different names: Ford of Pigeon (as travelers had to cross the Pigeon River to continue west); Vinson (after local postmaster Winfield Vinson); and Buford (after Algernon Sidney Buford, president of the Richmond & Danville Railroad, which became the Southern Railway system). These names failed to stick. As the story goes, local resident Cash Mingus was walking one day and came upon an iron-truss bridge built by a company in Canton, Ohio. Mingus proposed the name of Canton, which was approved sometime between 1893–1895. (Courtesy of the Canton Historical Museum.)

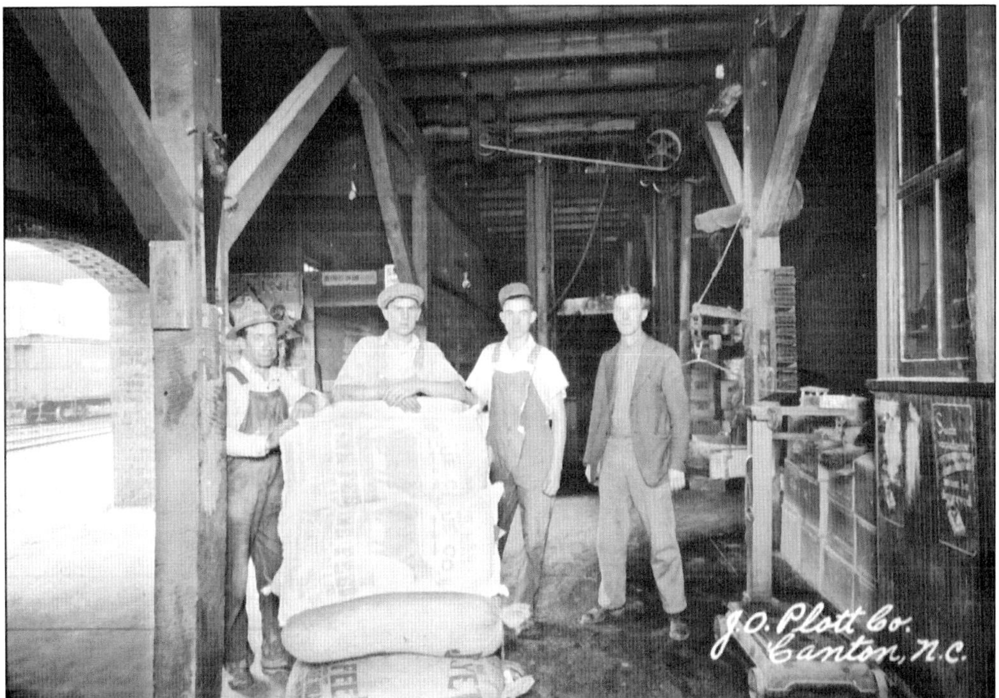

J.O. Plott Wholesale Grocery. In 1914, J.O. Plott took over the bottom floor of a three-story brick building on Main Street to use as a wholesale grocery store. Plott also ran the Pigeon Valley Mill, a feed store and sawmill. As a major wholesaler in the region, the Plott grocery served customers in western North Carolina from Asheville to Murphy. This building later became home to the So-Hy Chemical Products Company. (Courtesy of the Canton Historical Museum.)

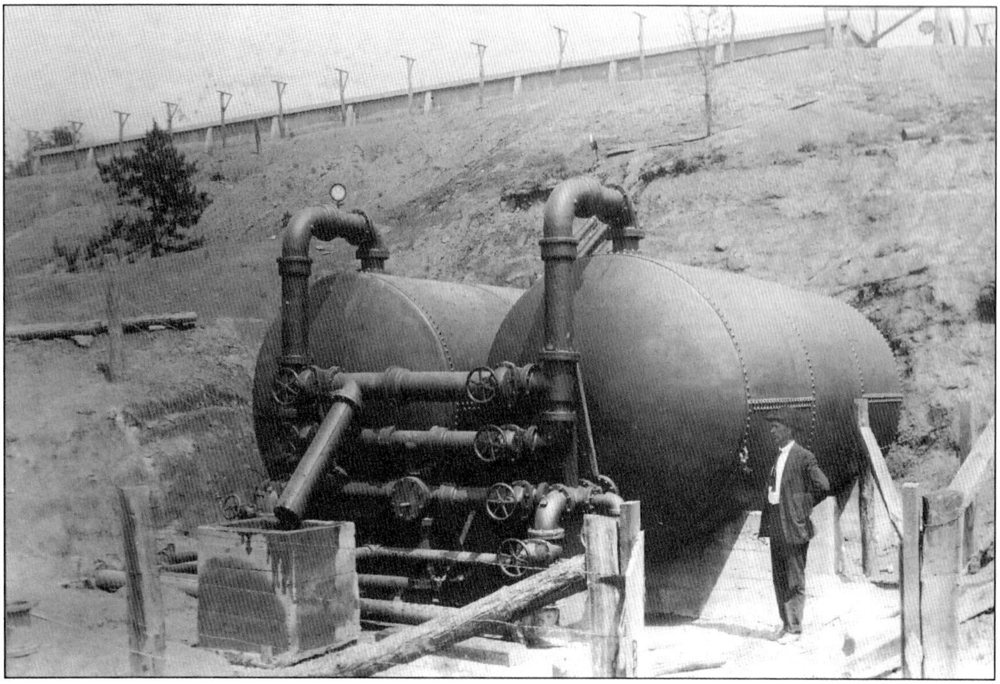

ROUGH CREEK RESERVOIR. This reservoir once served as the main water source for the town of Canton. The Rough Creek watershed lies north of town, and early settlers found fertile land nearby to farm, grow apple orchards, and raise livestock. Eventually, some of the families moved away and the farms gave way to wilderness, but the town took ownership of the watershed and kept it protected. When the federal government proposed a nuclear waste site in the area in the mid-1980s, Rough Creek residents launched a campaign to halt the plan and sent samples of its pure mountain water to Washington, DC, as evidence of the pristine resource that could be ruined by nuclear waste. The tactic worked, and the government looked elsewhere for a dump site. Today, the Rough Creek watershed is a peaceful, biodiverse 870-acre preserve with more than 10 miles of hiking trails open to the public. (Both, courtesy of the Canton Historical Museum.)

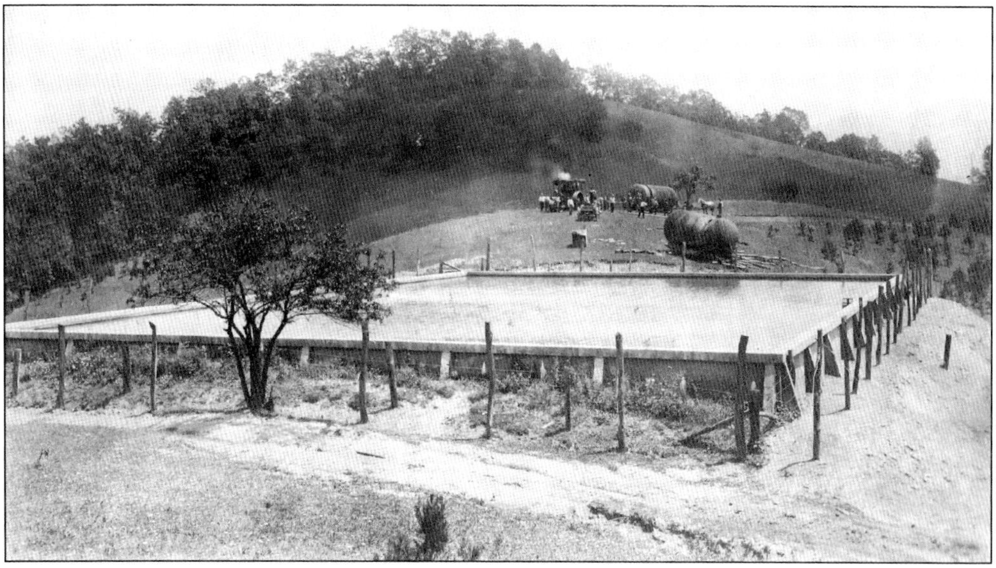

Two

CHAMPION

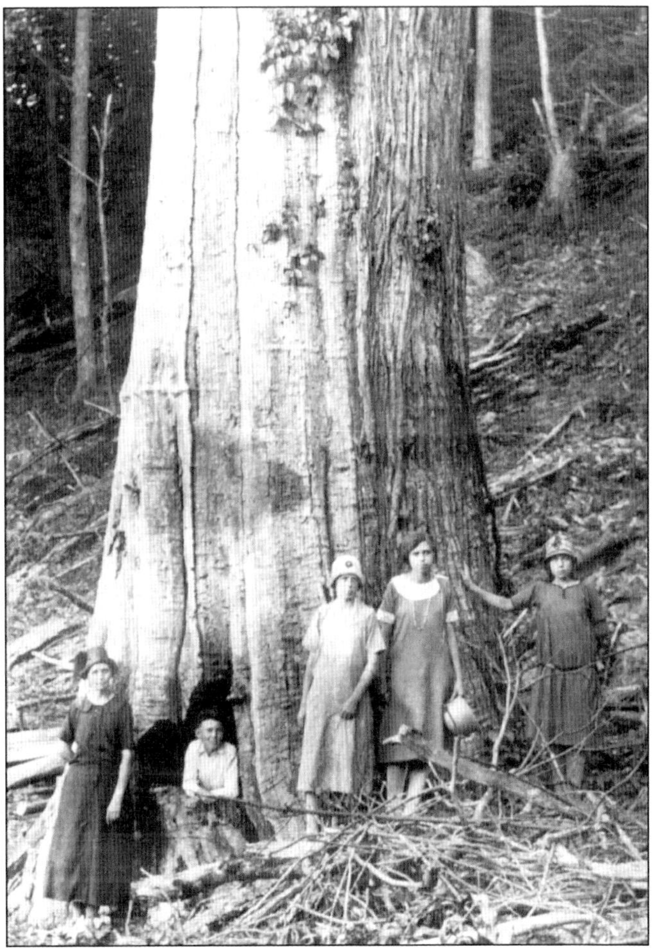

CHESTNUT TREE. Before a devastating blight fungus struck in the early 20th century, an estimated four billion American chestnut trees once grew in the eastern United States. The mighty chestnut was used widely for furniture, fences, floors, home construction, and telephone poles. Its nuts could be roasted or eaten raw. Chestnuts were also rich in tannins, and extract from their bark was used for tanning leather. This rich natural resource brought logging companies to the region and eventually lured Ohio industrialist Peter G. Thomson to Canton. (Courtesy of Great Smoky Mountains National Park Library.)

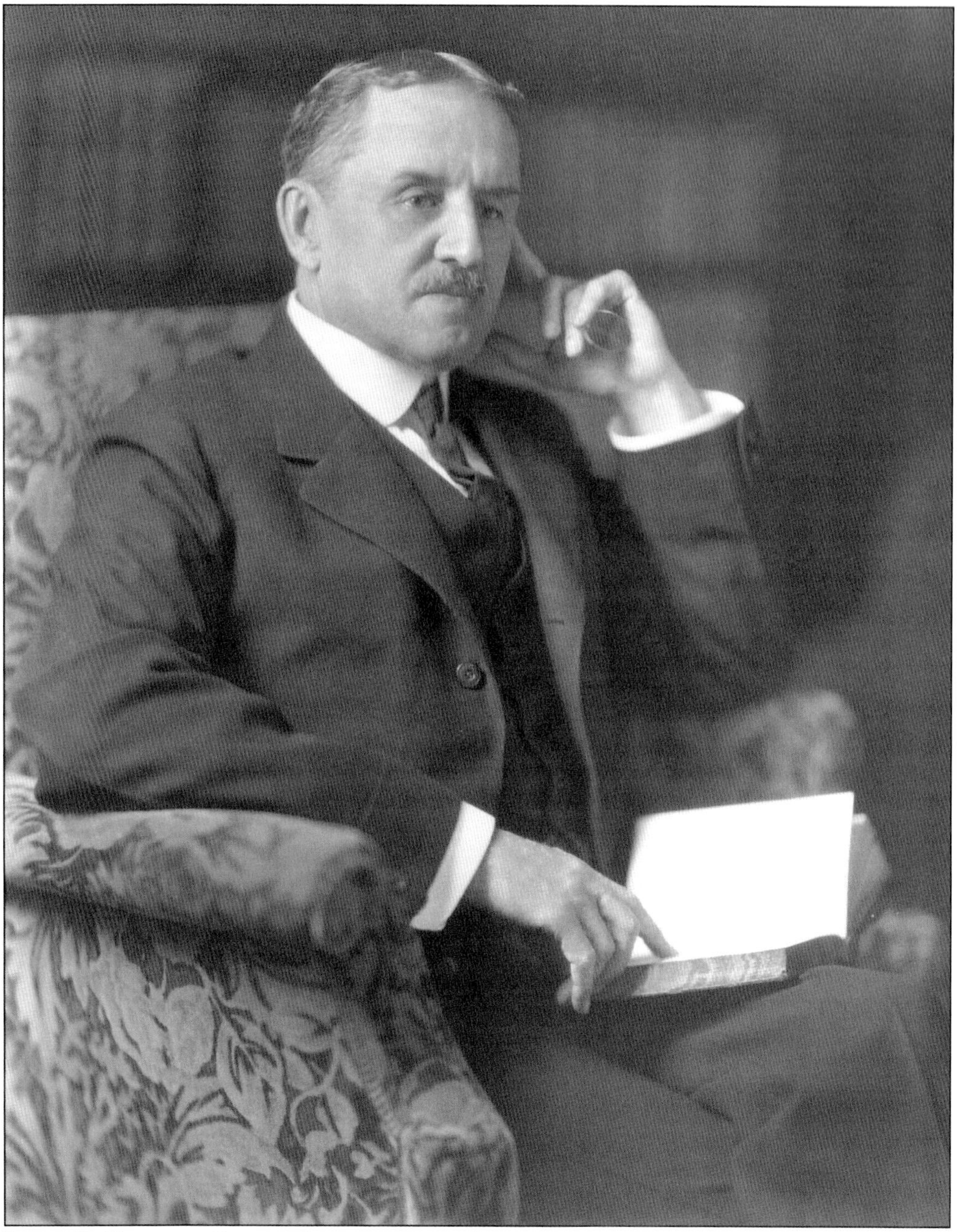

Peter G. Thomson. Born in Cincinnati in 1851 to immigrant parents, Peter Gibson Thomson quit school at age 14 to support his family after the death of his father and grandfather. He took business classes and found a job selling books. Borrowing money, he opened his own bookstore, collected rare books, and developed a successful printing company, which he sold to a New York firm. In 1893, he invested the money from this sale to create the Champion Coated Paper Company in Hamilton, Ohio. A health-conscious man who refused alcohol or smoking, he was a regular member of the Cincinnati Gym and once claimed to have deadlifted 1,260 pounds. Thomson died at the age of 79 in Cincinnati. His 20,000-square-foot mansion at Laurel Court in Cincinnati is now a historic site. (Courtesy of the Cincinnati Museum Center.)

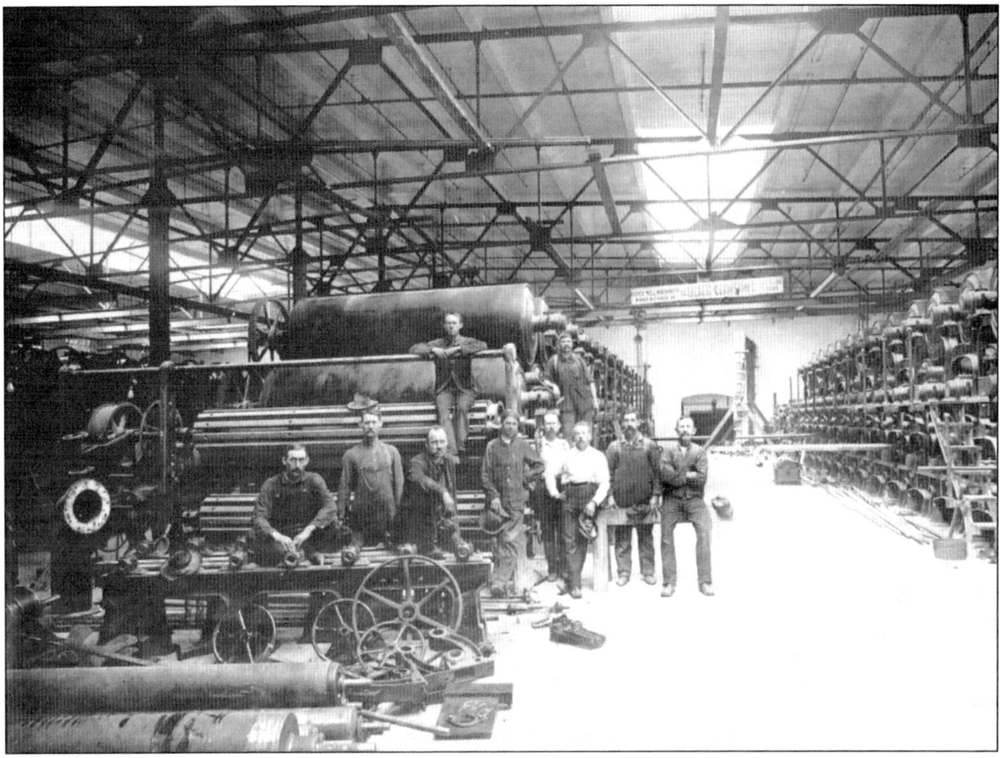

Paper Machines. By the end of the 1800s, Peter G. Thomson had a thriving papermaking business in Hamilton, Ohio. Machines like the ones seen here rolled out a handsome profit, but Thomson needed his own source of timber to continue making paper, and there were vast forests in western North Carolina. In 1905, while visiting his son Logan, who was attending the Asheville School for Boys, Thomson began investigating areas between Asheville and Andrews for a site to construct a new pulp mill. (Courtesy of the Canton Historical Museum.)

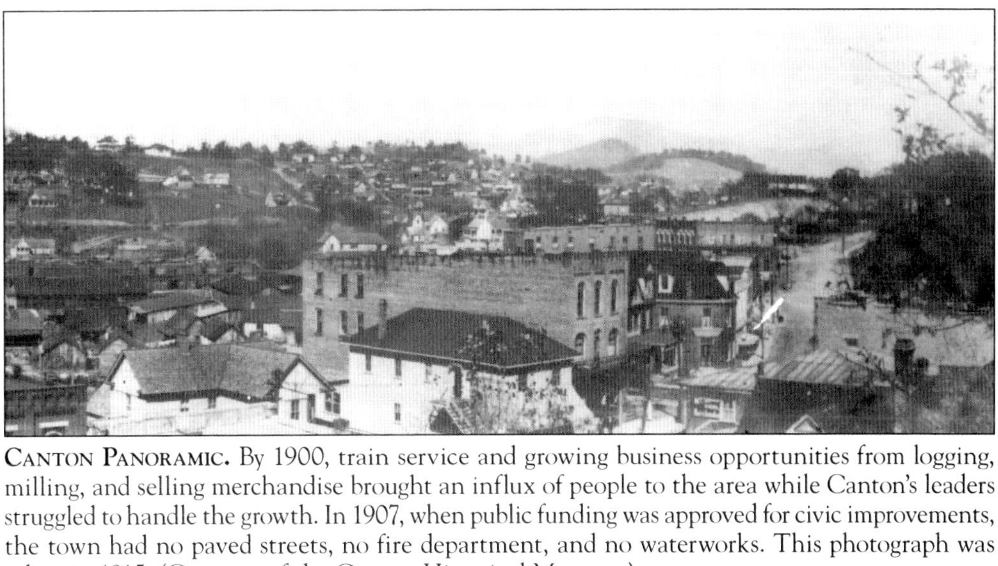

Canton Panoramic. By 1900, train service and growing business opportunities from logging, milling, and selling merchandise brought an influx of people to the area while Canton's leaders struggled to handle the growth. In 1907, when public funding was approved for civic improvements, the town had no paved streets, no fire department, and no waterworks. This photograph was taken in 1915. (Courtesy of the Canton Historical Museum.)

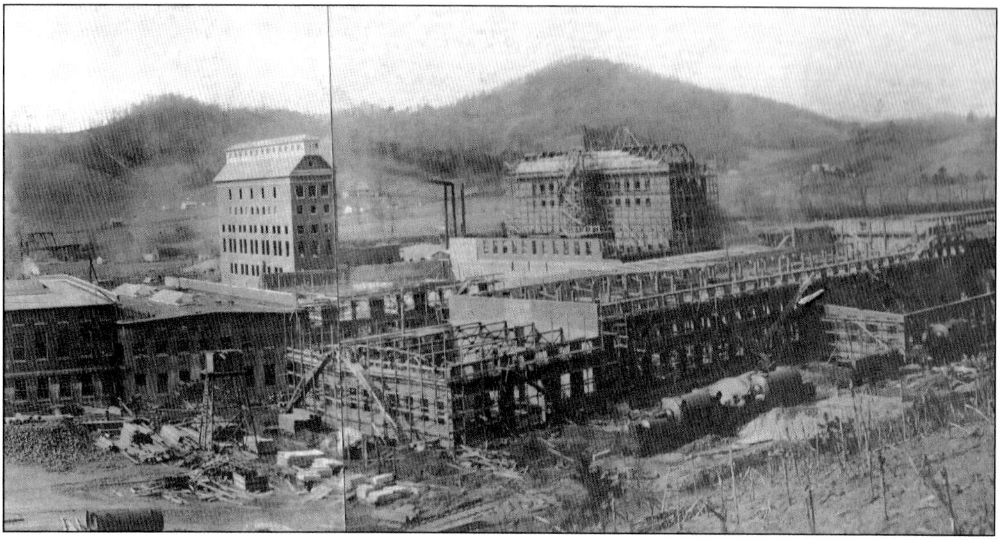

Champion Under Construction. Ignoring the recommendations of architects, Peter G. Thomson chose a swampy cornfield along the Pigeon River in Canton as the place to build his new pulp mill. Canton's mayor, "Squire" J. Nelson Mease, sold Champion the plot of land for $4,000. Construction began in 1906. However, heavy rains and a national banking crisis stalled efforts to complete the project. Local farmers hired for the construction often had to leave work and tend to their own farms, delaying the mill's construction even further. Thomson turned to his son-in-law Reuben B. Robertson, a lawyer from Cincinnati, to oversee the project. By January 1, 1908, Canton's mill finally opened. Champion invested $2 million to create what became one of the largest pulp mills and tannic operations in the world. (Both, courtesy of the Canton Historical Museum.)

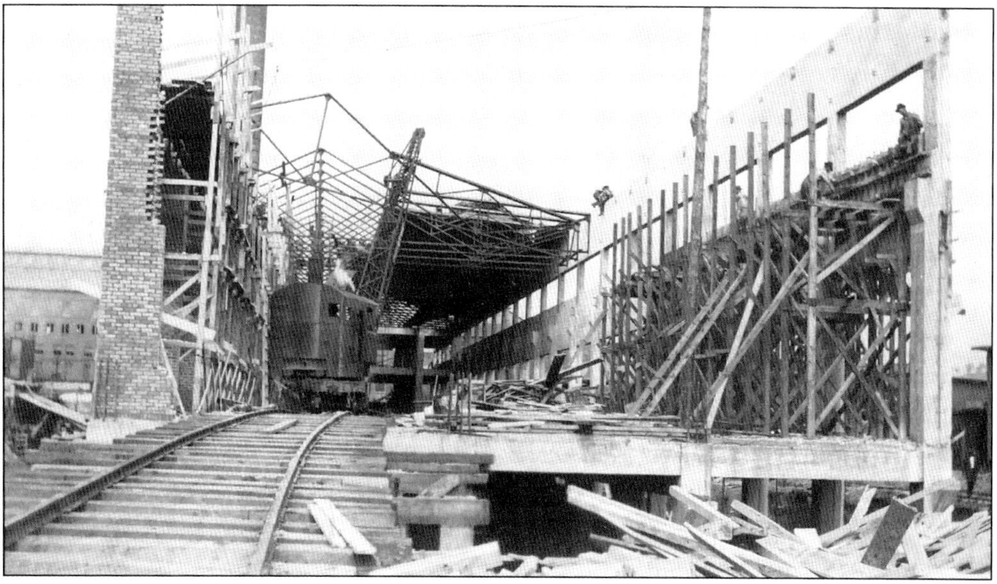

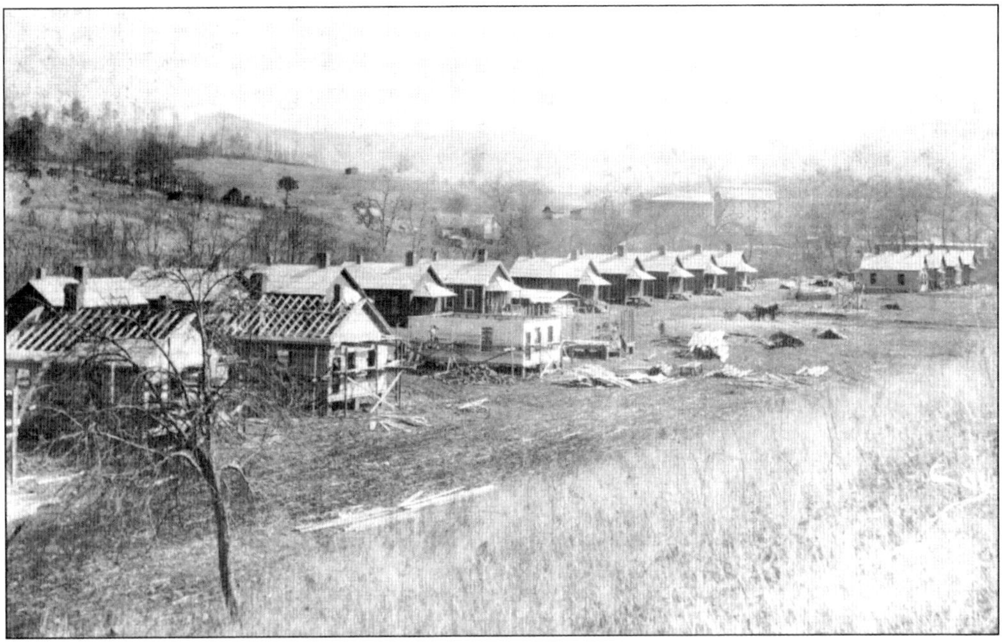

FIBREVILLE. As the Champion Fibre Company began, the company built houses (above) for some of its workers in a neighborhood near the mill known as Fibreville. Its main street, Woodview Drive, ran parallel to the Pigeon River. The simple, one-floor designs made them look like shotgun houses, but Champion offered cash prizes for tenants who beautified and landscaped their yards. Because the homes were built so close to the river, they were easy targets for floods, which inevitably wreaked havoc on the community. Devastating storms in 1940 and 2004 flooded many of the homes, which were subsequently torn down. Thomas Marr (right), a native of Virginia, was hired to oversee the construction of Fibreville. He later became chief of the tannin extract operation. (Both, courtesy of the Canton Historical Museum.)

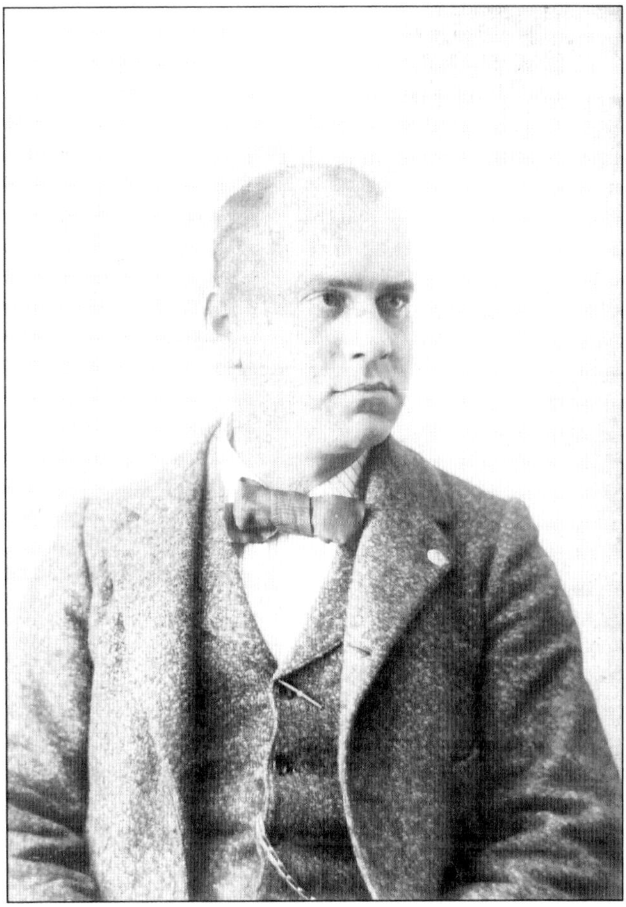

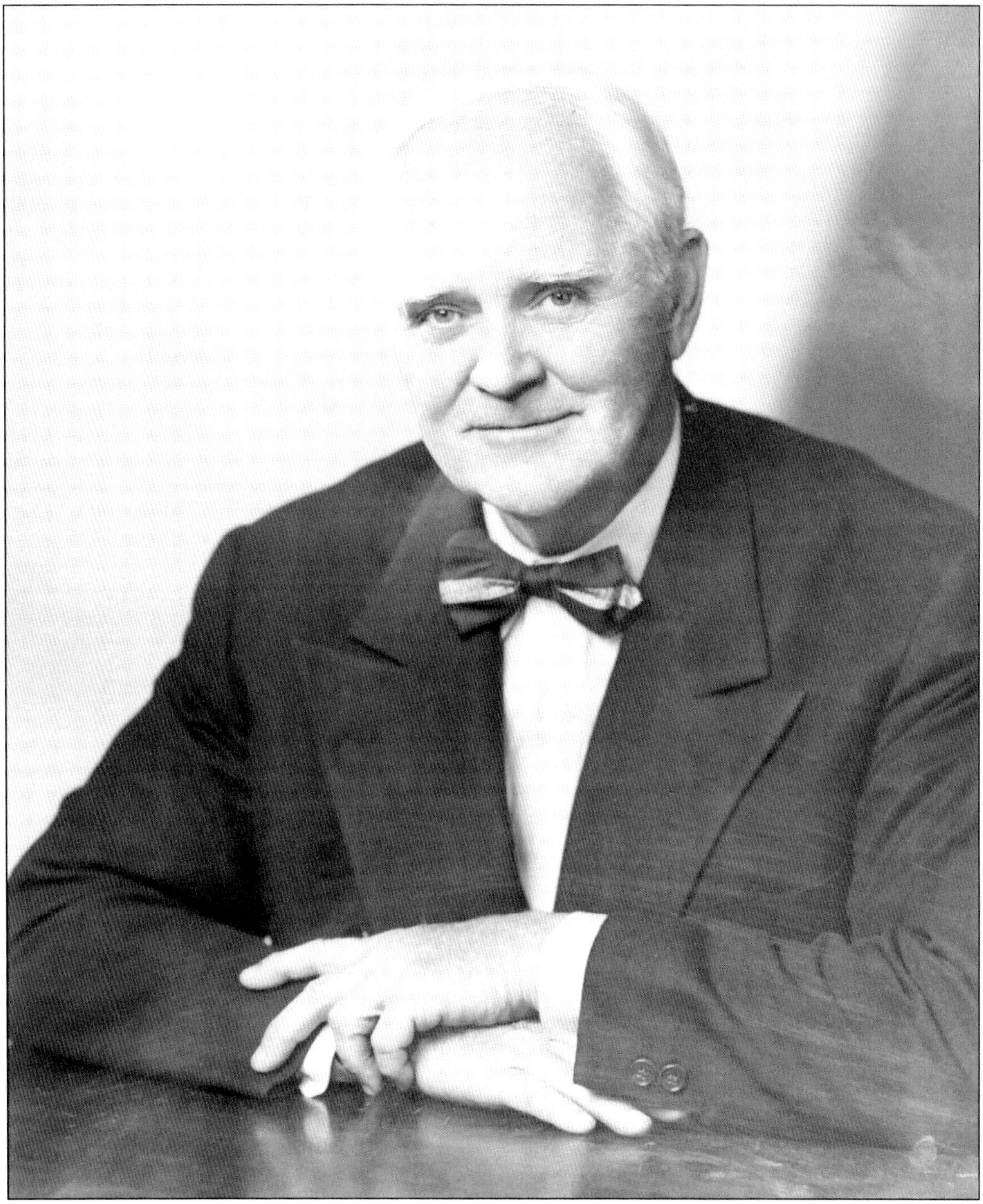

Reuben B. Robertson. Born in Cincinnati, Ohio, in 1879, Reuben Buck Robertson graduated from Yale University with a law degree and married Peter G. Thomson's daughter Hope in 1905. Soon after, Thomson hired Robertson to oversee the Champion paper mill construction. Robertson became a fixture in Canton, serving as the mill's plant manager and rising to become Champion's president. Affectionately known as "Mr. Champion," Robertson offered an open-door policy to all employees at the Canton mill. Though he fought for decades against workers forming a union, he strongly supported employees and the Canton community. He helped establish the Champion YMCA, began the Snug Harbor Center for Champion retirees, and donated land for the Canton Public Library. Robertson died in 1972 at the age of 93. A North Carolina State University professorship and a Western Carolina University dormitory are named in his honor. (Courtesy of the Canton Historical Museum.)

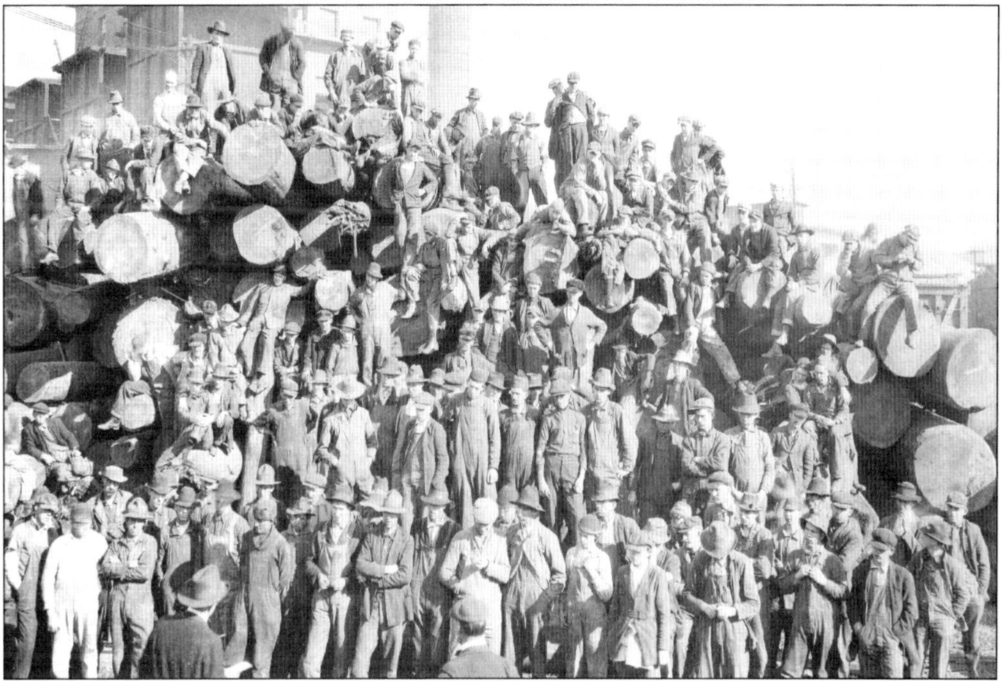

WORKFORCE. When the Champion mill first opened in 1908, it employed about 650 people. Workers came from all over the United States, Canada, and Europe, giving Canton one of the most diverse populations in western North Carolina and one of the highest median incomes in the region. Under Peter G. Thomson's progressive leadership, employees received free life insurance, access to a free medical clinic, and a pay raise every five years. Below, Champion workers pose for a photograph inside the mill's boiler room around 1910. (Both, courtesy of the Canton Historical Museum.)

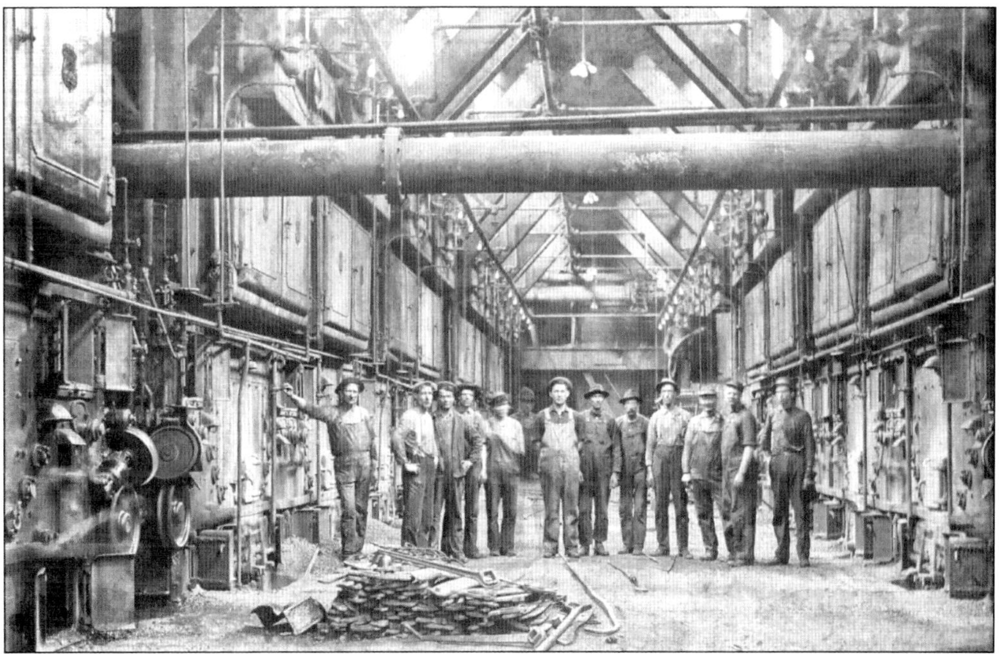

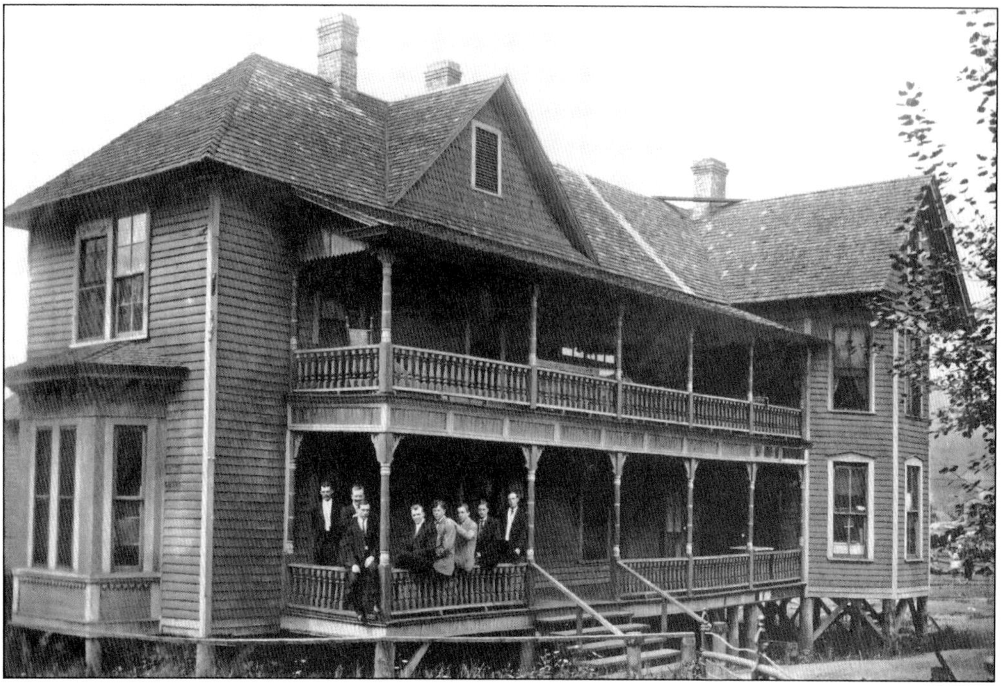

Champion Office. This building, erected in the late 1800s, served as the original main office for Champion Fibre Company's administrators. It was torn down and replaced in 1918 with a three-story, flat-roofed, square building designed by Asheville architect W.H. Lord. Located on the eastern side of the mill, it still stands today. (Courtesy of the Canton Historical Museum.)

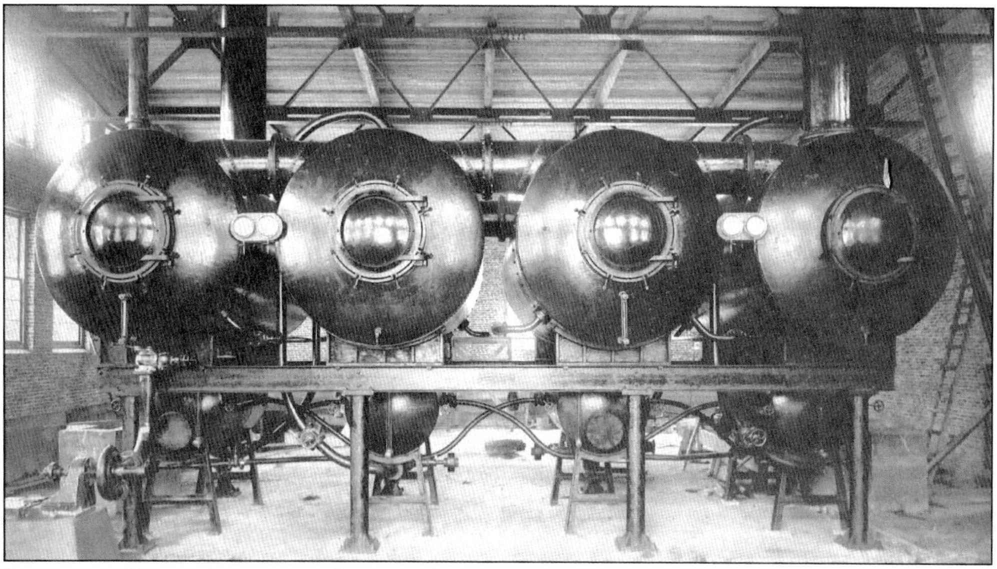

Generator Room. A massive mill required a powerful source of electricity to run lights, machinery, and office equipment. In its early days, Champion had two work shifts: an 11-hour day shift and a 13-hour night shift. Each weekend, the entire mill shut down for 24 hours to make repairs and adjustments. Eventually, the mill converted to three eight-hour shifts, resulting in increased productivity, minimal changes to payroll, and an end to the weekly shutdowns. (Courtesy of the Canton Historical Museum.)

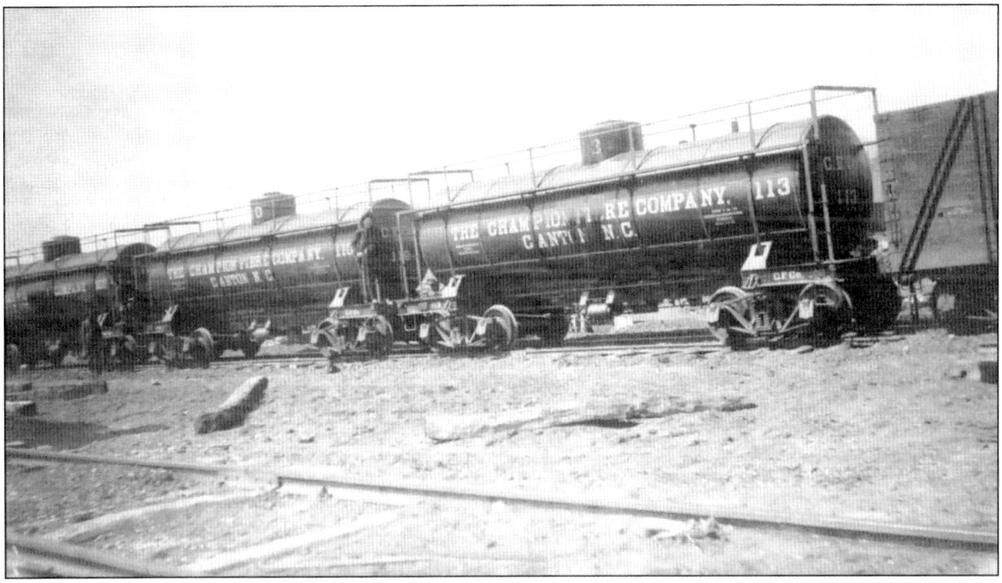

EARLY TRAIN. As one of the busiest stops on the Southern Railway system, the Champion mill kept a steady traffic of train cars, importing logs, coal, and other raw materials and exporting chestnut extract, caustics, and paper. (Courtesy of the Canton Historical Museum.)

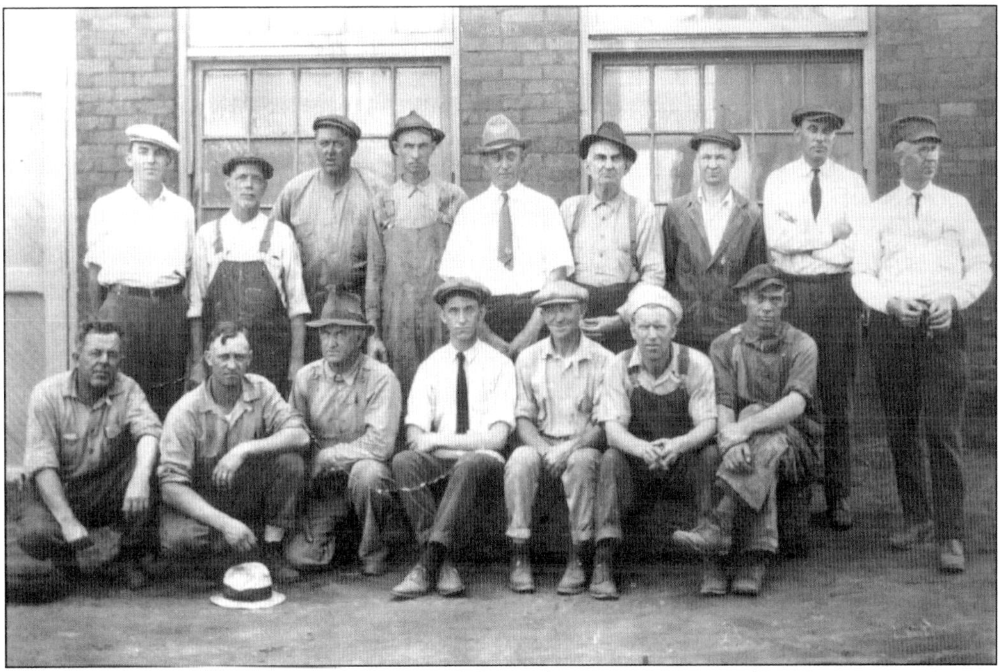

MILL WORKERS. Champion developed many different departments at its mill, with a variety of teams in both blue-collar and white-collar jobs. In the beginning, its main operations were producing pulp from spruce, poplar, and chestnut wood and extracting tannin from chestnut, which was used for tanning leather. By 1921, the mill installed machinery to produce paper. As the first operation of its kind in the South, it became one of the main suppliers of paper for publications like *Life* magazine. (Courtesy of the Canton Historical Museum.)

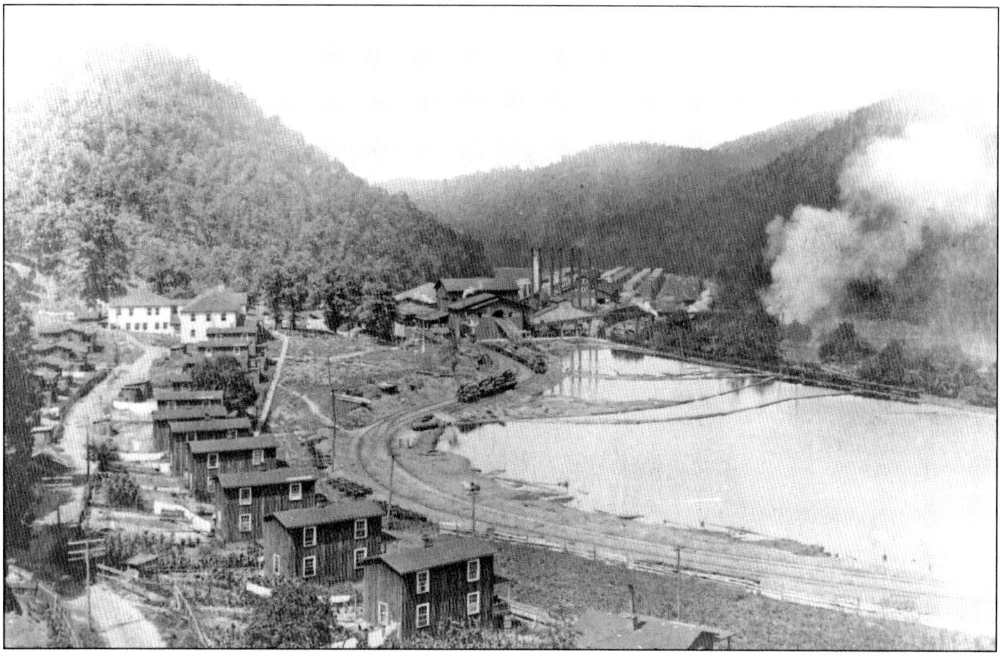

Sunburst. To supply its mill, Champion purchased 40,000 acres of forestland in nearby communities like Sunburst, south of Canton. Originally, Peter G. Thomson's idea was to float logs from the Sunburst community down the Pigeon River to Canton, but the waterway was too shallow. Nevertheless, a booming logging community of 500 men took root. Sunburst got its name from the view of morning sun bursting over the mountains. (Courtesy of the Canton Historical Museum.)

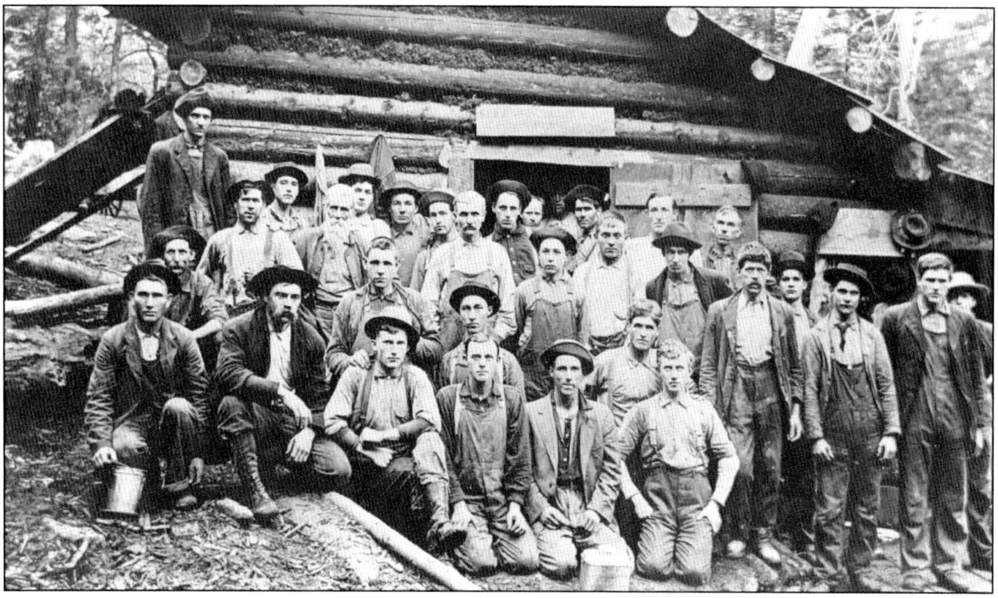

Logging Camp. For this logging camp, located west of Sunburst, jobs were highly specialized so that groups of men had assigned tasks, such as carving out skid trails, operating machines, loading logs onto flumes, cutting wood, and watching out for potential hazards like fires or log spills. Yoked oxen and trains hauled logs and supplies up and down the rugged mountain slopes. (Courtesy of the Canton Historical Museum.)

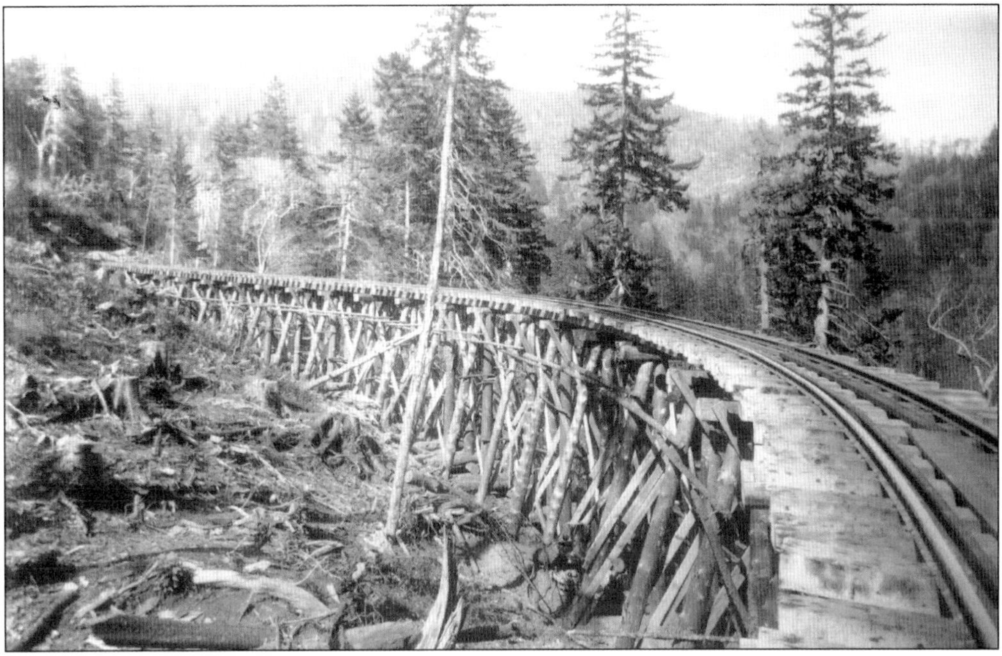

Trestle. As a logging operation progressed, train tracks had to be laid through forests to carry workers, logs, and supplies. The support frame, or trestle, would often be made of the timber harvested from the surrounding forest. Timber trestles tended to be temporary structures. After a logging operation finished with a given area, these structures could be disassembled and hauled to another viable logging site. (Courtesy of the Canton Historical Museum.)

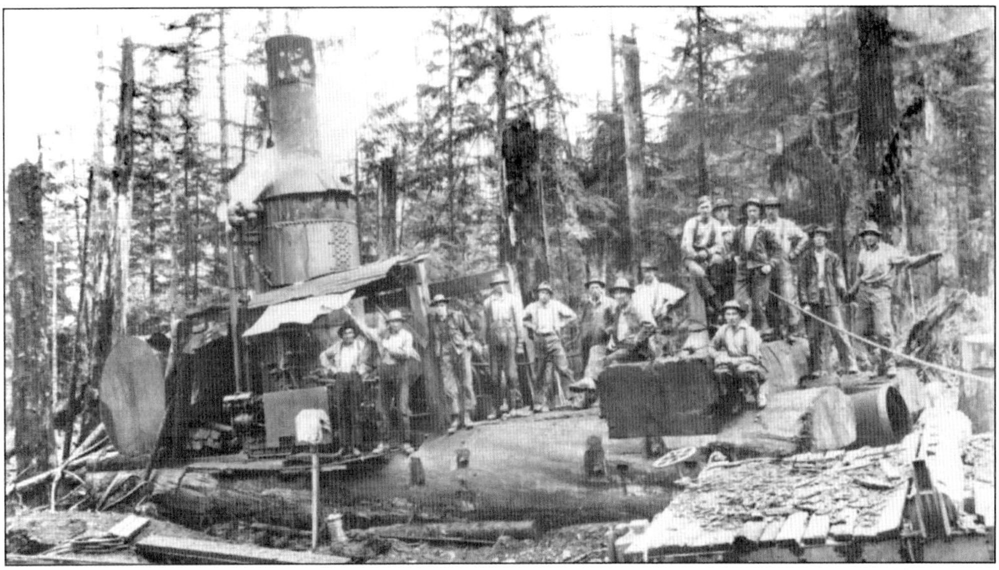

Logging Crew. Before 1900, logging in and around Canton had primarily been a local business, with landowners selecting large, mature trees for sawmills. With the coming of the railroad, larger companies came with plenty of capital. Trains made rugged terrain more manageable, especially with the use of gear-driven Shay locomotive engines, which were lighter and more maneuverable than conventional steam trains. Champion quickly contracted with Sunburst and other logging companies in the region. (Courtesy of the Canton Historical Museum.)

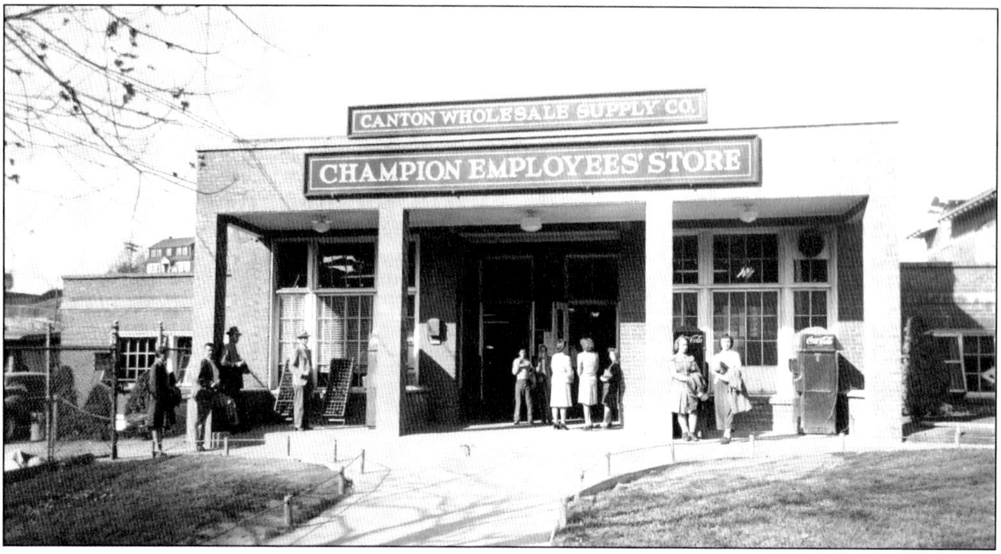

Champion Company Store. The Champion company store opened in 1926 to offer groceries and dry goods for mill employees. It functioned much like a general store, except that employees were allowed to purchase items with company scrip, a currency substitute used as a form of credit. This payment system was often used in mill or mining towns. Champion employees could pay for their groceries using pre-paycheck credit, with a limit of no more than 25 percent of the paycheck. In the store's early days, customers would pick out the items they wished to purchase and the store would deliver them to their homes using a fleet of service trucks. Later on, customers bought items at the store and took them home themselves. Each year during Christmas season, employees were given a dividend allowing them to purchase approximately two weeks worth of groceries at the store. Such policies helped create strong loyalty between the mill's management and its employees. (Both, courtesy of the Canton Historical Museum.)

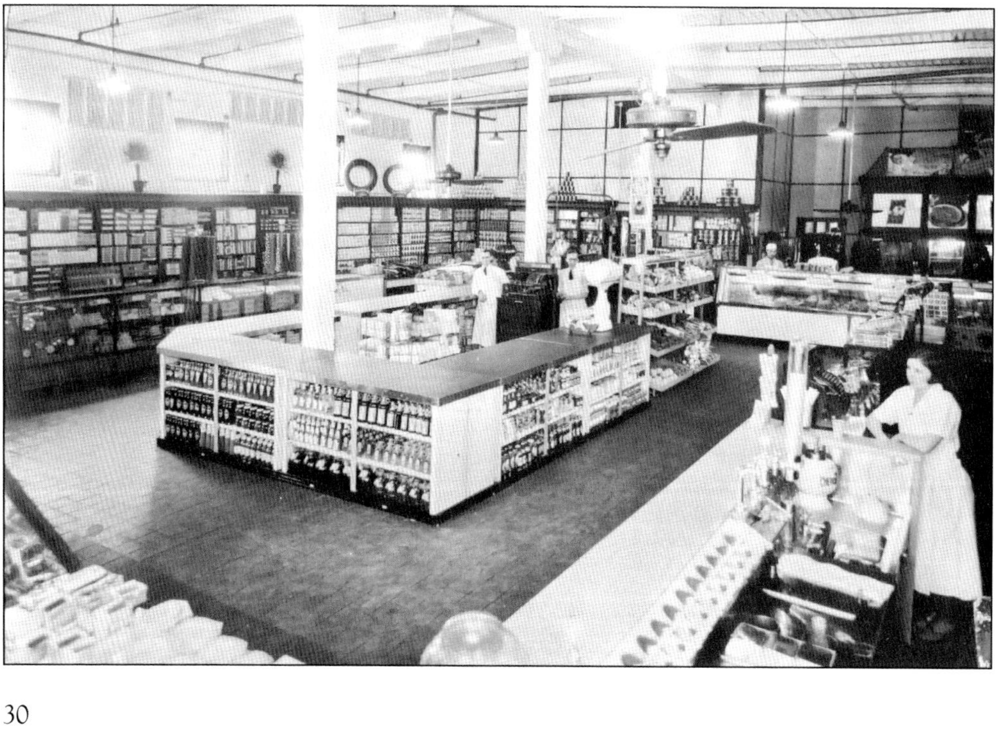

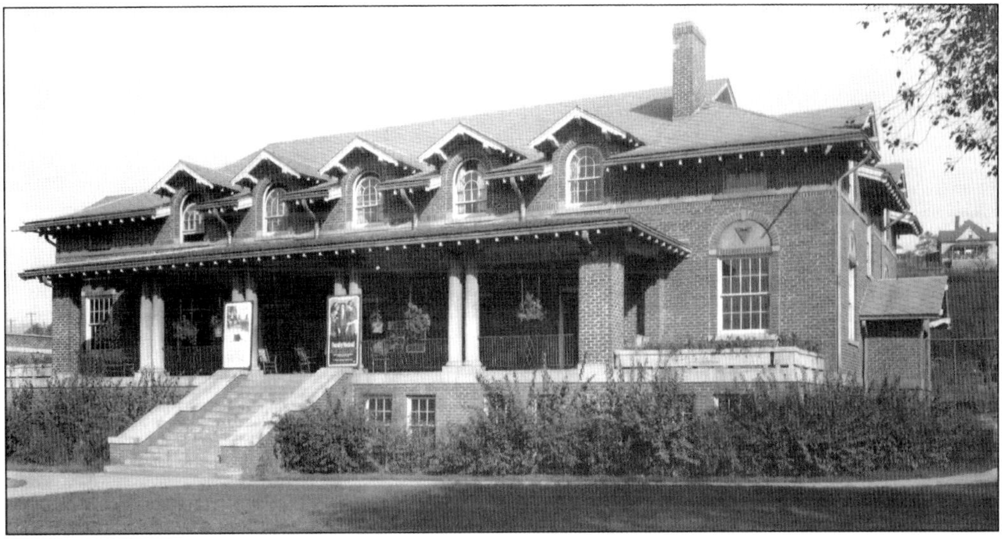

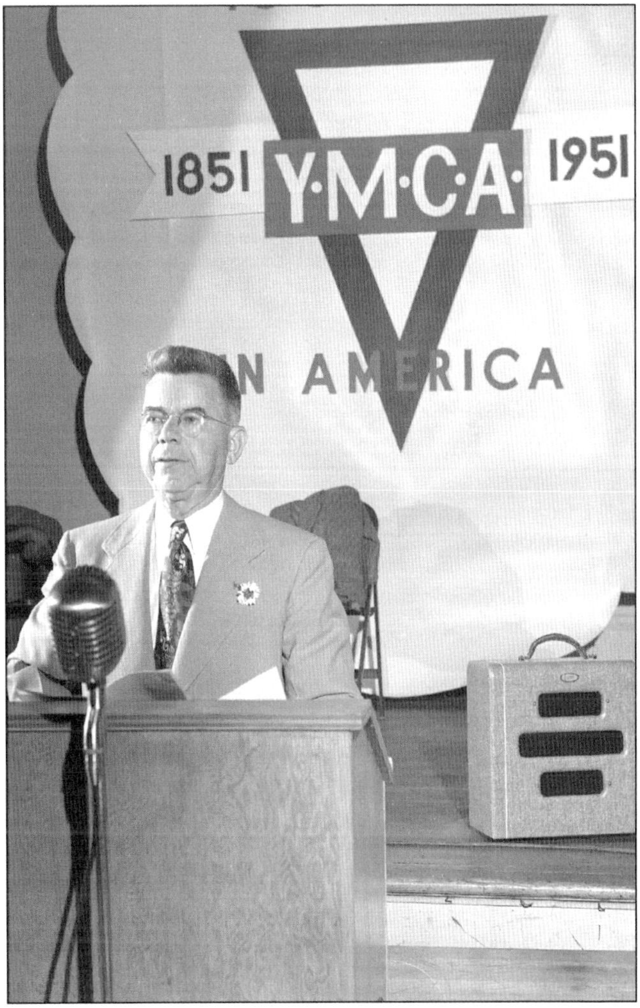

Champion YMCA. Perhaps no single civic institution was as influential to Canton's social life as the Champion-sponsored YMCA, which opened in 1920 as the largest facility of its kind in western North Carolina west of Charlotte. The family-oriented recreation center (above) included a gymnasium, two bowling alleys, a swimming pool, locker and shower rooms, a library and reading room, a billiard room, various offices, and a kitchen. The original YMCA was torn down in the 1960s to build Machine No. 19 at the Champion mill. A second facility, the Reuben B. Robertson Memorial YMCA, was dedicated in 1965. Today, it is the site of Bethel Christian Academy. Grover Suttles (right) served as director of the Champion YMCA from 1929 to 1954 and was a key force behind its success, as an administrator, coach, and instructor. An active man who hiked and stayed healthy, Suttles lived to be 100 years old. (Both, courtesy of the Canton Historical Museum.)

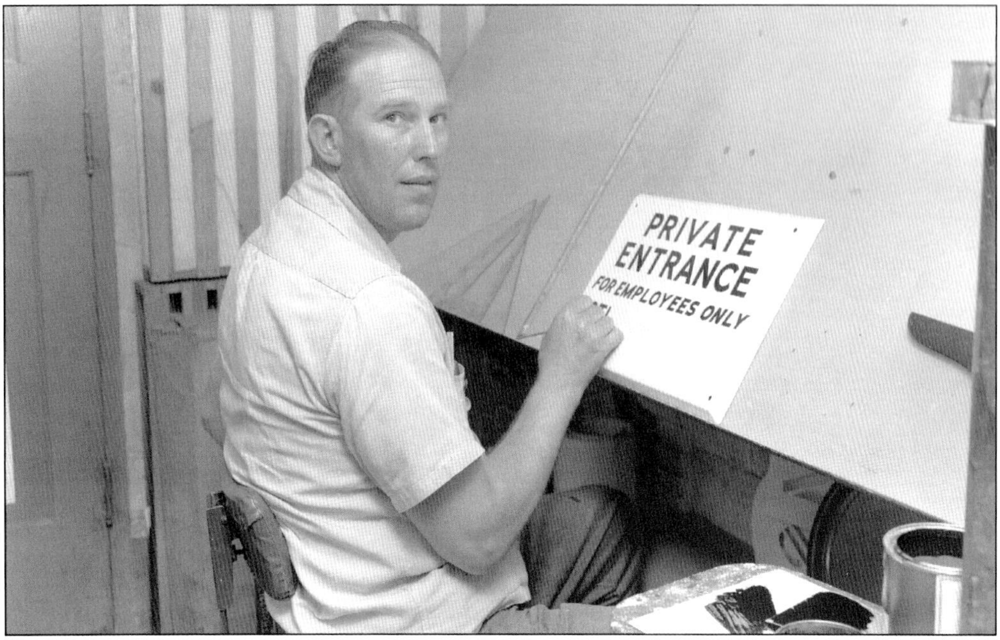

ARTIST AT THE MILL. Marshall Cooper was the artist behind many of the logos, displays, and signs that Champion produced in the mid-1900s. He traveled the country painting Champion logos on cars and planes, decorated Champion's Labor Day floats, and designed the first logo for Canton's rescue squad. He served in the Navy in World War II and remained in the Naval Reserve for 30 years. (Courtesy of the Canton Historical Museum.)

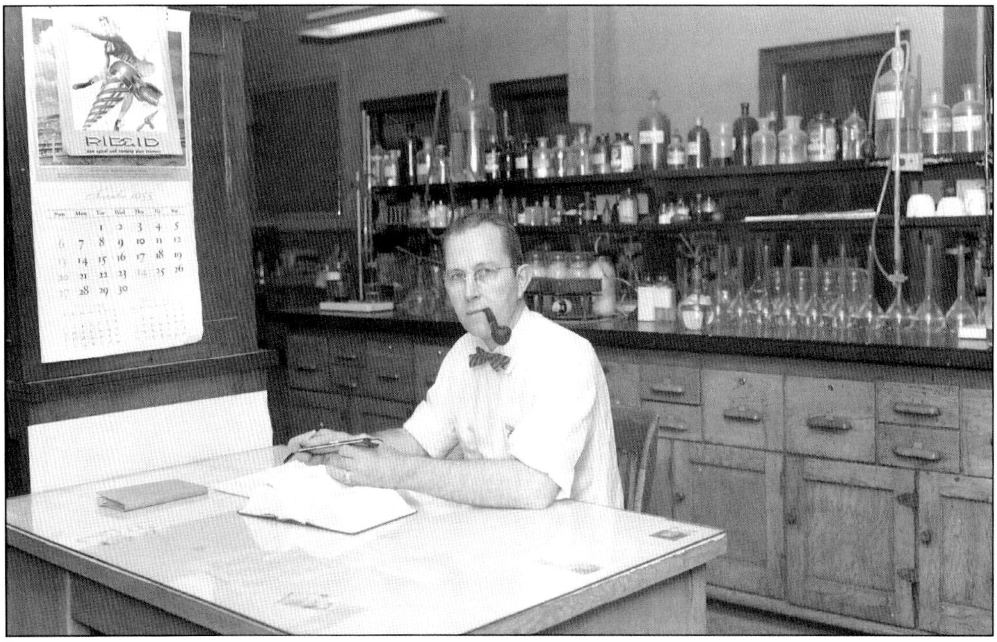

CHEMIST. Champion became the first company to make bleached white paper from southern yellow pine, a plentiful, fast-growing tree in the Southeast. Champion chemists like Louis Gates, seen here in 1955, studied and developed the chemical processes for converting trees into paper products. (Courtesy of the Canton Historical Museum.)

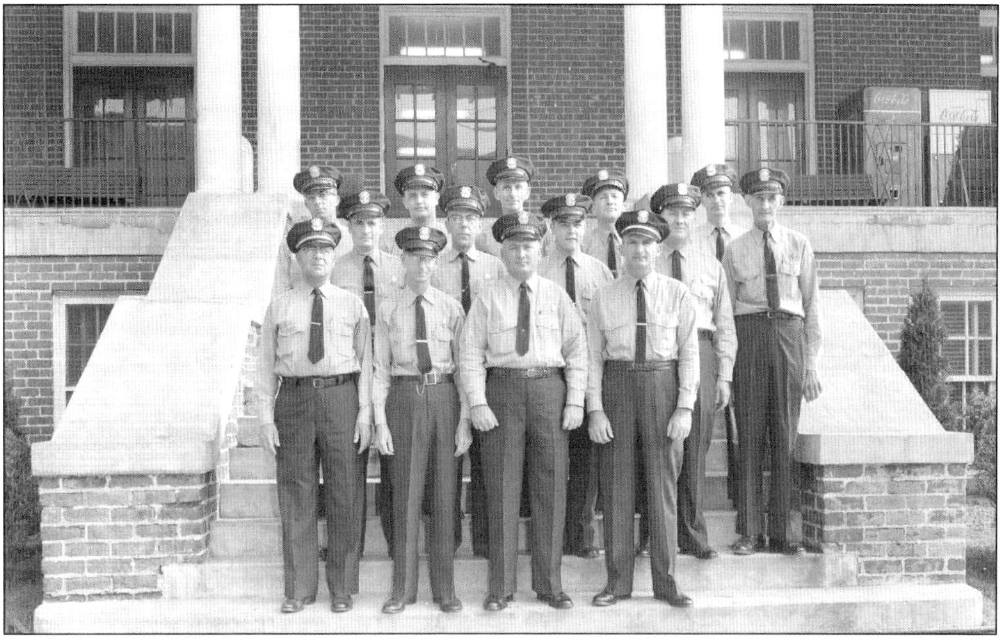

Mill Police. The Champion mill had its own police force, with officers guarding the company gates and checking for proper identification for incoming and outgoing vehicles. According to a 1926 *Canton Enterprise* article, police arrested a 13-year-old boy after he stole a Ford towing car from a parking lot at the Champion plant. Turning a corner at the Hipps store on Main Street, he ran into a gas pump and did considerable damage while trying to make his way to Asheville. (Courtesy of the Canton Historical Museum.)

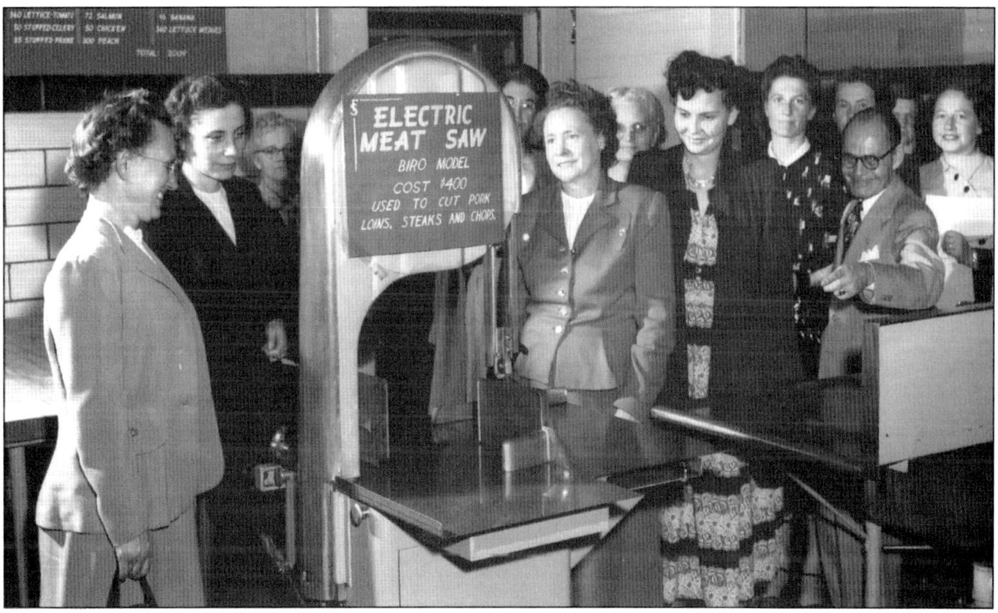

Cafeteria Open House. With hundreds of employees spread across a sprawling campus, Champion needed a full-service cafeteria. Most likely, the company's cafeteria had more regular business than the restaurants in town. This 1950s open house showcased a newly installed meat slicer. (Courtesy of the Canton Historical Museum.)

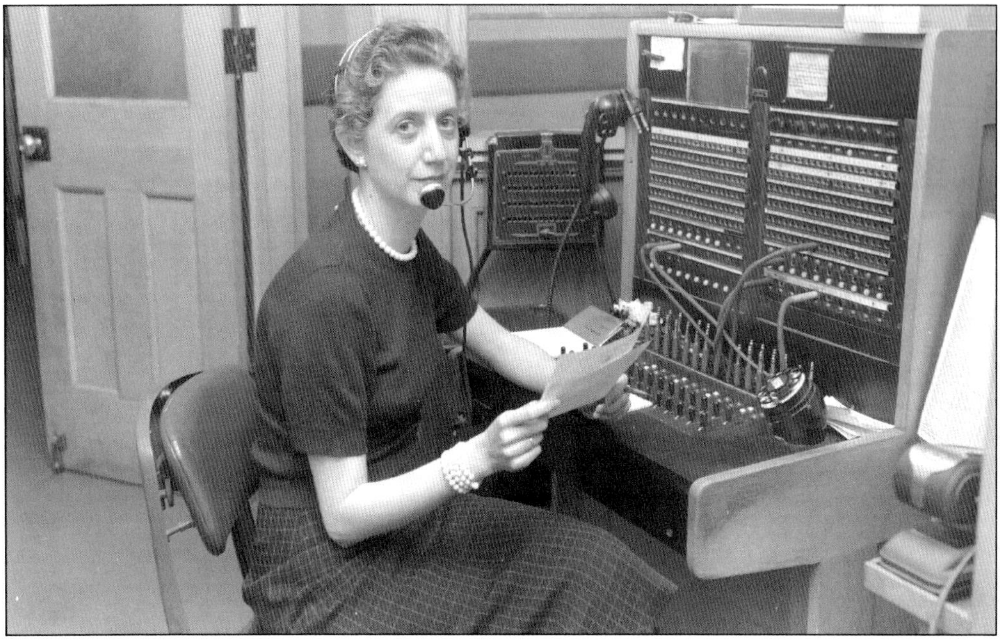

SWITCHBOARD. Not all jobs at the mill involved working around heavy machinery. In fact, the mill required plenty of desk jobs, like tabulating figures, processing paperwork, and typing up reports. Norma Briggs worked as a receptionist and operated a switchboard at the main office, greeting visitors and directing incoming calls to the various departments at the Champion complex. (Courtesy of the Canton Historical Museum.)

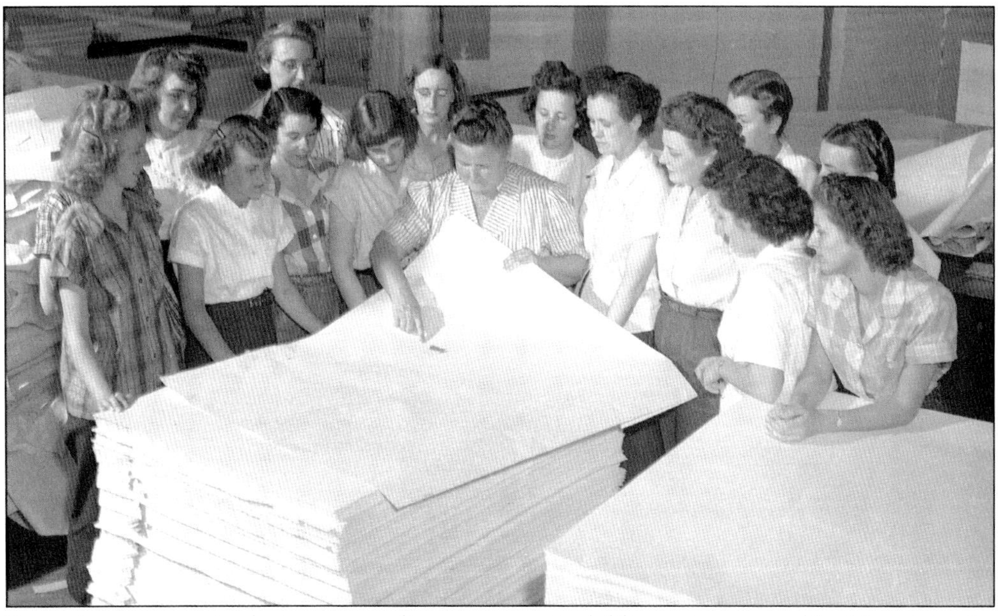

PAPER INSPECTION. Producing top-quality paper required diligent inspectors like Nannie Styles (center), who were trained to spot paper defects such as holes, stains, or poor texture. Styles worked as a supervisor in the inspection department and was a respected forelady. She also taught Sunday school at First United Methodist Church of Canton. (Courtesy of the Canton Historical Museum.)

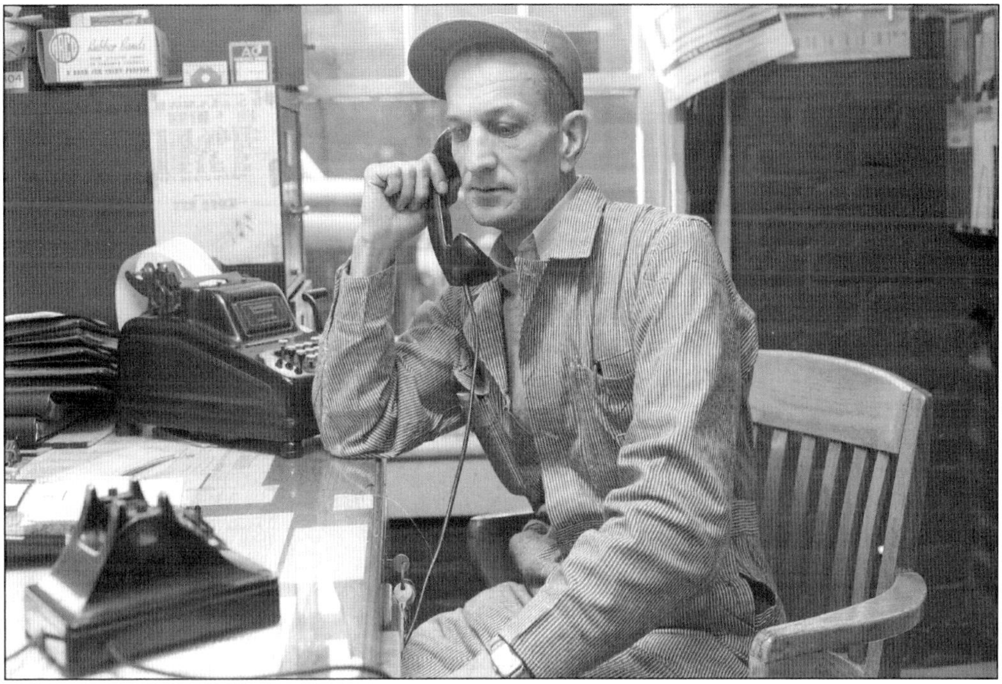

Garage. Champion's operations included a fleet of vehicles that required ongoing maintenance and upkeep. Moody Hyatt managed a retail service station and garage at the Champion mill, which offered gas, oil changes, tune-ups, and other car and truck service, just like a regular auto service station. (Courtesy of the Canton Historical Museum.)

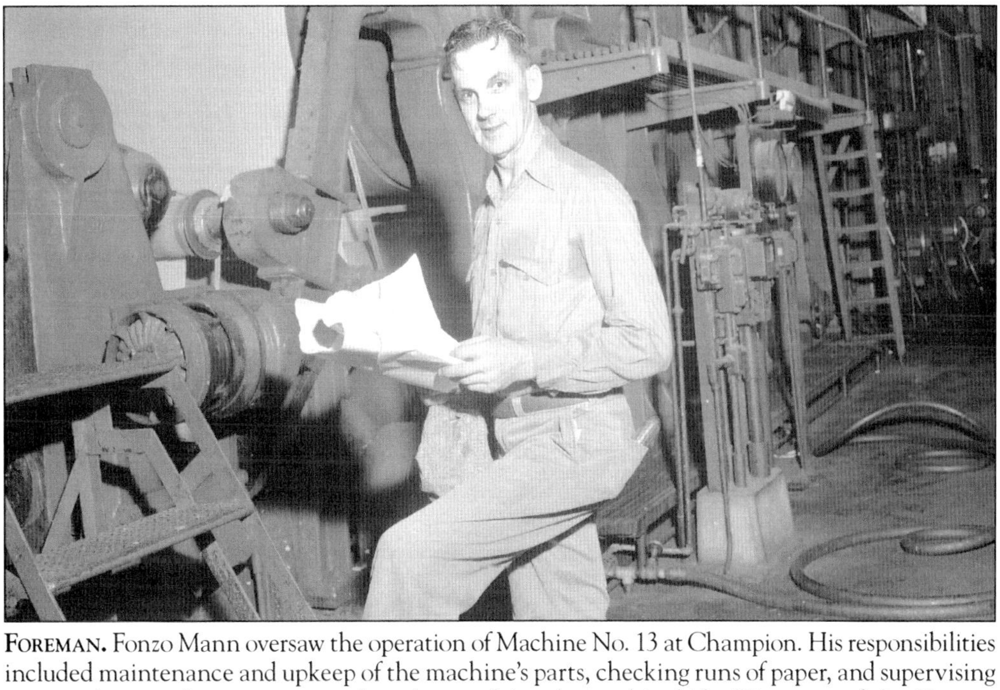

Foreman. Fonzo Mann oversaw the operation of Machine No. 13 at Champion. His responsibilities included maintenance and upkeep of the machine's parts, checking runs of paper, and supervising any employees who were assigned to the machine during his shift. (Courtesy of the Canton Historical Museum.)

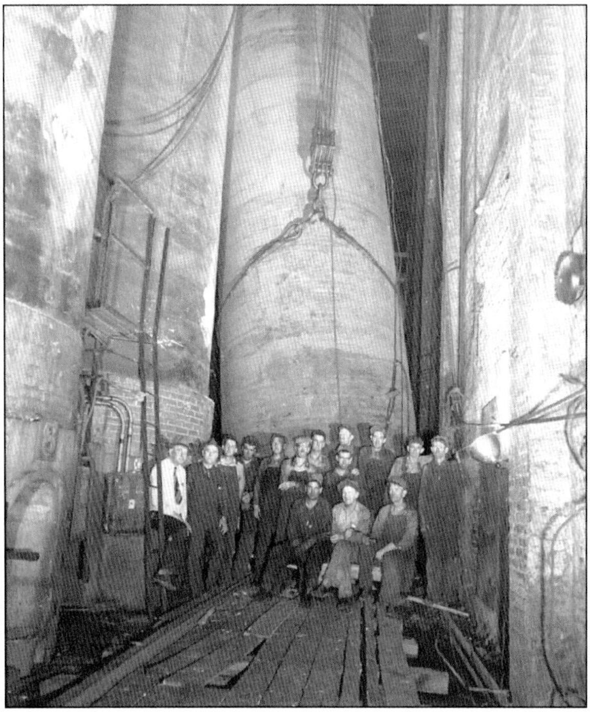

DIGESTER. Wood chips at Champion are digested by being loaded into a steam-pressured vessel that is injected with chemicals to break down the wood's cellular composition into a liquid pulp. The pulp is then pumped through a series of tanks, washed, and processed before turning a shade of white that becomes suitable for making paper. Here, workers pose for a photograph while changing out a towering digester. (Courtesy of Zelda Ponder.)

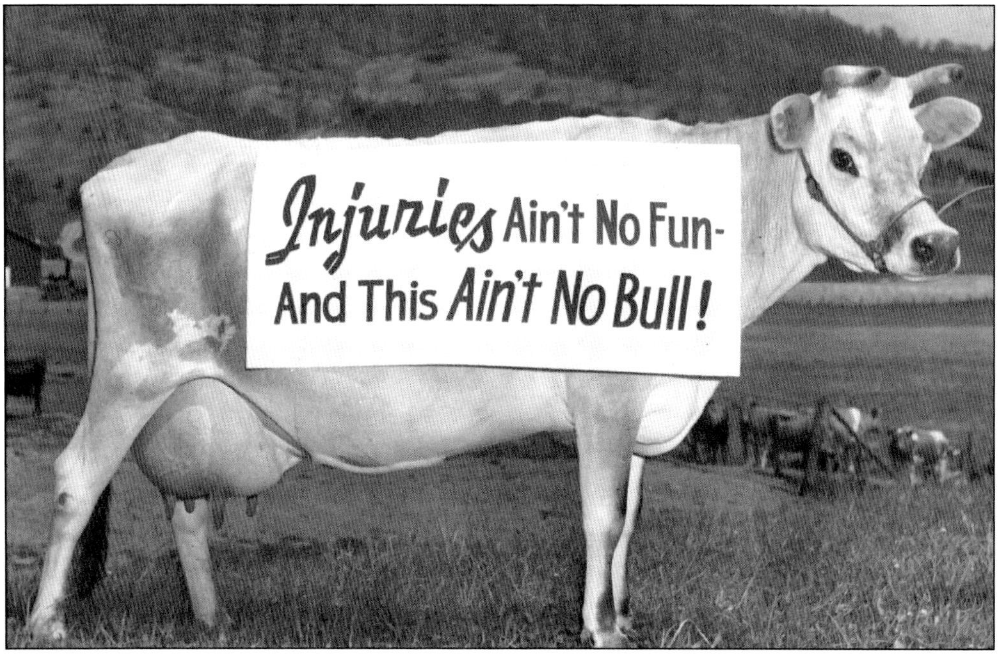

ACCIDENTS. With its complex machines, mill work could be dangerous at times, and Champion pushed hard to enforce workplace safety, tallying injury-free days on a board and keeping up signs as reminders to stay alert. Despite the safety-conscious environment, some workers lost limbs, suffered severe injuries, and even died in accidents. A 1919 report of one such accident involved a man who was hospitalized after being hit by falling building material. He suffered broken ribs, a fractured spine, a bruised head, and a cut over his left eye. (Courtesy of the Canton Historical Museum.)

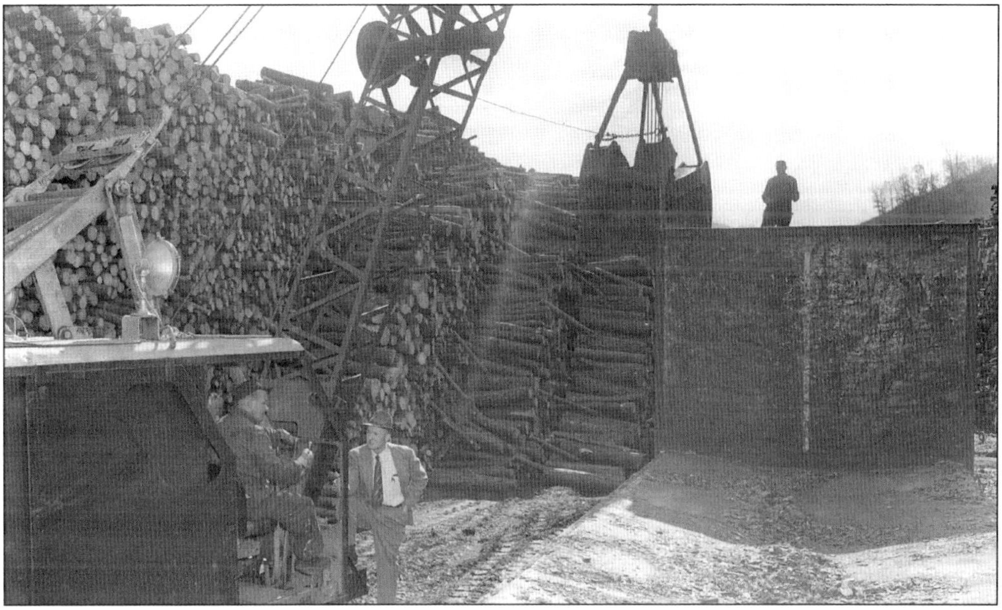

Wood Products. Incoming train cars loaded with wood had to be carefully measured before entering machines. Champion's chestnut extract production ended on June 11, 1951, after a devastating chestnut blight wiped out much of the American chestnut trees in the eastern United States, depleting supplies for Champion. The Canton mill was once the world's largest producer of 25-percent chestnut extract, shipping to 12 foreign countries, including China, Japan, South Africa, and New Zealand. In its prime, the extract operation at Champion churned out 300 barrels of extract every 24 hours. Over its 43 years, the mill produced more than 2.58 billion pounds of extract, enough to fill 32,500 train carloads. Seen below on their last day on the extract crew are, from left to right, (first row) J.L. Ledford, Dan Stockton, J.M. Taylor, R.M. Plemmons, and Jim Nanney; (second row) B.W. Medford, N.K. Drake, and superintendent W.C. Moody. (Both, courtesy of the Canton Historical Museum.)

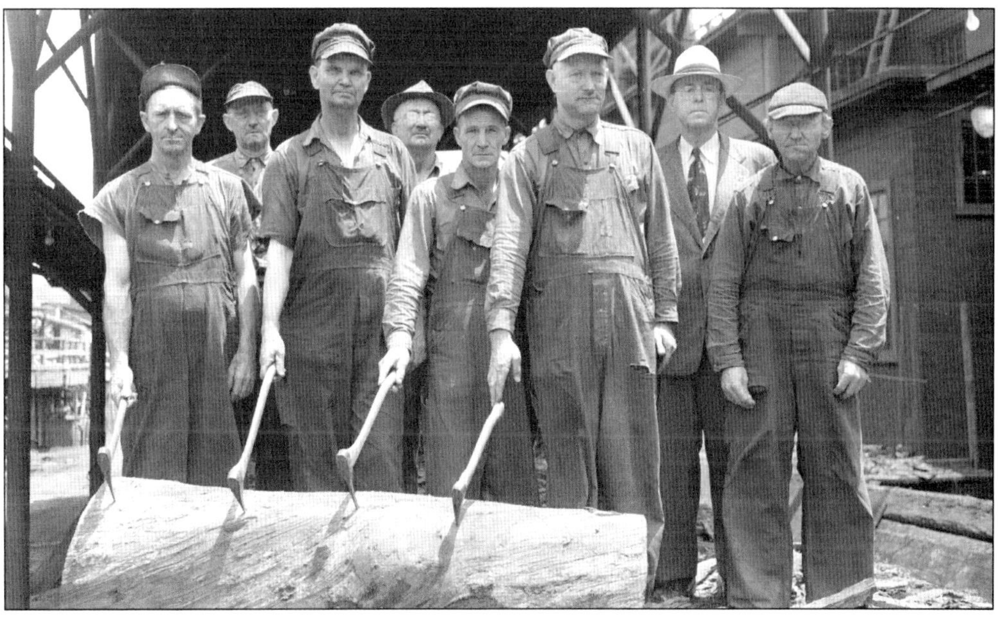

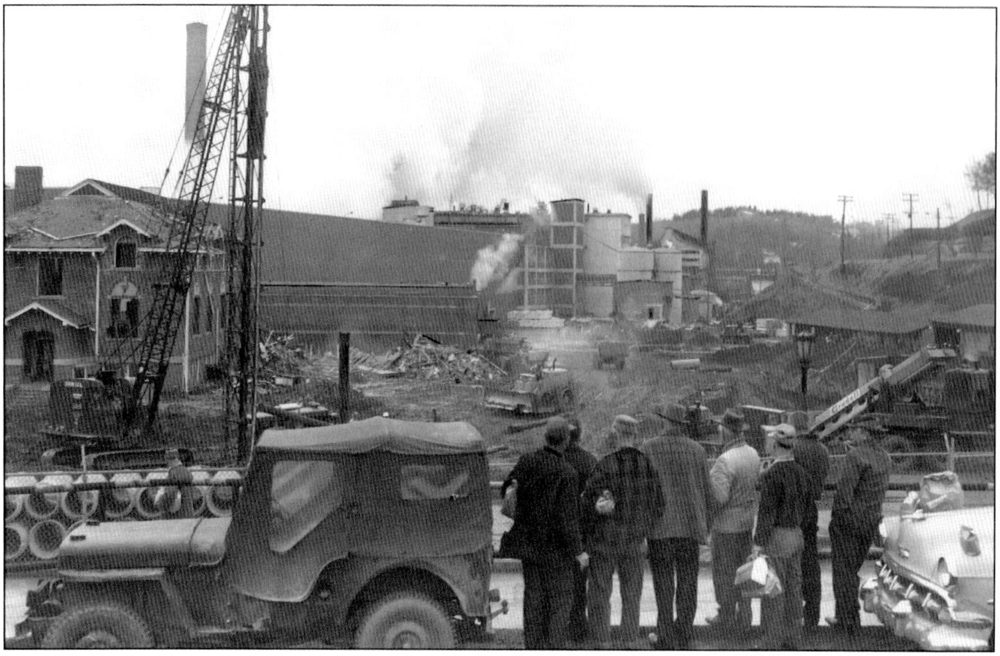

Machine No. 19 Construction. This view of the construction site in January 1964 shows plans for Champion's continual upgrades and expansion. However, in this case, the addition of a major machine in the mill also meant the demolition of one of Canton's beloved icons, the Champion YMCA building (left). With a sizable contribution from Reuben B. Robertson, a second YMCA was built on Park Street, on the current site of Bethel Christian Academy. (Courtesy of the Canton Historical Museum.)

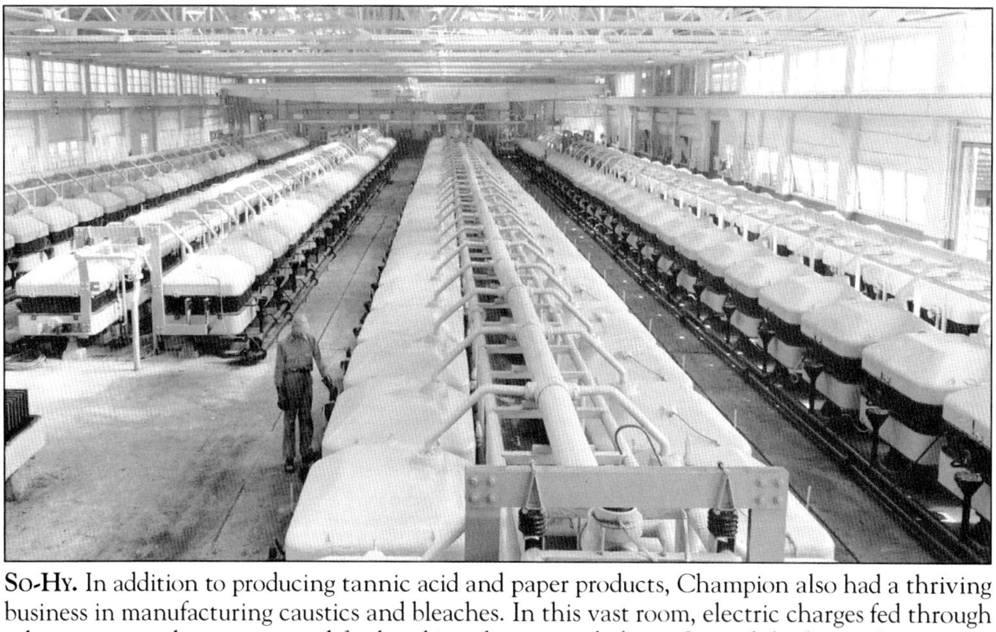

So-Hy. In addition to producing tannic acid and paper products, Champion also had a thriving business in manufacturing caustics and bleaches. In this vast room, electric charges fed through saltwater created a caustic used for breaking down wood chips. One of the by-products was a bleach that Champion sold under the name So-Hy. It was marketed and shipped throughout the Southeast. (Courtesy of the Canton Historical Museum.)

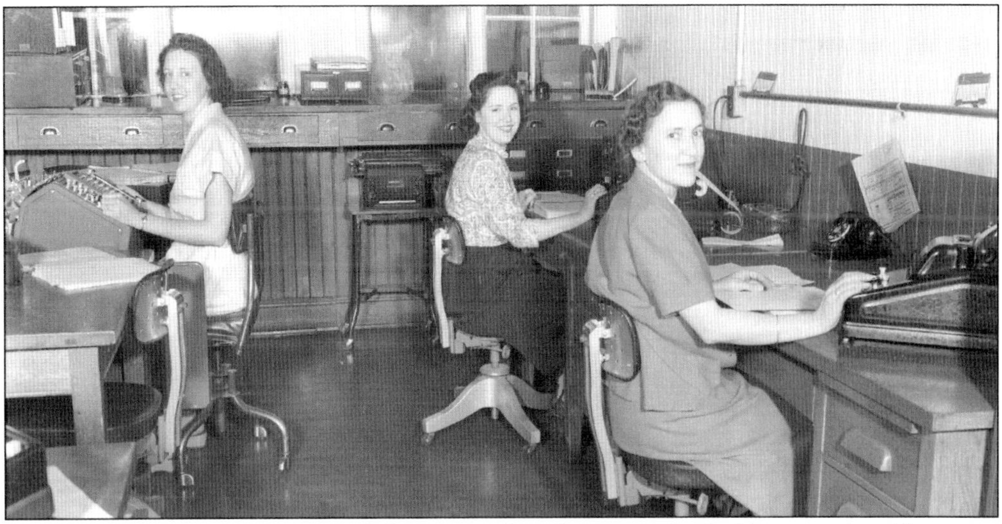

CHAMPION CREDIT UNION. Founded in 1932, the Champion Credit Union is the oldest non-postal credit union of its kind in North Carolina. While many of its original members were Champion employees and its original offices were at the mill to provide customer convenience, the credit union is open to the general public. Its headquarters are in downtown Canton, and its more than 20,000 customers live throughout western North Carolina. (Courtesy of the Canton Historical Museum.)

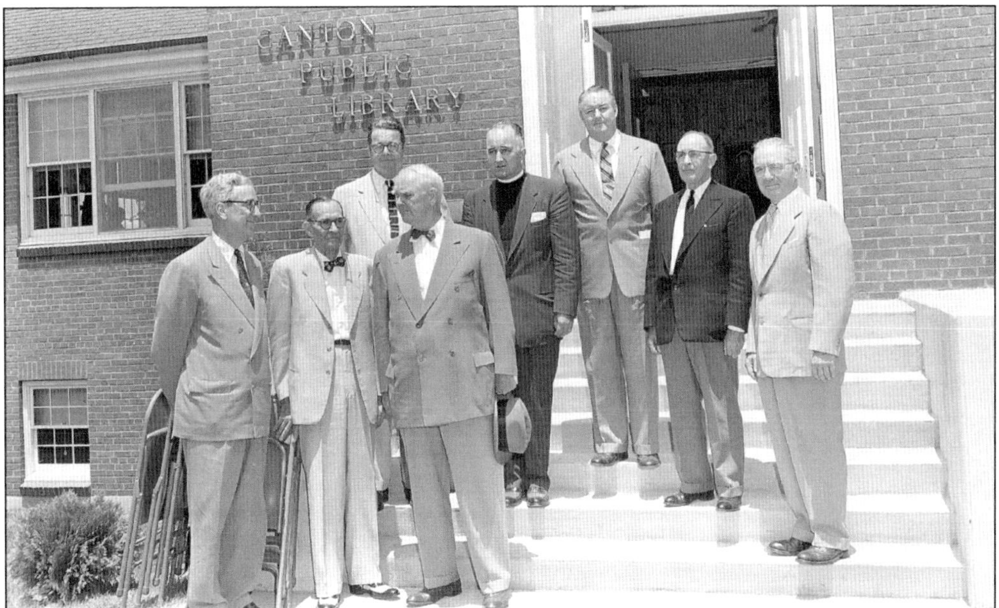

CANTON PUBLIC LIBRARY OPENING. Under Reuben B. Robertson's leadership, Champion funded many community programs, including the donation of land for the town's library. Among the dignitaries who gathered at the 1954 opening of the library on Park Street are, from left to right, (first row) North Carolina treasury secretary Brandon Hodges, North Carolina governor William Umstead, and Robertson. Third from the right on the steps is Reuben B. Robertson Jr. The library building is now the home of the Canton Historical Museum. (Courtesy of the Canton Historical Museum.)

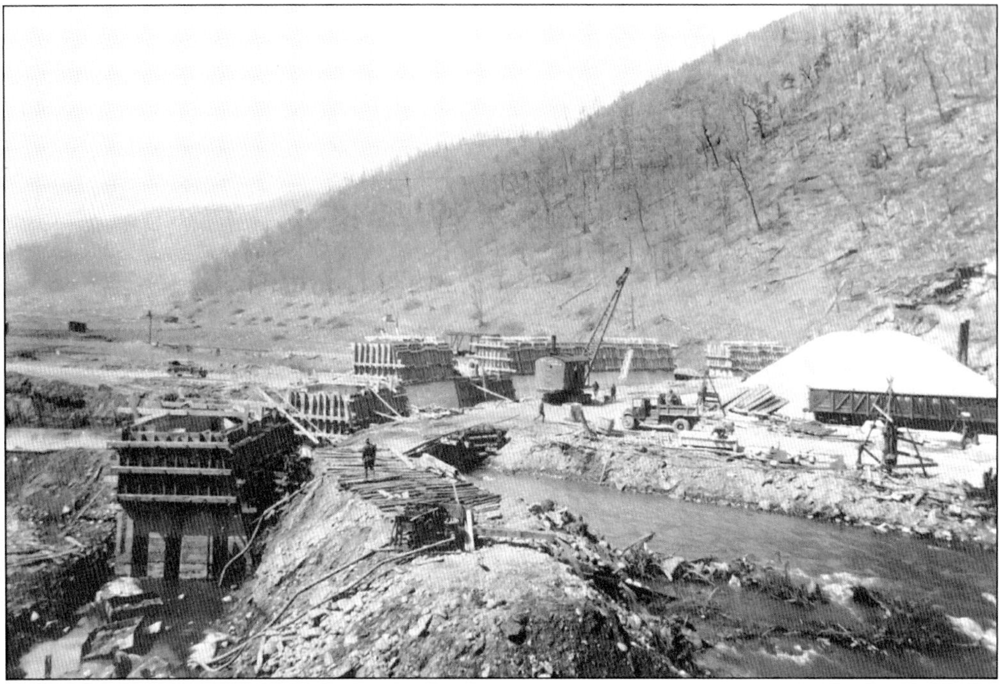

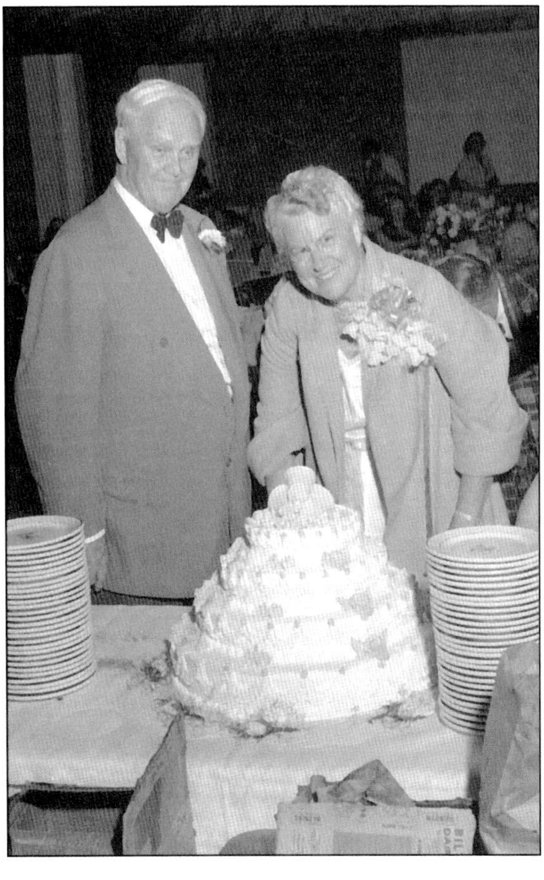

LAKE LOGAN. Champion sold approximately 90,000 acres of forest to the federal government to help create the Great Smoky Mountains National Park. Money from that sale helped to pay for the Lake Logan dam construction, shown in this 1932 photograph. Lake Logan, named after Peter G. Thomson's son, served as a water source for paper operations at the Champion mill in Canton. Today, it is a recreational site for a conference center run by the Episcopal Diocese of Western North Carolina. (Courtesy of the Canton Historical Museum.)

HOPE ROBERTSON. Reuben B. Robertson's wife, Hope, was a constant source of strength and support for the Champion executive. In 1953, the Robertson family dedicated Camp Hope in honor of her, pictured here. The 101-acre site along the East Fork of the Pigeon River became a scenic getaway for generations of Canton residents and a popular place for banquets, Boy Scout gatherings, sports camps, and company-related events. (Courtesy of the Canton Historical Museum.)

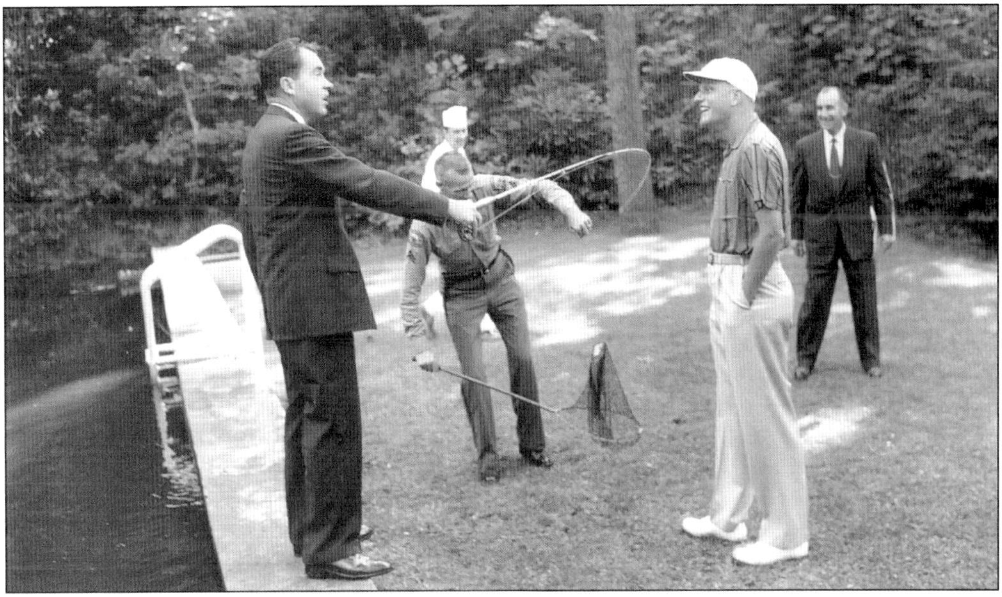

Politics at Play. In 1955, Vice Pres. Richard Nixon (above, far left) came to western North Carolina and addressed religious assemblies at Montreat, Ridgecrest, and Lake Junaluska during a two-day visit. He also met with Christian evangelist Rev. Billy Graham (above, second from right) at Lake Logan. Nixon may have been plotting his presidential future at the time. From 1955 to 1957, Reuben B. Robertson Jr. (second from left below, with Champion employees) served as the deputy secretary of defense in Pres. Dwight D. Eisenhower's administration and was considered a possible vice presidential candidate on the Republican ticket when Nixon eventually ran for president in 1960. However, those plans ended tragically when the younger Robertson was struck by a car and killed instantly after stopping to check on people involved in a car accident on March 13, 1960. (Both, courtesy of the Canton Historical Museum.)

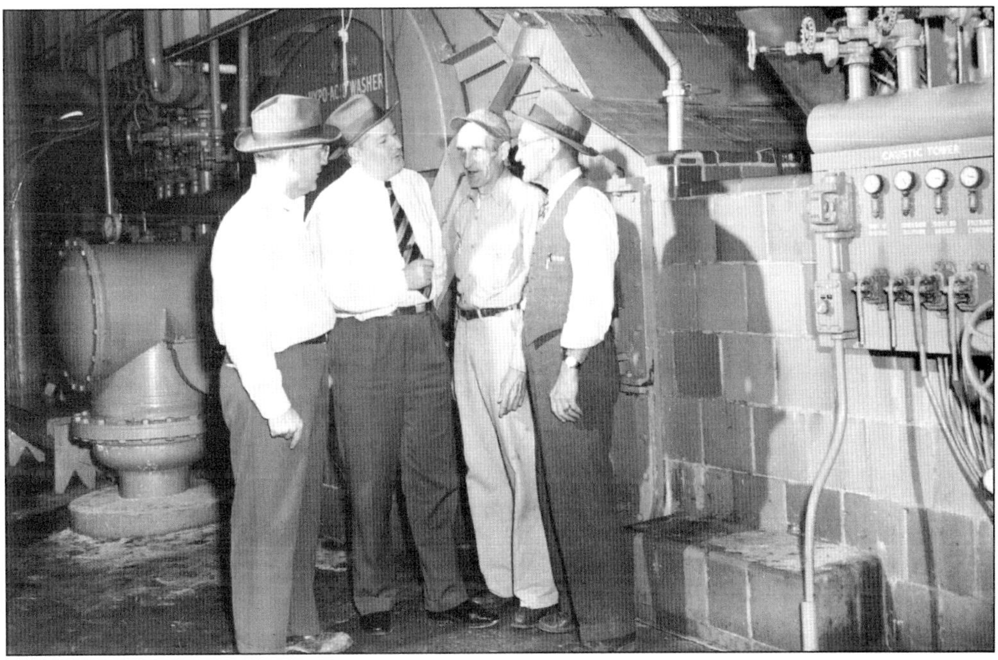

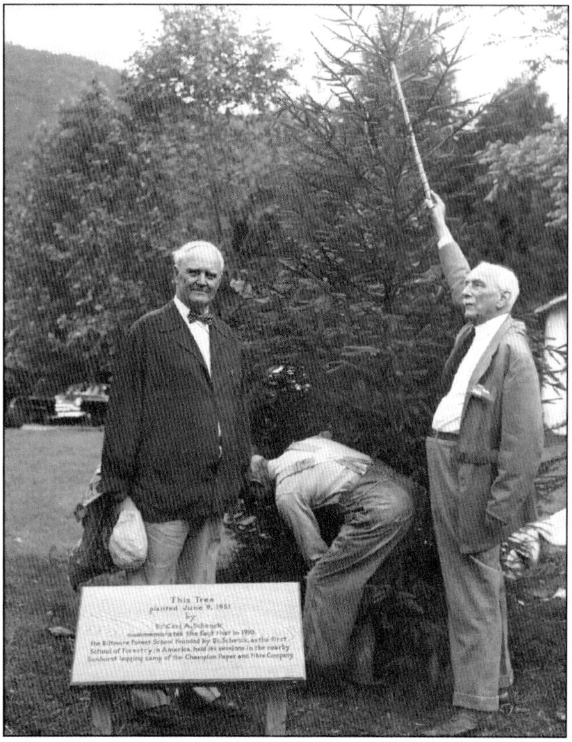

CRADLE OF FORESTRY. In 1910, German-born forester Dr. Carl Schenck (right) established the Biltmore Forest School, the first forestry school in the United States, on the grounds of the Biltmore Estate, the home of the famously wealthy George Vanderbilt. After a falling-out with Vanderbilt, Schenck left the estate and taught sessions at various locations, including Sunburst, which was owned by Champion. This 1951 photograph with Reuben B. Robertson (left) shows a tree that was planted to commemorate the founding of the forestry school. (Courtesy of the Canton Historical Museum.)

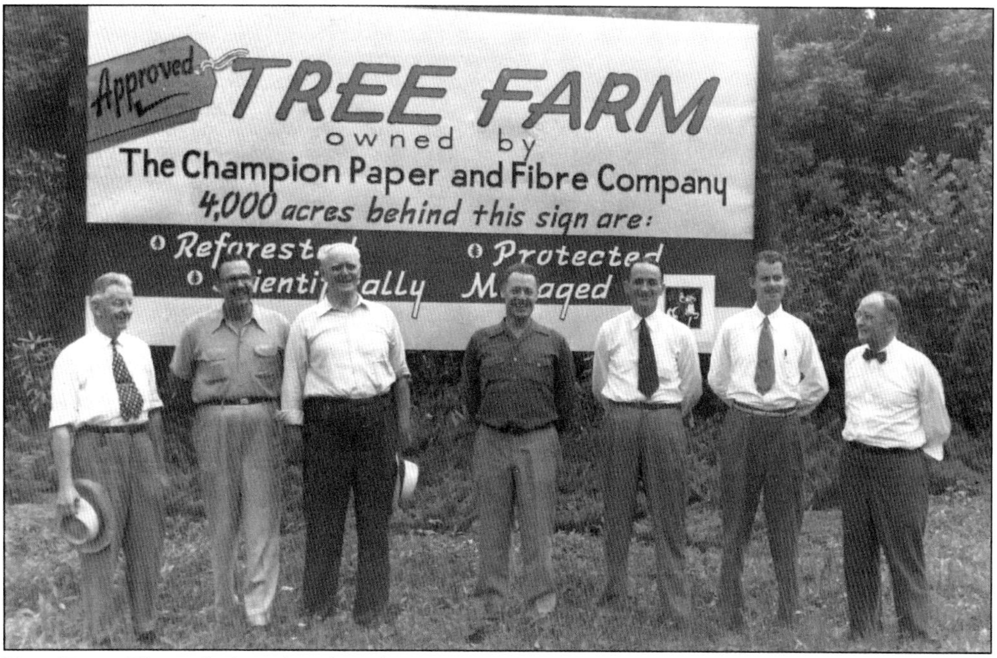

TREE FARM. Through their decades of operation, Champion executives understood that a business reliant on trees meant they had to be replenished, making them a renewable resource for the future. For every tree the company cut down, more had to be planted in its place. As this sign proclaims, Champion set aside thousands of acres of its holdings to manage and reforest. (Courtesy of Zelda Ponder.)

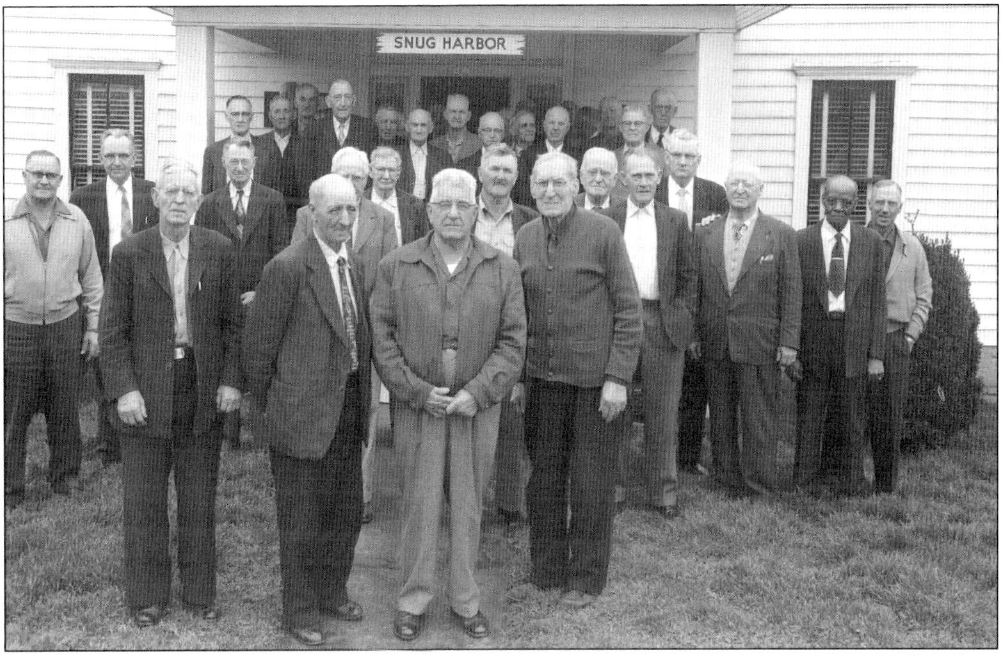

SNUG HARBOR. In 1953, Champion retirees were given a place to come together for fellowship, shared meals, games of shuffleboard and horseshoes, and well-deserved hours of relaxation. Reuben B. Robertson Sr. established the building as a way of honoring loyal employees. A car was even made available to visit Snug Harbor members who were homebound or sick. (Courtesy of the Canton Historical Museum.)

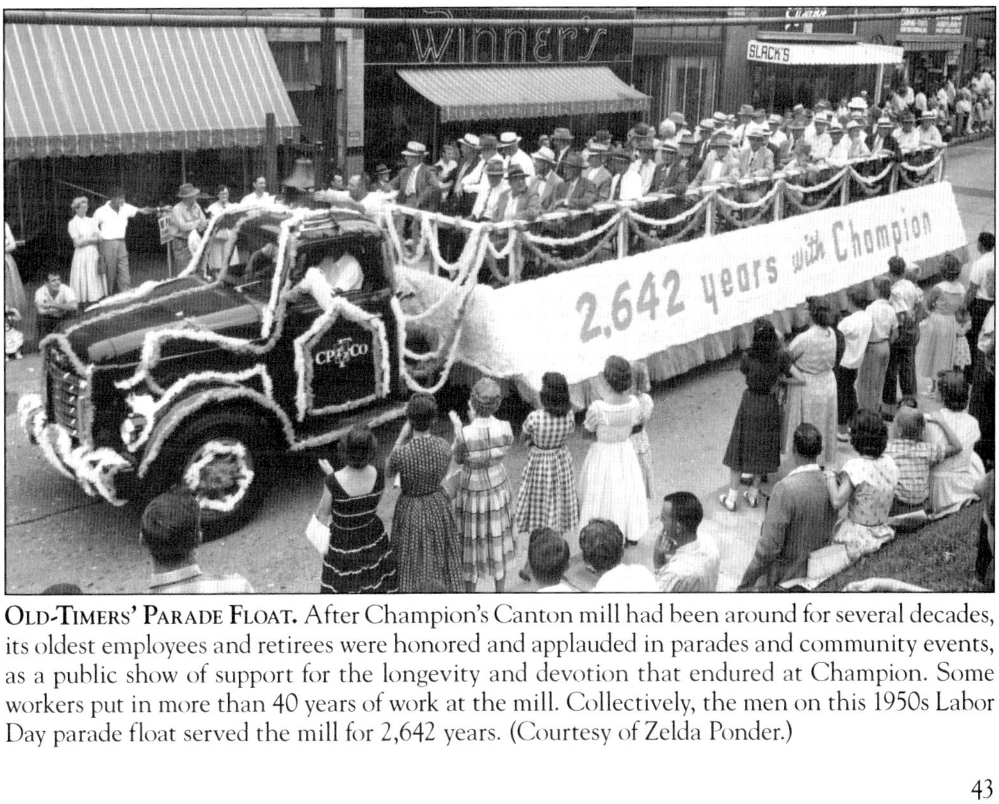

OLD-TIMERS' PARADE FLOAT. After Champion's Canton mill had been around for several decades, its oldest employees and retirees were honored and applauded in parades and community events, as a public show of support for the longevity and devotion that endured at Champion. Some workers put in more than 40 years of work at the mill. Collectively, the men on this 1950s Labor Day parade float served the mill for 2,642 years. (Courtesy of Zelda Ponder.)

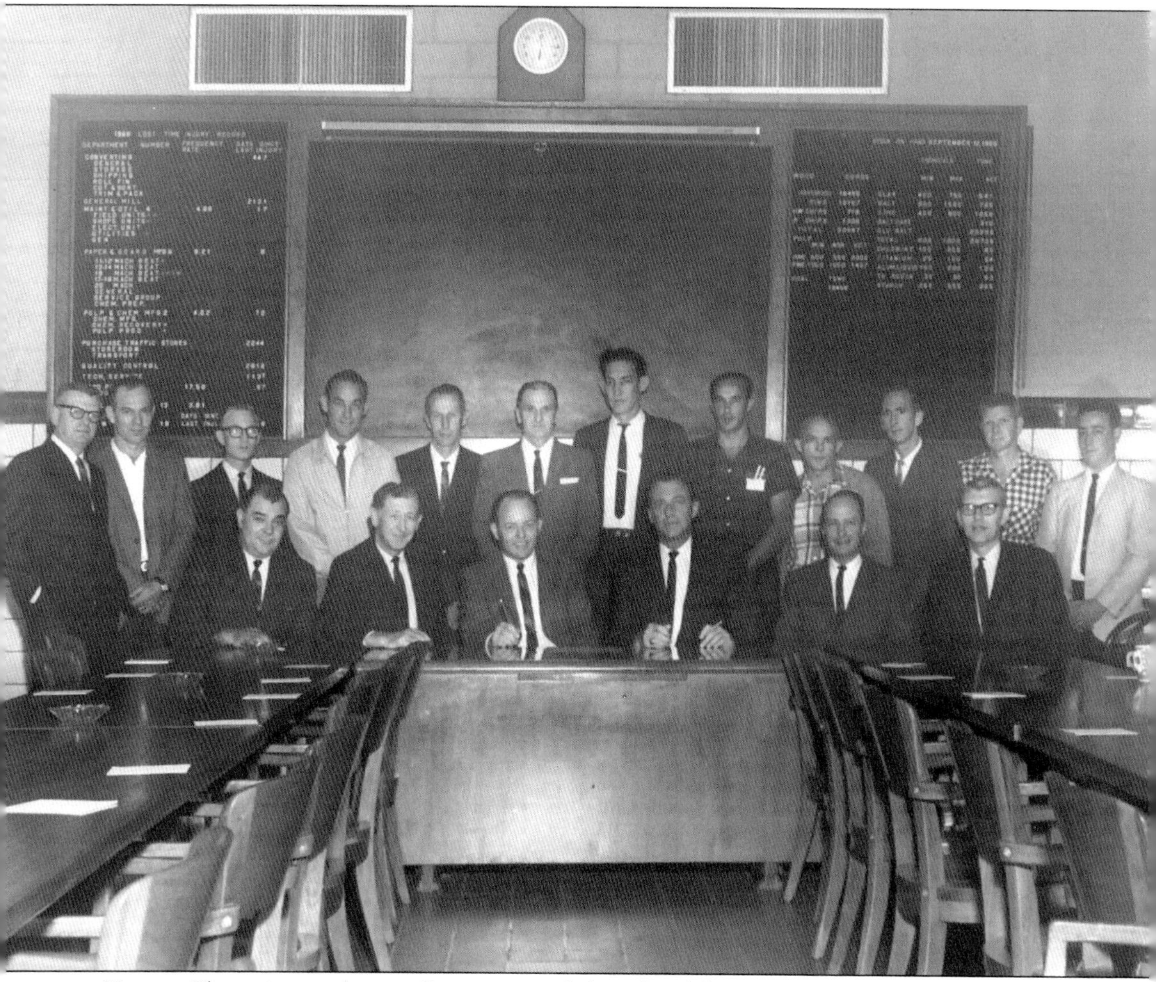

Union. Champion workers in Canton signed their first labor agreement in 1966 after a vote of 841-726 in favor of forming a union, Smoky Mountain Local 507, which became part of the AFL-CIO. Charlie Cable (seated in front, third from left) served as Local 507's first president from 1966 to 1970. A longtime Champion employee, Cable represented Canton's union at international conferences and later became an ordained Baptist minister. Champion vice president Robert Longbine (seated to the right of Cable) later became Champion's president from 1980–1987. Meeting in Canton, the union used the old Chevrolet dealership building and a lot on the old Sluder Furniture site as its headquarters. For decades, Champion executive Reuben B. Robertson Sr. fought warily against the union effort. In the winter of 1923–1924, after Champion cut wages and reduced hours during an economic downturn, workers went on strike. The plant halted operations. Robertson restored pay, welcomed back employees, and all was forgiven—as long as workers agreed not to unionize. Even after Robertson retired, he railed against unions forming at Champion. Workers often sought unions when job security was not assured. When Champion changed leadership in 1960 after the sudden death of Reuben B. Robertson Jr., the new president, Karl Bendetsen, signed off on cutting about a third of the workforce. March 31, 1961, would be known as "Black Friday" among Champion workers, who were let go through a series of severance packages and early retirements. (Courtesy of the Canton Historical Museum.)

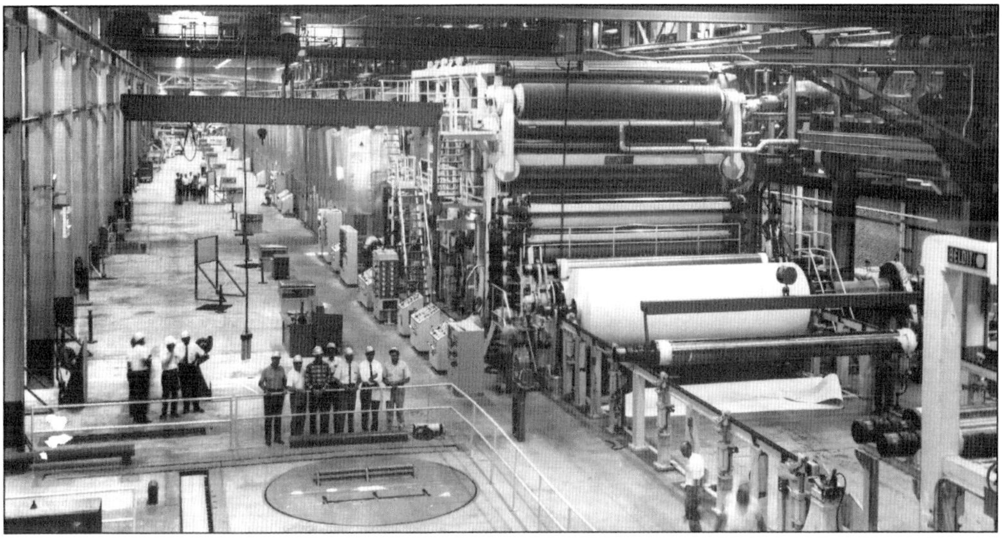

Pollution and Politics. From its earliest days, Champion's paper mill in Canton discharged waste into the Pigeon River, killing fish and turning the water a coffee color. By the 1970s, environmentalists and the newly formed Environmental Protection Agency mobilized to speak out against pollution. However, tougher regulations were viewed locally as a threat that could shut down the mill, which employed nearly 3,000 workers at its peak. People living around Canton came to know the mill's foul odor as the "smell of money." North Carolina politicians such as Jim Hunt, seen below campaigning for governor and shaking hands with Champion employee Fred Riley, spoke in favor of keeping the Canton mill open. By the mid-1990s, Champion cut its Canton workforce to about 1,650 workers and invested $330 million to modernize the Canton mill and clean up the Pigeon River. Two decades later, the river is clean enough to run whitewater-rafting trips. Environmental watchdog groups continue to push for efforts to keep the river clean. (Both, courtesy of the Canton Historical Museum.)

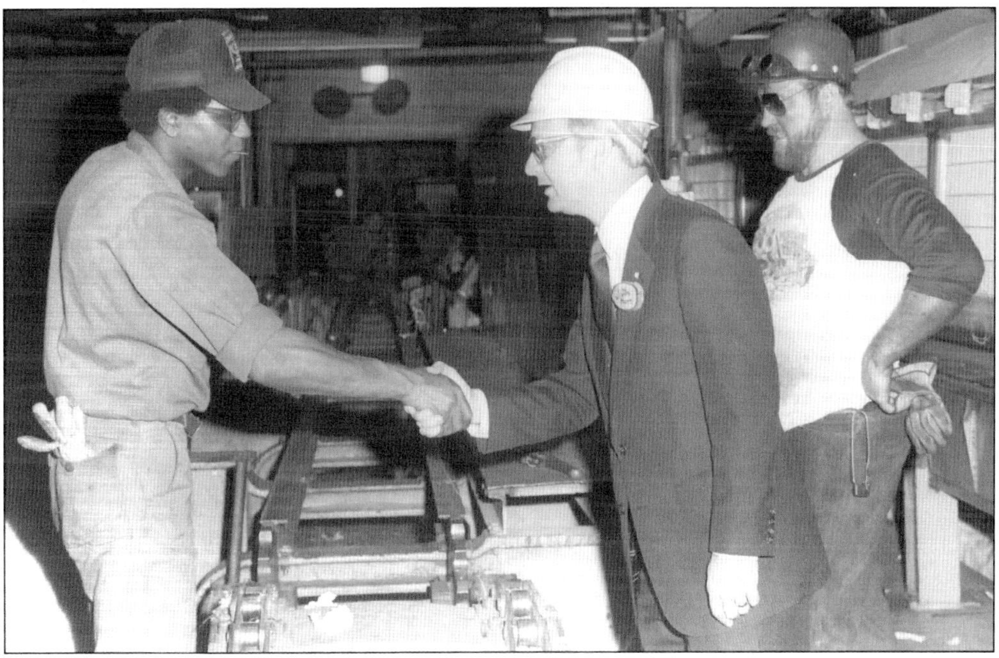

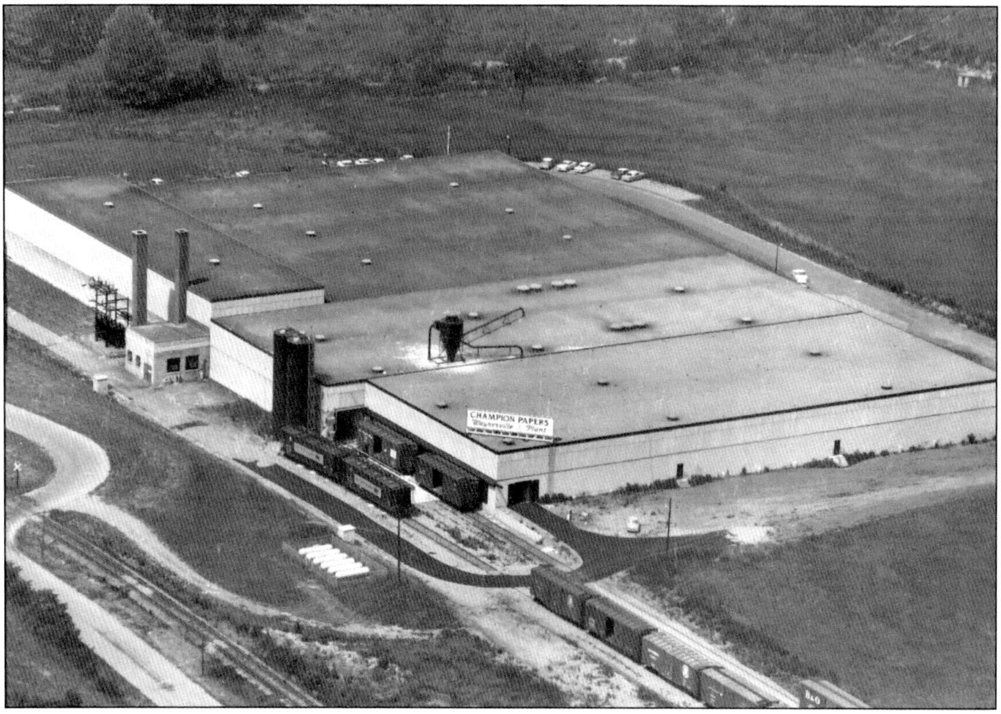

LITTLE CHAMPION. In June 1959, Champion purchased a packaging plant in Waynesville that would become known as Little Champion. In 1966, a majority of workers at this plant voted in favor of forming a union and merged with Local 507 in 1969. Little Champion would continue to be linked with the Canton mill in the following decades. (Courtesy of the Canton Historical Museum.)

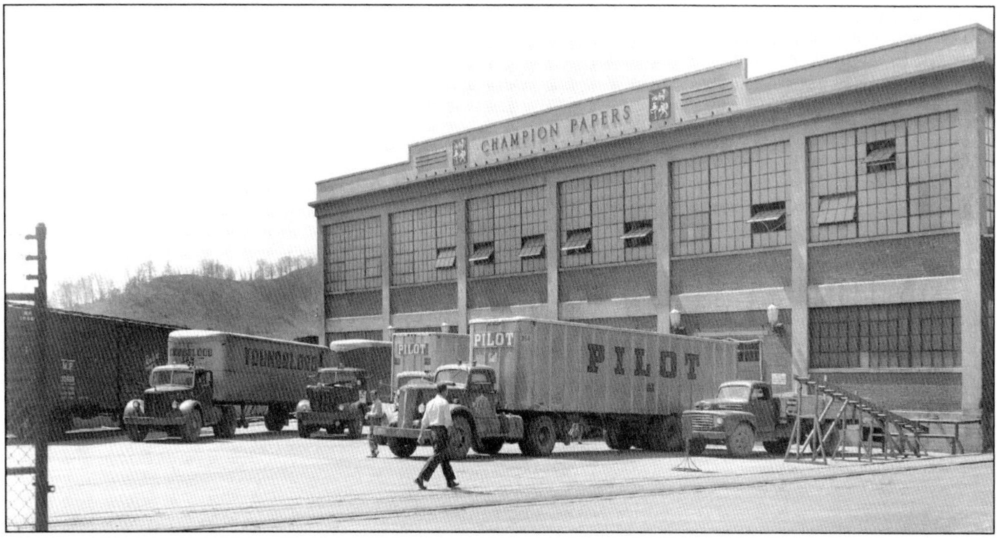

CHANGES. By the 1990s, Champion Fibre Company became Champion International. As the industry changed and out-of-state executives made decisions in faraway boardrooms, the Canton mill was put up for sale. In 1999, Canton's mill workers and management united with a New York City–based private equity firm to buy the mill and create a new name, Blue Ridge Paper Products, Inc. In 2007, the mill was sold once again to a global conglomerate known as Evergreen Packaging, headquartered in Memphis, Tennessee. (Courtesy of the Canton Historical Museum.)

Three

CHURCHES

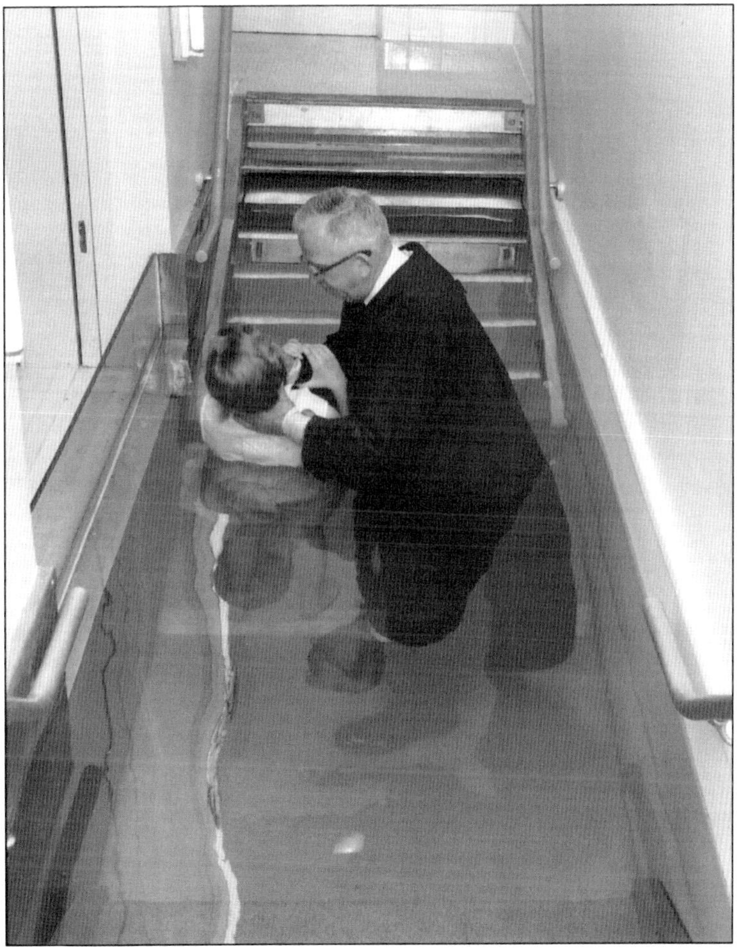

BAPTISM. Rev. Horace Smith, pastor of First Baptist Church of Canton, submerges a congregation member in the baptismal pool as one of the most sacred acts of the Christian faith. Early churches in the Canton area performed such baptisms in nearby creeks and rivers, with the entire congregation in attendance. (Courtesy of the Canton Historical Museum.)

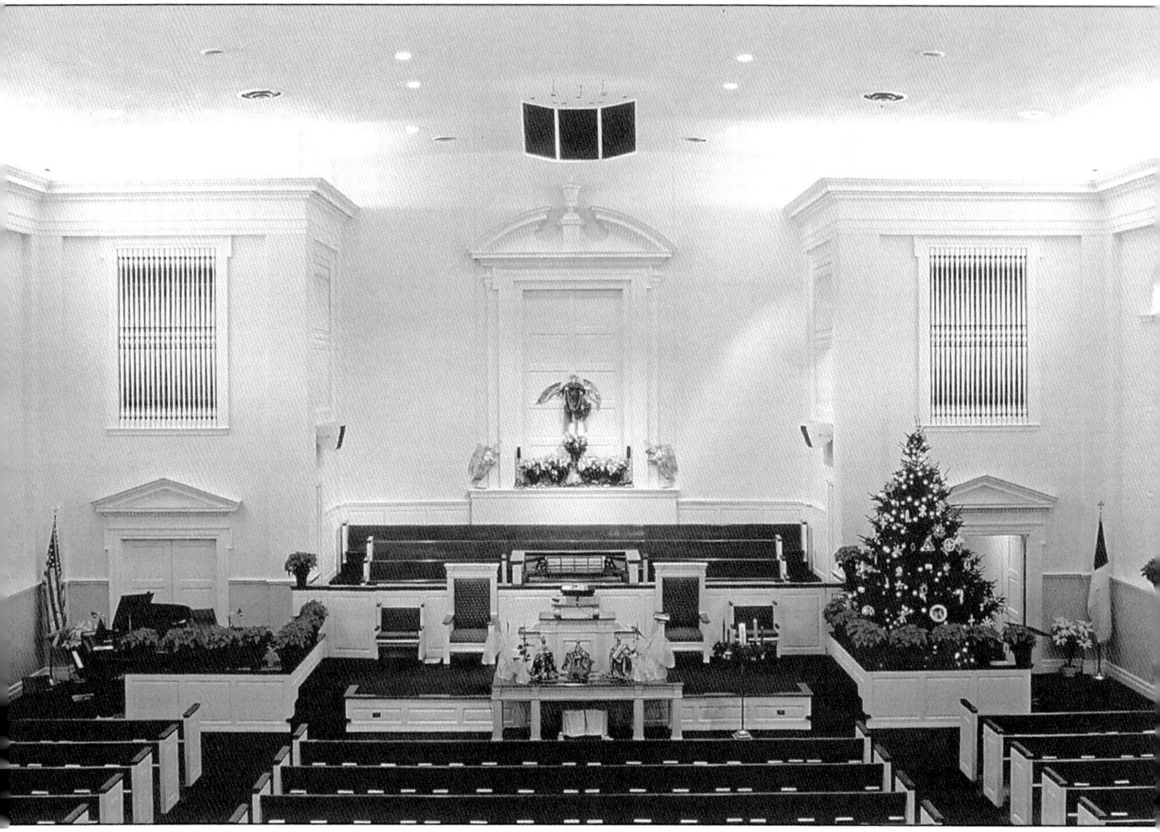

First Baptist Church of Canton. Organized in 1803, this congregation was one of the first denominations of any kind established in western North Carolina west of the French Broad River. Its first church structure was a simple log cabin built on a hill overlooking Canton, where the Locust Fields Cemetery is today. A second structure was built nearby, and a third church structure included a student academy, which is the origin of Academy Street, which passes by the cemetery. As the Champion mill attracted hundreds of employees and their families, Canton's population soared in the early 1900s. Between 1910 and 1915, the Locust Field Church was torn down and replaced by a larger brick church located down the hill. The growing congregation then took on the name First Baptist Church of Canton. In 1958, the church celebrated its newest building in the more spacious sanctuary seen here, which is still home to the congregation's worshippers. (Courtesy of Roland Osborne.)

Central United Methodist Church. Founded in 1875, Central United Methodist Church is the second-oldest church congregation within Canton's town limits. John Reno donated land for worshippers to hold meetings in an old school on Newfound Street. Reno also provided land for a Methodist campground along what is present-day Trammel Street. A fire in 1882 damaged some of the structures at this campground, which was a popular summer setting for weeklong meetings. The congregation moved into a brick building in 1910, seen below behind a women's church group in the 1920s, which was about the same time that the congregation adopted the name Central Methodist Church. In 1949, the present-day brick church, at right, was built. A blockish educational building was added in 1956. (Both, courtesy of Central United Methodist Church of Canton.)

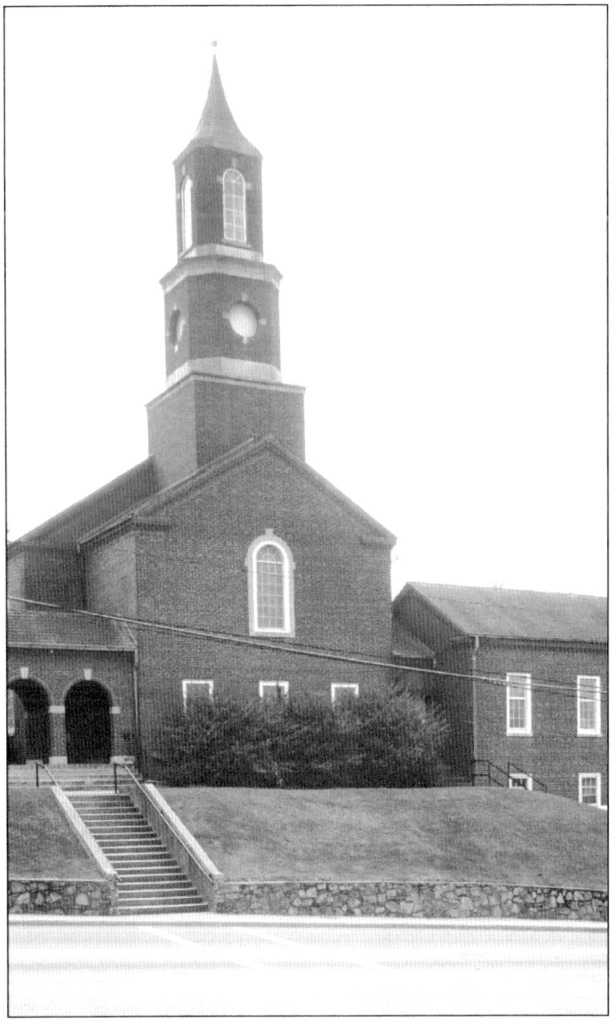

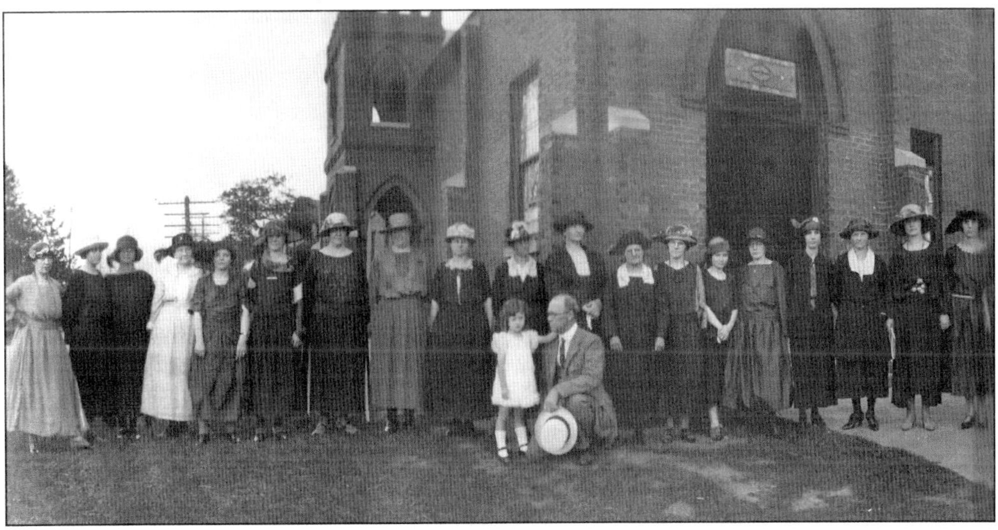

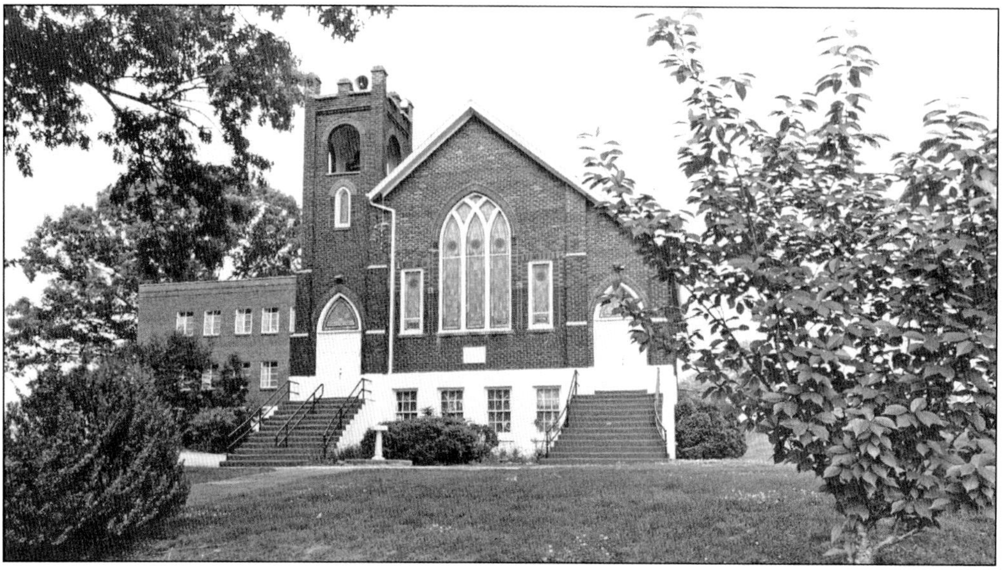

Morning Star United Methodist Church. Organized in the Dutch Cove community by German Lutherans in 1825, this church began under the direction of Rev. Nehemiah Bonham, a traveling preacher originally from Virginia. The original structure was a log house, which was replaced by other structures over the years. In 1866, the congregation decided to change over to the Methodist denomination. More than a century later, in 1968, it took on its present name, Morning Star United Methodist Church. (Courtesy of Roland Osborne.)

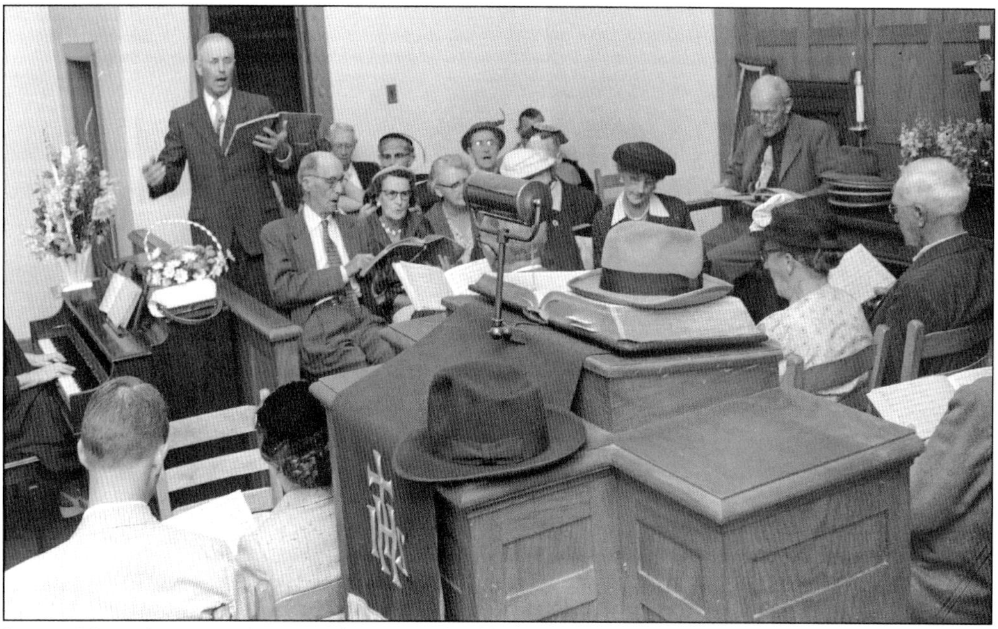

Shape-Note Singing. As part of its annual Old Folks Day celebration at Morning Star Church, the choir sings hymns in the Christian Harmony shape-note tradition. This singing program originally began at Locust Old Fields Church as early as 1891 and shifted to Morning Star around 1910. Shape-note singing uses geometrical shapes as notes on a musical scale. The choir finds harmony by singing the musical "do-re-mi" syllables first and then sings the lyrics to the hymns. (Courtesy of the Canton Historical Museum.)

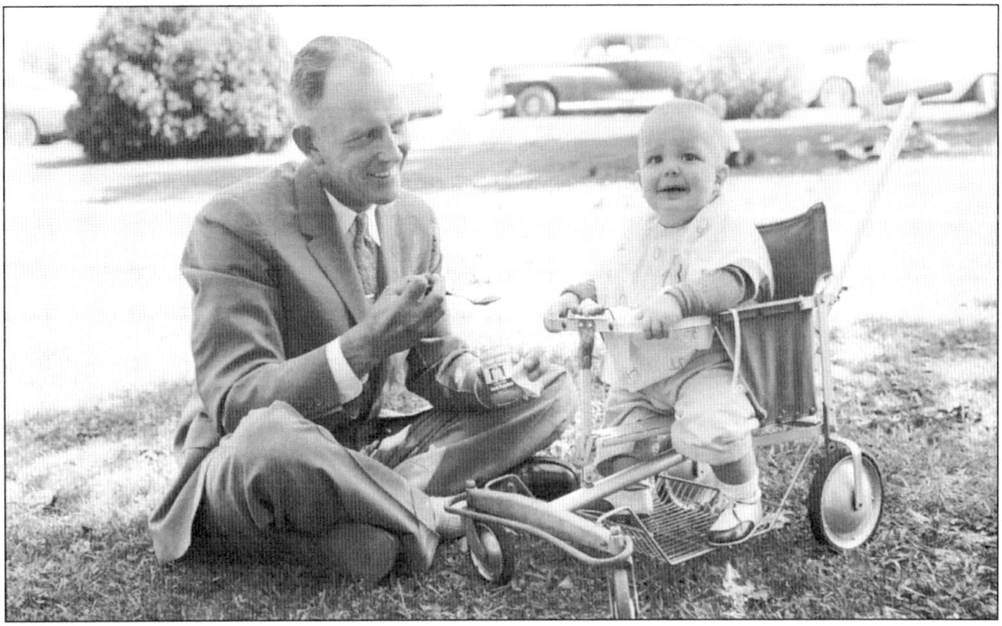

OLD FOLKS DAY. As part of a time-honored tradition at Morning Star United Methodist Church, members of the congregation in Dutch Cove hold a special celebration each year on the second Sunday in September to recognize the elders of the community, share fellowship with a picnic lunch, and sing hymns. After the church service, the congregation feasts outside, with a bountiful spread of chicken and dumplings, beef, garden vegetables, platters of biscuits, and plenty of homemade pies and cakes. The program at Morning Star has become a popular annual event, drawing people from all over the United States. (Both, courtesy of the Canton Historical Museum.)

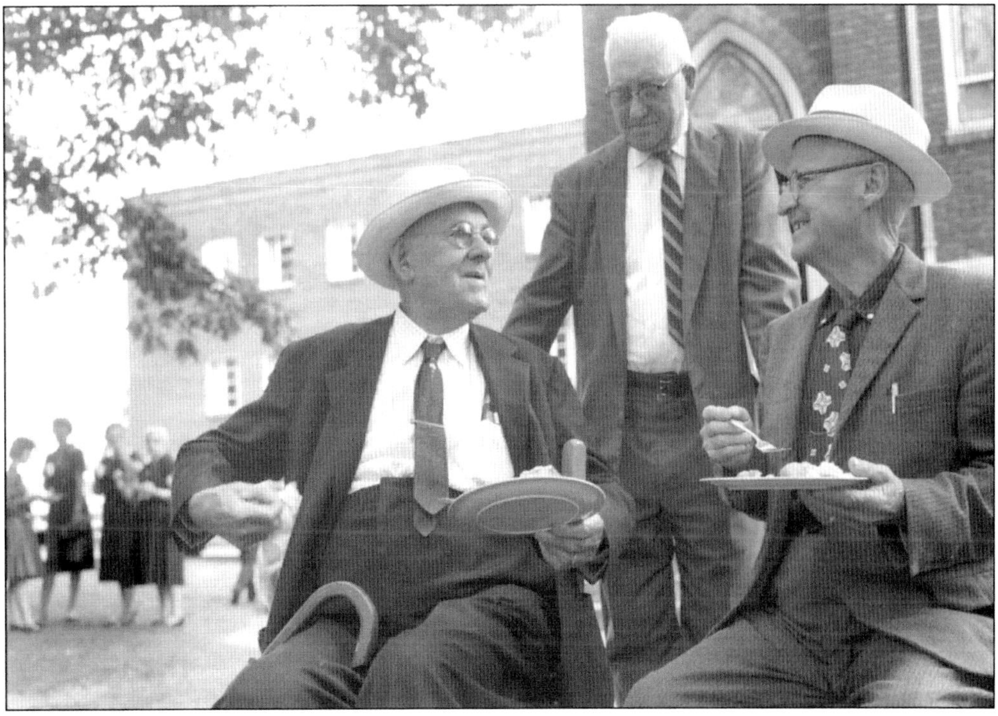

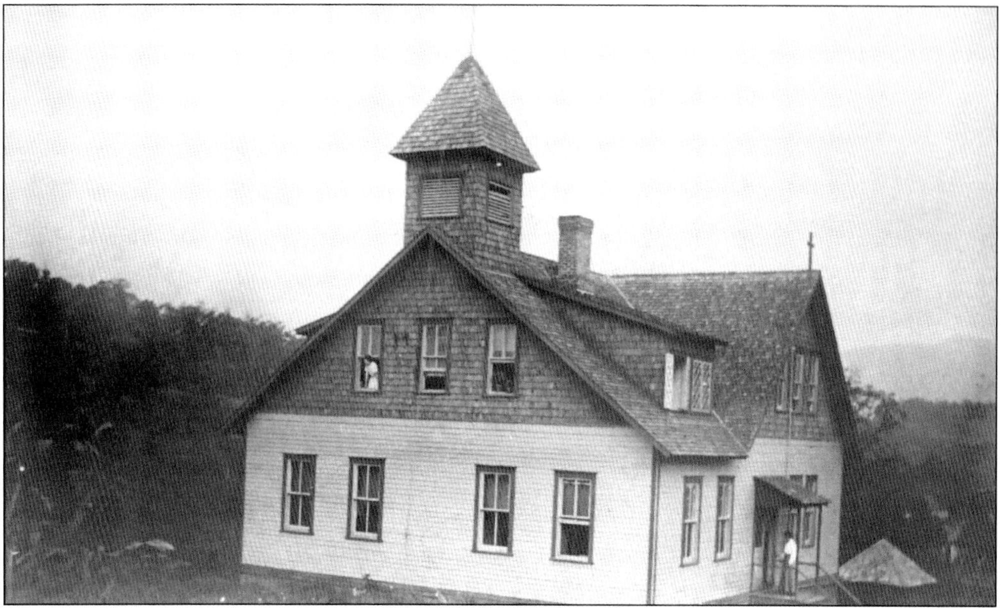

St. Andrew's Episcopal Church. An Episcopal mission church and school (above) began in the Fibreville section of Canton in 1906 to minister to incoming mill workers. After an outbreak of typhoid fever, the mission house was sold to Champion and converted into a hospital. The congregation found a new home on its current site on Academy Street. Men of the church traveled to Sunburst and loaded up river rock, which was hauled by train to build the new church (below) in the early 1920s. Stained-glass windows are found over the altar and at the rear of the sanctuary. St. Andrew's earned parish status in 1960. Though a small congregation, the church is active in local charities and continues its outreach missions in the community. (Above, courtesy of the Canton Historical Museum; below, courtesy of Roland Osborne.)

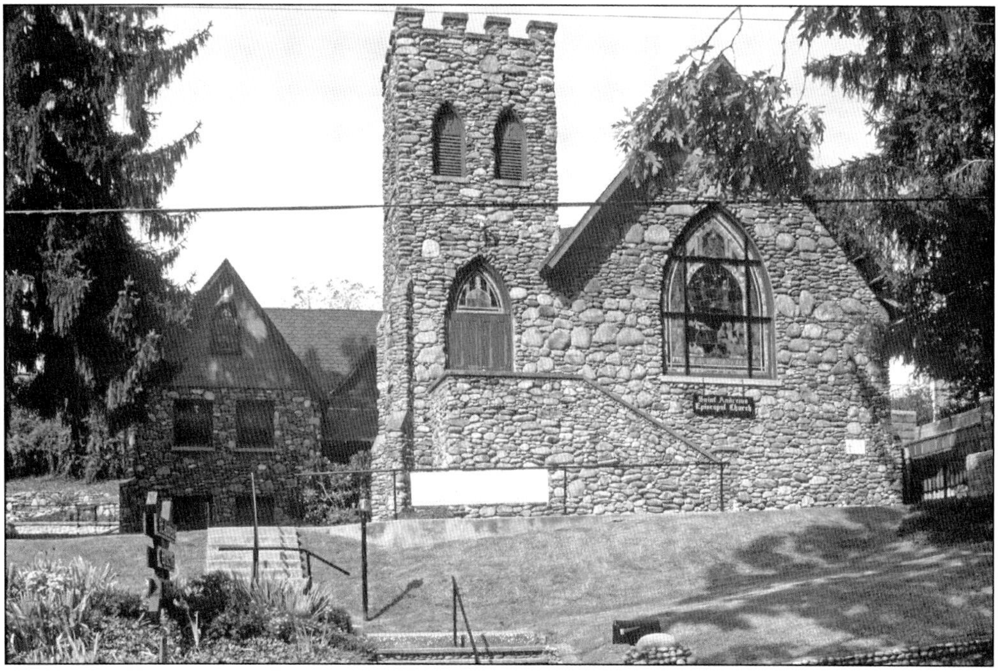

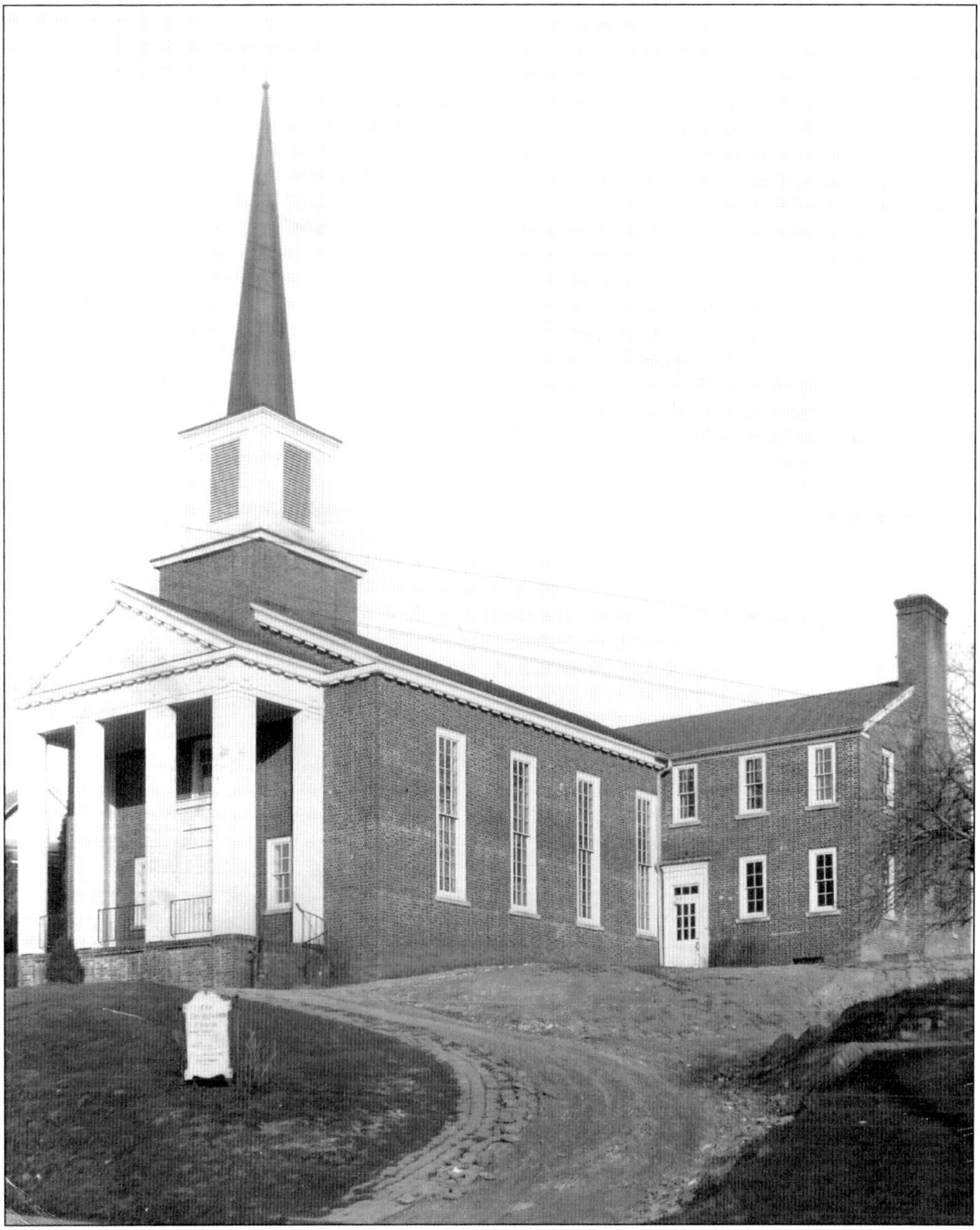

Canton Presbyterian Church. Organized in 1904 by a commission of eight charter members, the original Canton Presbyterian Church was a modest building that included a pyramidal roof and bell tower. Before a church building could be constructed, however, members of the congregation met at a store on Main Street in downtown Canton. Rev. J.C. Hardin served as the church's first pastor from 1904 to 1907. Mary Fuller was the mission school's first teacher. As the congregation grew, a second structure, located at its present-day site, was built in the late 1930s. Rev. George Bradley Hammond, the church's pastor at the time and also an architect, designed the plans. Rev. J.C. Lime served the church's longest-running pastorate from 1950 to 1970. During his tenure, a Sunday school building was added to the side of the church in 1958. (Courtesy of the Canton Historical Museum.)

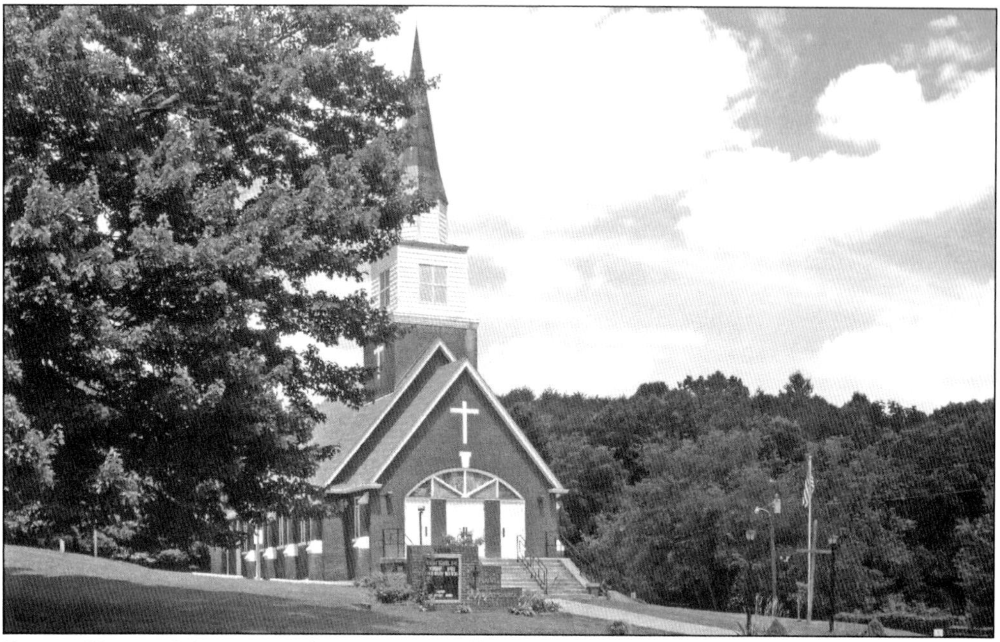

Plains United Methodist Church. Arnold Plains Church dates back to 1842, when Enoch Hall provided six acres to build a log cabin church on the eastern side of Canton. Part of the congregation moved in 1875 to establish what would become Central United Methodist Church. Another faction moved to establish Harmony Grove Methodist Church in the late 1800s, but later reunited with Plains in 1941. The present-day Plains United Methodist Church building was completed in 1951. (Courtesy of Roland Osborne.)

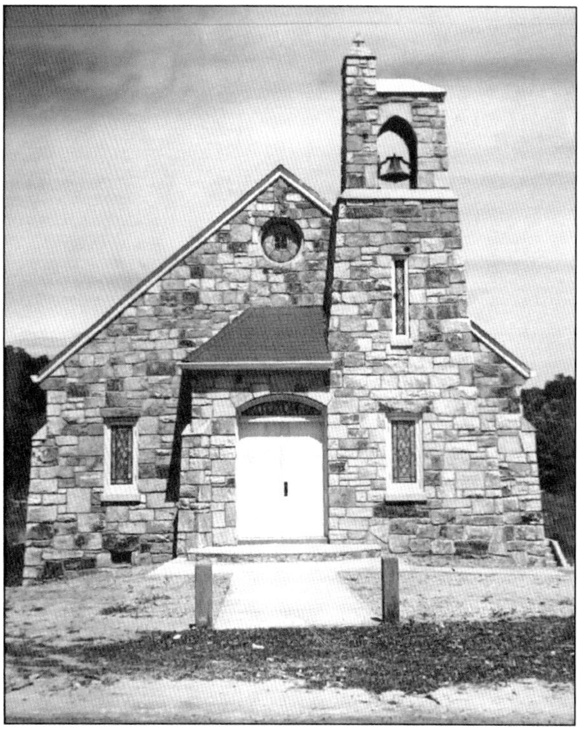

Rockwood United Methodist Church. In 1893, Calvin Clark donated a plot of land for a church that became known as Clark's Chapel. The church operated within the Canton, Bethel, and Clyde circuits until 1939, when new land was found to build another church. The new church received a new name, Rockwood Methodist Church. An educational wing was completed in 1979. (Courtesy of the Canton Historical Museum.)

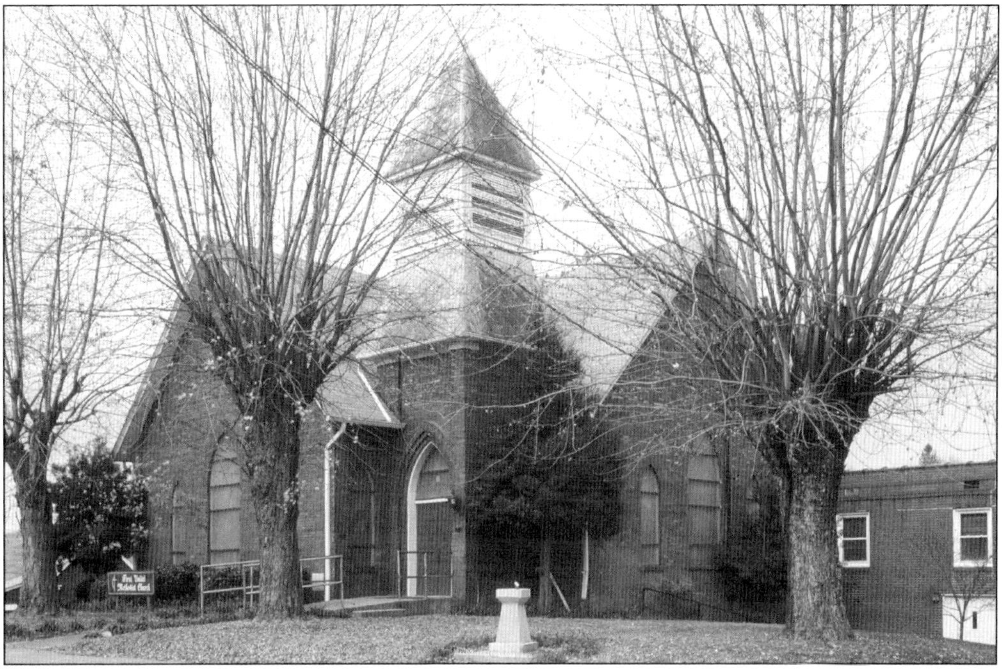

First United Methodist Church. This congregation, formed in 1906, originally met for worship at Canton Presbyterian Church, joined the Blue Ridge Conference in 1907, and erected its sanctuary two years later. The brick building is believed to be one of the oldest surviving church structures in Canton. Located on Newfound Street, the Gothic Revival–style church includes a bell tower and stained-glass windows. Subsequent interior renovations took place in 1946 and 1959. (Courtesy of Roland Osborne.)

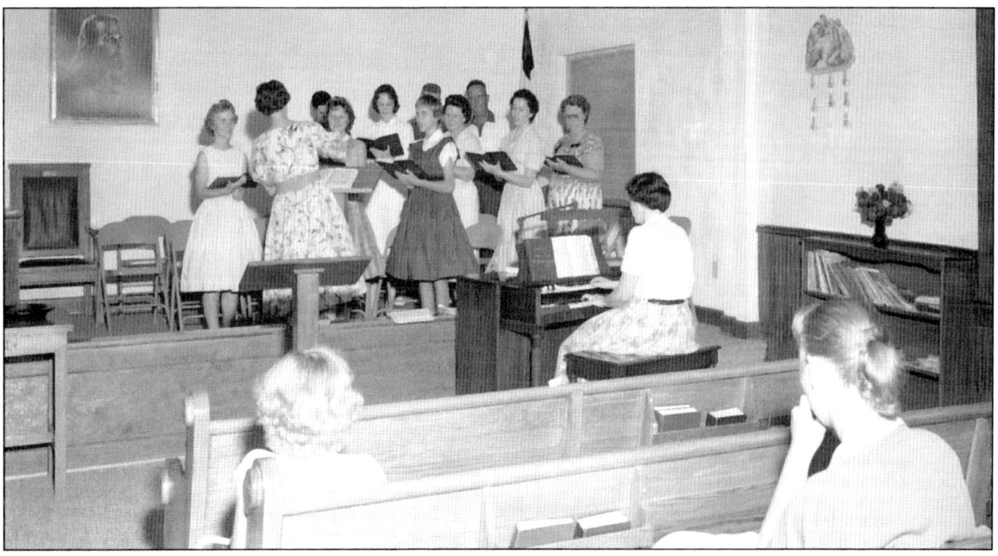

Wesleyan Church. The Wesleyan Church of Canton began in the midst of the Great Depression, with 12 charter members at a tent meeting on July 16, 1934. A church was built within a year and a parsonage stood by 1941. Subsequent additions, such as a youth building, nursery, classrooms, and a pastor's study, were added in the 1950s. This photograph features a church choir rehearsal from June 1960. (Courtesy of the Canton Historical Museum.)

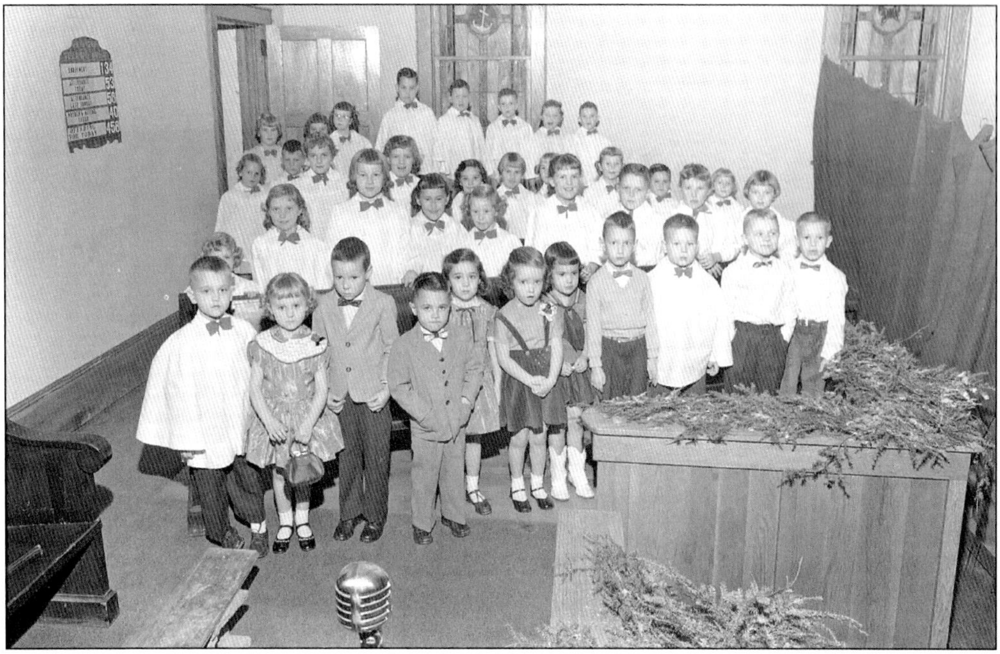

West Canton Baptist Church. This church began in 1916 as a missionary Baptist church. A two-room building known as the "sheep pen" provided worship services and Sunday school classes. The church's children's choir is seen above. West Canton Baptist Church held a service on January 7, 1917, with 33 people and a humble offering of 77¢. By the following year, a new church was erected in the Phillipsville community, with services held on the second and fourth Sundays of each month. The congregation continued to grow, and expanded in 1922. A larger church was built in 1946 (below) on Lowe Street in west Canton. (Both, courtesy of the Canton Historical Museum.)

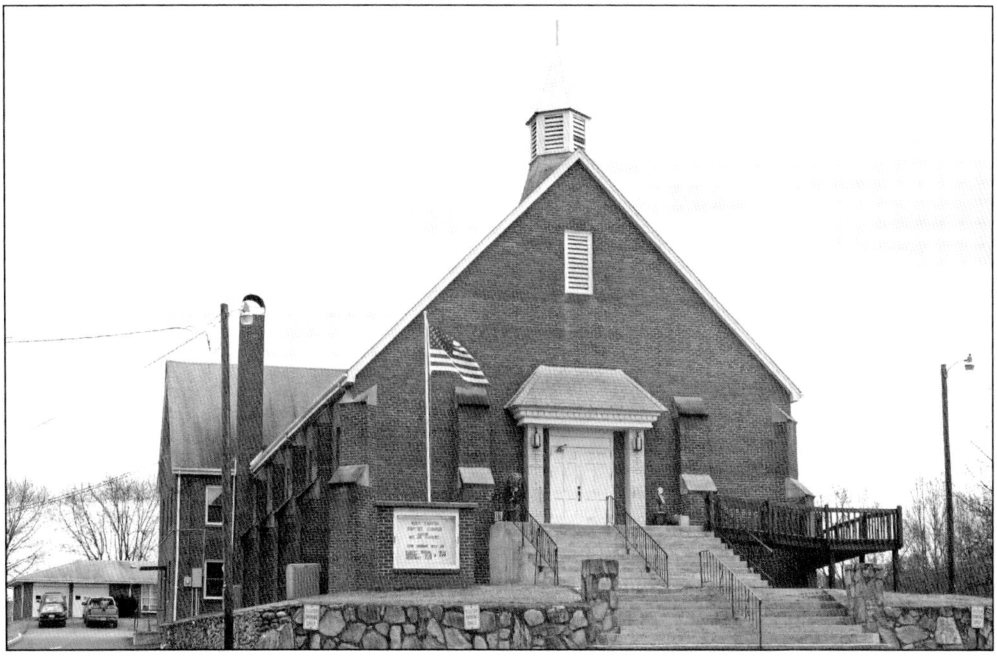

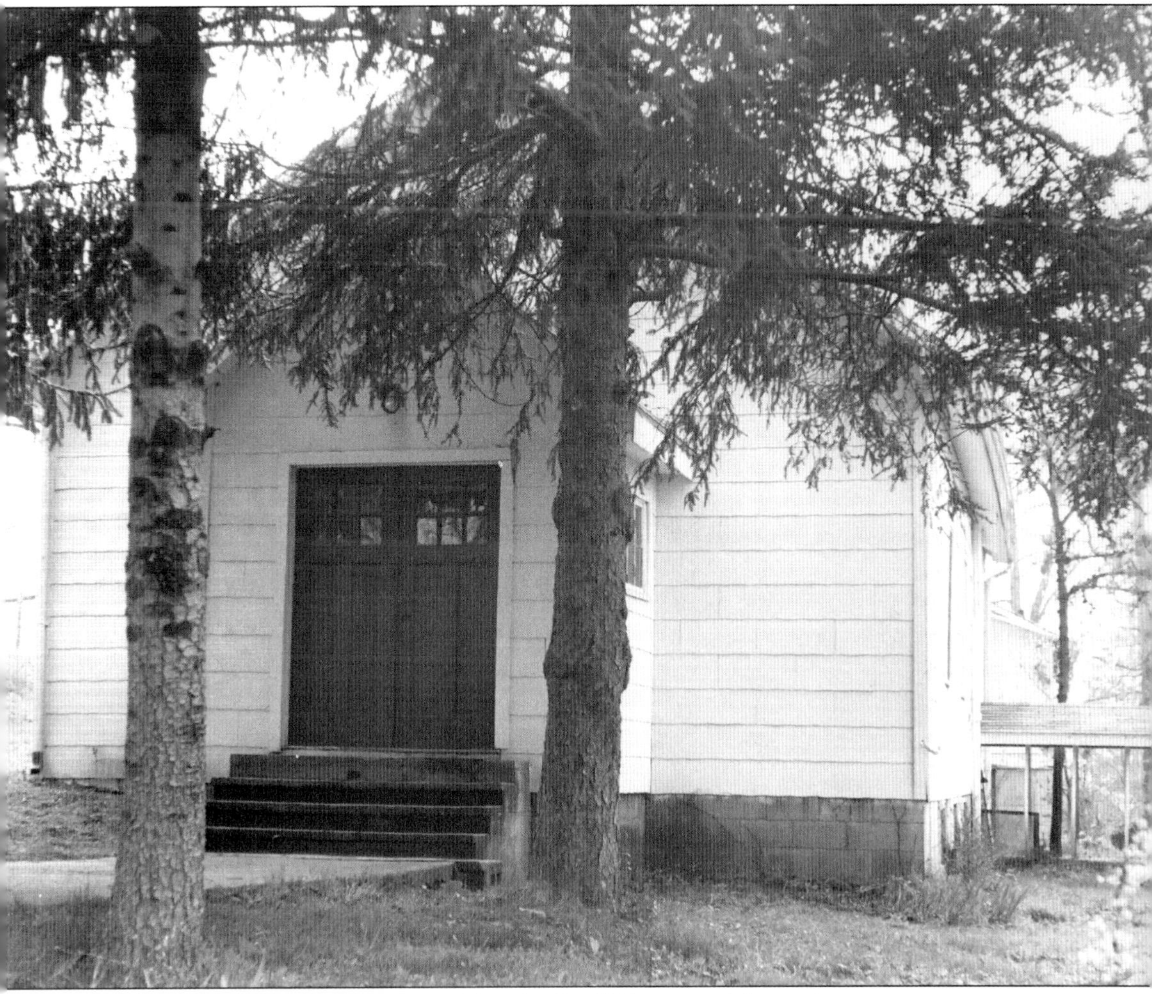

Harris Chapel AME Zion Church. After the Civil War, many African American congregations in the South formed their own churches rather than continue to be segregated within existing predominantly white churches. This one-story African Methodist Episcopal chapel, at 96 Prospect Street, near the Canton Public Library, began as a congregation in the late 1800s on a site in what is now downtown Canton. It was a small building erected by H.A. Osborne, who owned a lumber company in town. Black Baptist and Methodist congregations alternated Sunday worship services in this building until expanding businesses forced both congregations to relocate. In 1930, a group of trustees purchased land on the church's current site and named the church Harris Chapel after Cicero Richardson Harris, a bishop and a key figure in organizing Livingstone College, a private, historically black four-year college in Salisbury. In the winter of 1984, the old church building was torn down and replaced with a new sanctuary, which was dedicated in the spring of 1985. (Courtesy of the Harris Chapel AME Zion Church.)

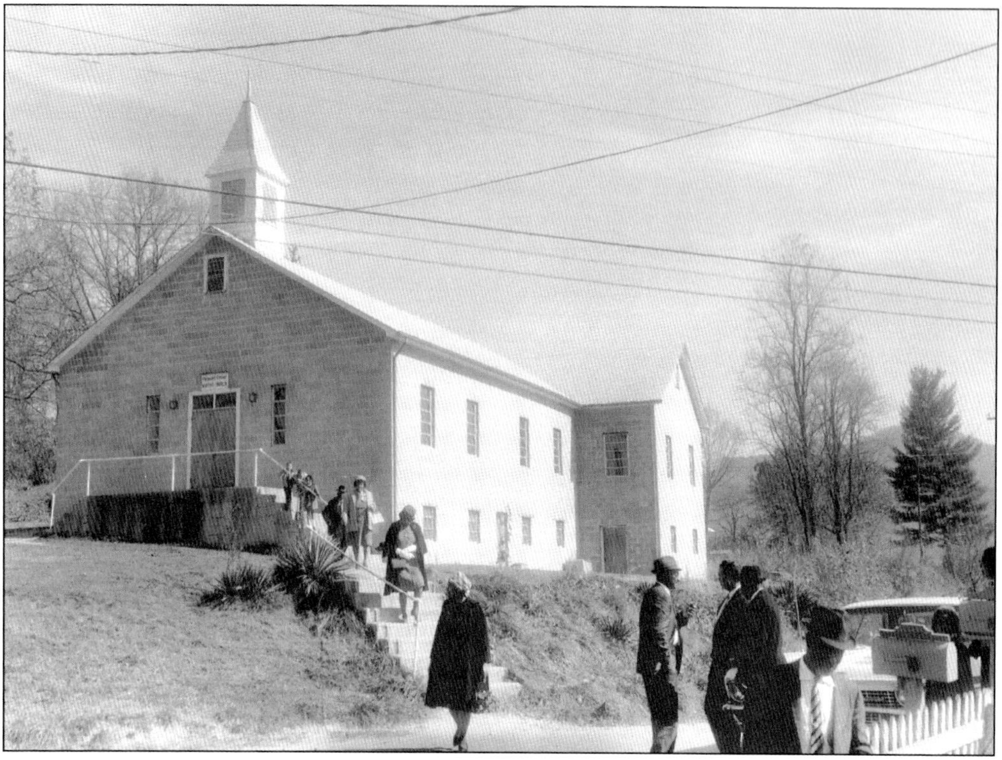

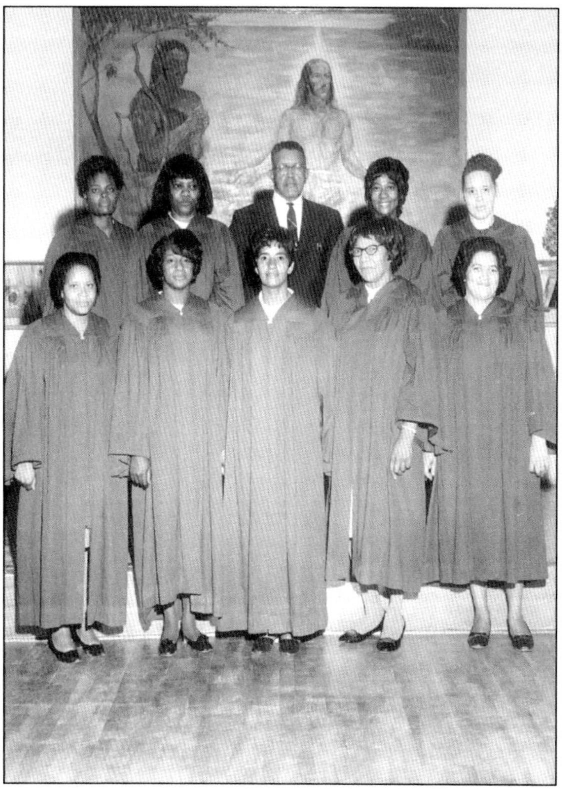

Pleasant Grove Baptist Church. The Pleasant Grove congregation had its roots in downtown Canton, sharing a church building with the Methodist congregation that became Harris Chapel. Expansion forced both congregations to move to Baptist Hill, where they shared another building. Pleasant Grove's first church was built in 1911, and a new building in the Gibson Town community replaced it in the 1950s. For its first 65 years, Pleasant Grove held services twice a month. Then, in the fall of 1967, the church hired its first full-time ordained minister. Behind the church is a small cemetery with some of the oldest African American graves in Haywood County. The Gibson Town community is named after the Gibson family. (Both, courtesy of the Canton Historical Museum.)

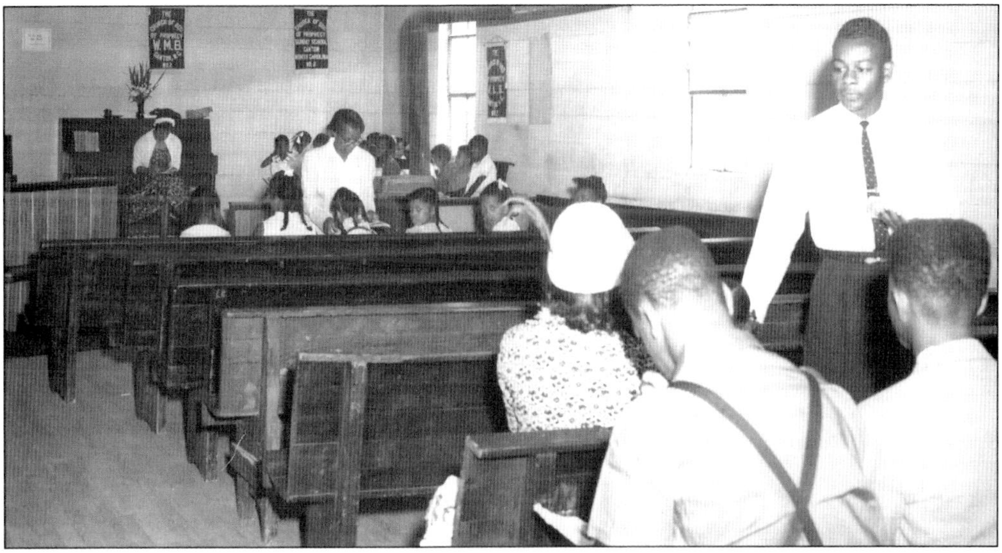

Church of God of Prophesy. Established in 1941 through the leadership of Rev. James Conley, this African American church congregation is currently located in Gibson Town. The Church of God denomination was originally referred to as Christian Union, and had its origins in 1886 on the North Carolina–Tennessee border. (Courtesy of the Canton Historical Museum.)

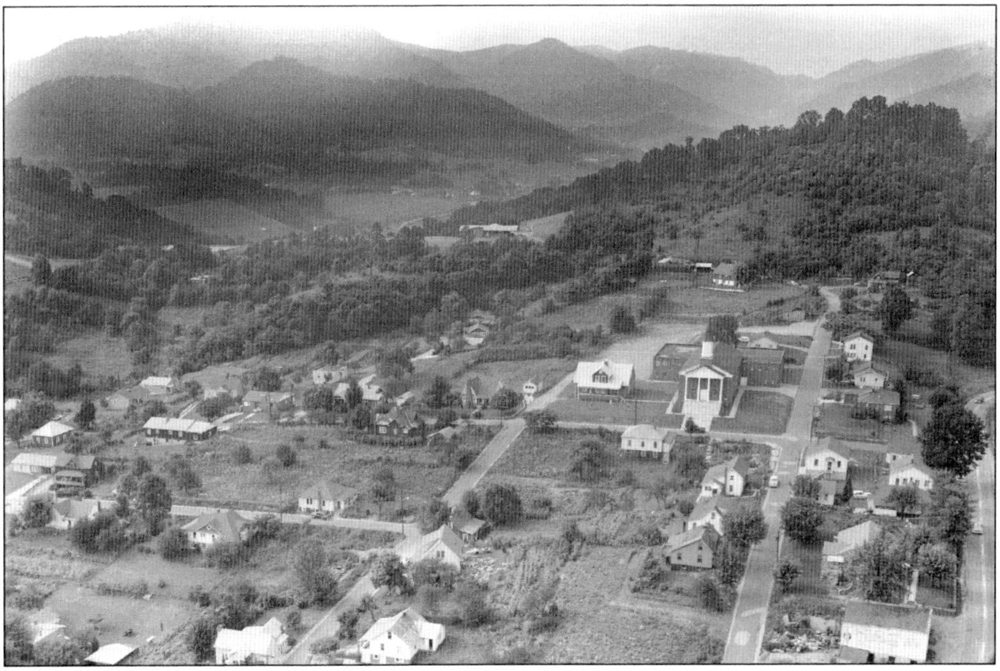

Calvary Baptist Church. In 1918, a group of teenagers from Plains Methodist Church started a Sunday school on Sunday evenings. They met in local homes, and as the group grew, they raised money and bought a house on the corner of what are now Spruce and Phillips Streets in Canton. The meetinghouse was called Ferguson Town Union Church. The congregation established itself as the East End Baptist Church by 1921, and changed its name again in 1940, to Calvary Baptist Church. In the fall of 1954, the congregation moved into its current sanctuary, which is seen in this aerial image of east Canton and Beaverdam. (Courtesy of the Canton Historical Museum.)

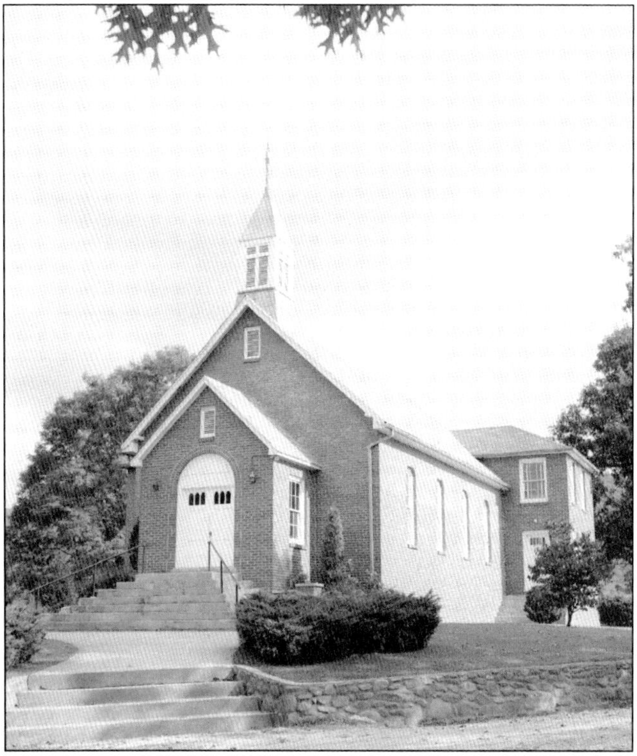

Oak Grove Baptist Church. Established in 1899, this church is on the northwestern side of Canton in the Thickety community. The one-story A-frame structure was built of brick with a single bell tower and includes a two-story educational wing to the rear of the sanctuary. (Courtesy of the Canton Historical Museum.)

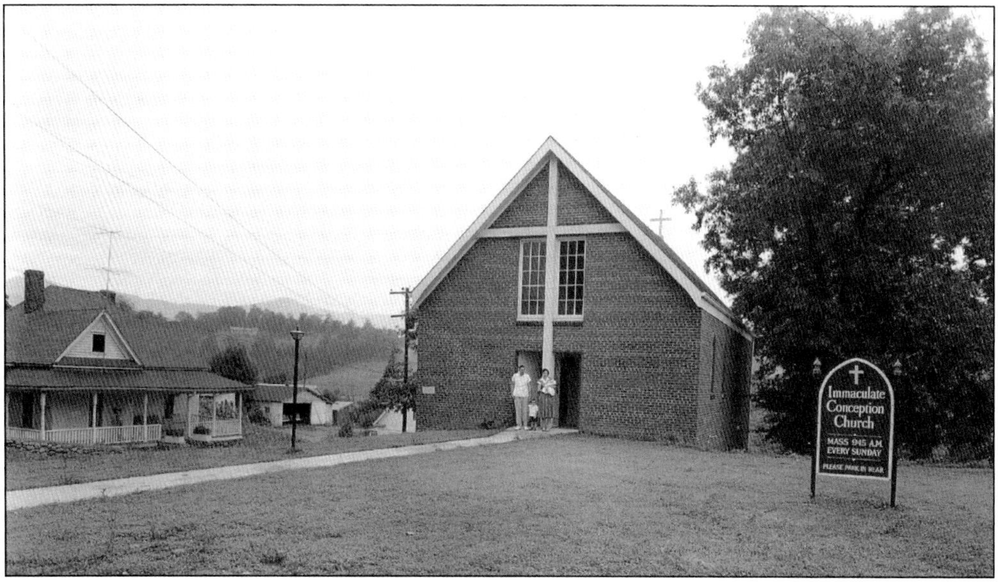

Immaculate Conception Catholic Church. As the Champion mill in Canton brought in new workers in the early 1900s, some of these employees were of the Catholic faith. With no Catholic church in Canton, they attended mass at St. John's Catholic Church in Waynesville. During World War II, when gasoline had to be rationed, a St. John's school bus carried Canton parishioners to and from the Waynesville church on Sundays. After the war, Canton Catholics met at the YMCA for worship until the current Immaculate Conception Church was built in 1954. (Courtesy of the Canton Historical Museum.)

Four

EDUCATION

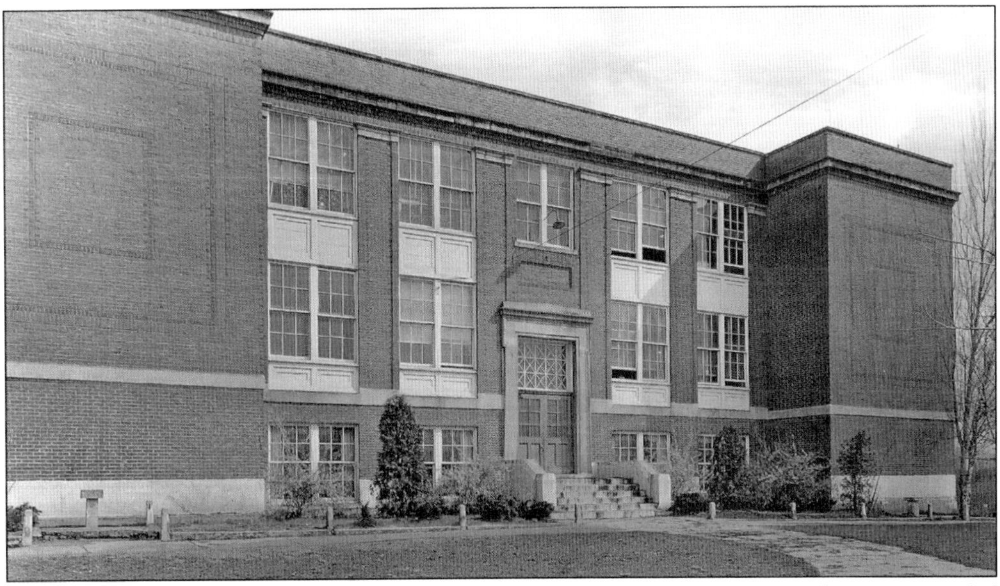

CANTON GRADED SCHOOL. Located on Mease Hill overlooking the Champion mill, Canton Graded School was the town's first public school, opening in 1909. The rectangular brick building, completed at a cost of $25,000, served as the main public school in town until Canton leaders approved funding for two additional schools in 1922. (Courtesy of the Canton Historical Museum.)

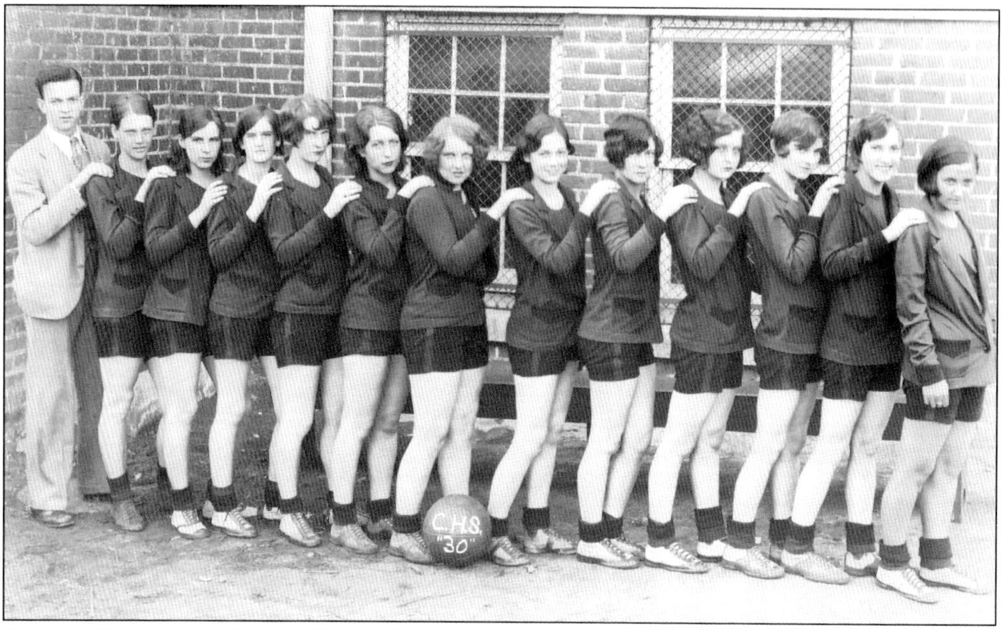

CANTON BASKETBALL TEAM. Canton has a long and storied sports history, with its high school teams winning state championships in football, softball, basketball, and wrestling. Canton High School fielded its first basketball teams in 1930, including this ladies' team. (Courtesy of Edie Burnette.)

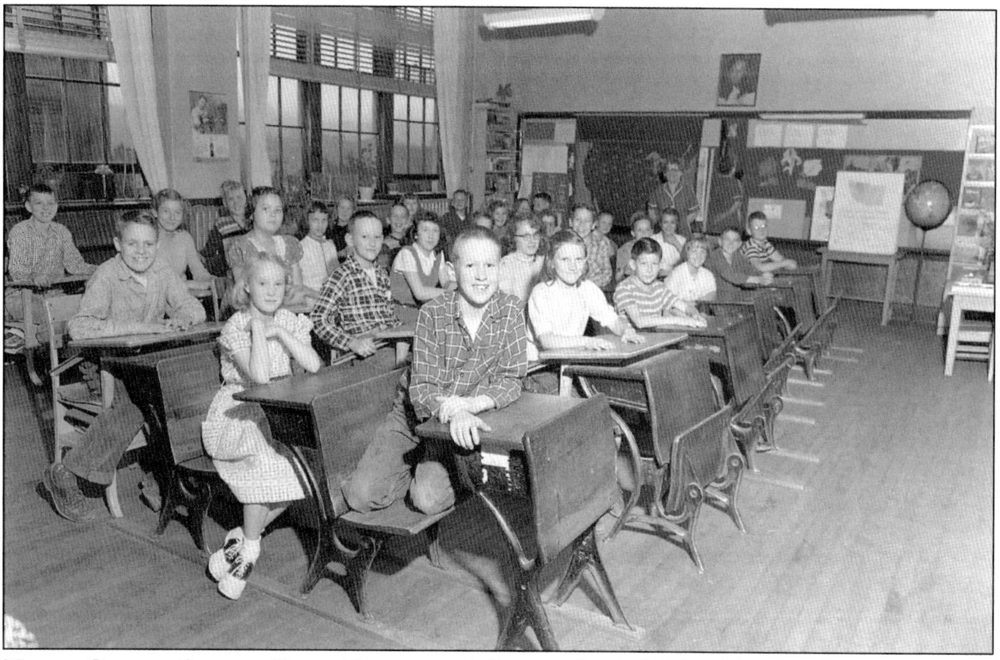

NORTH CANTON SCHOOL CLASS. The original Canton Graded School became known as North Canton School and housed elementary school classes. A new North Canton Elementary School was later built on Thompson Street, on the northeastern side of town, and the old North Canton School building was converted into a storage facility for Champion. The sixth-grade class in 1955–1956 is seen here. (Courtesy of the Canton Historical Museum.)

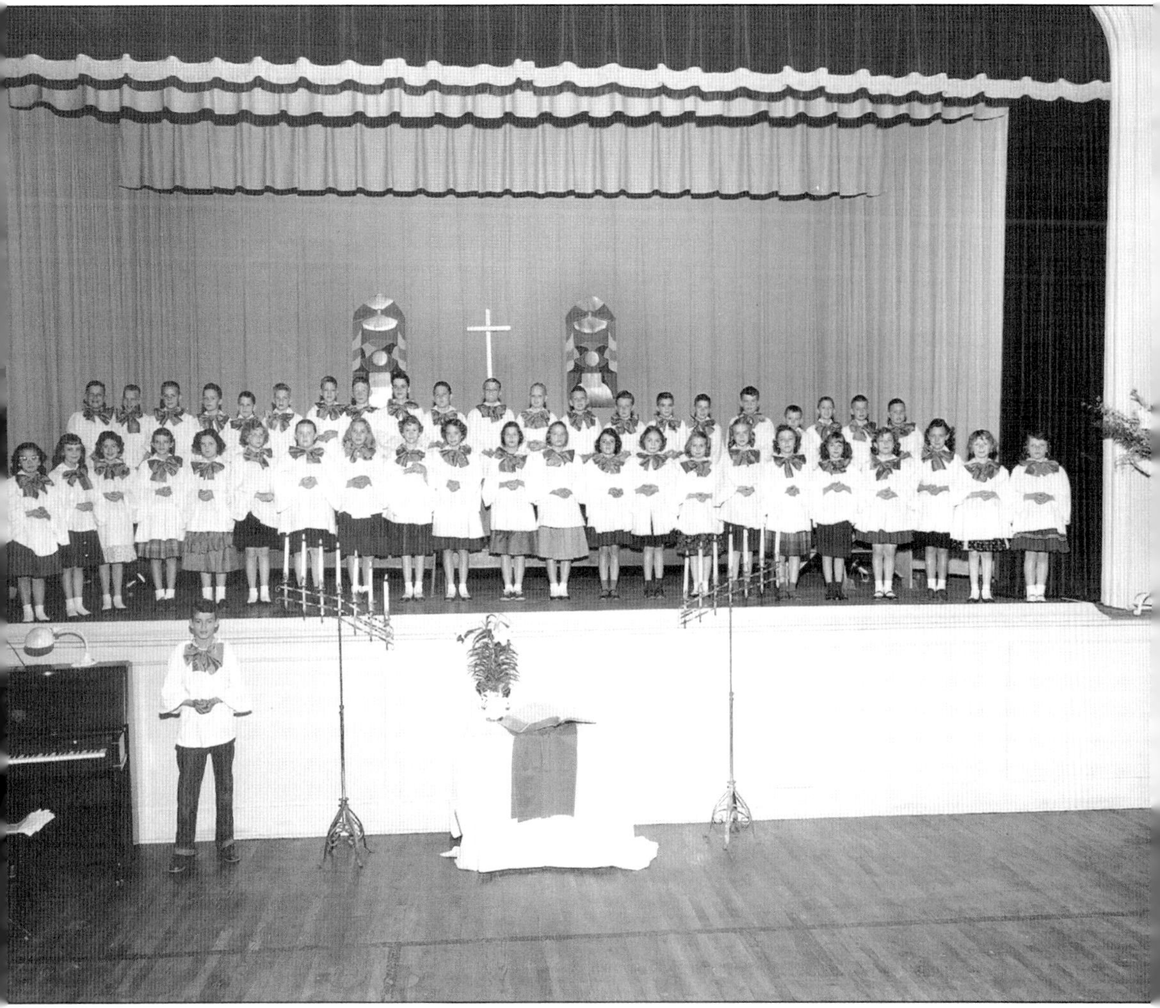

Glee Club. These stage performers are students at Pennsylvania Avenue School, a former elementary school once located at the current site of the Canton Public Library. The school's street name came from Champion professionals, such as chief chemist George Trotsel, who moved to the Canton neighborhood from Pennsylvania. As Canton's population grew, the town approved a 1922 bond to provide money for school construction. The H-shaped, flat-roofed brick building opened in the spring of 1923 with eight classrooms for grades one through five. J.C. Brown served as the school's first principal, and enrollment that first year included 329 students. By 1938, six additional classrooms were added, as well as a library and an auditorium. (Courtesy of the Canton Historical Museum.)

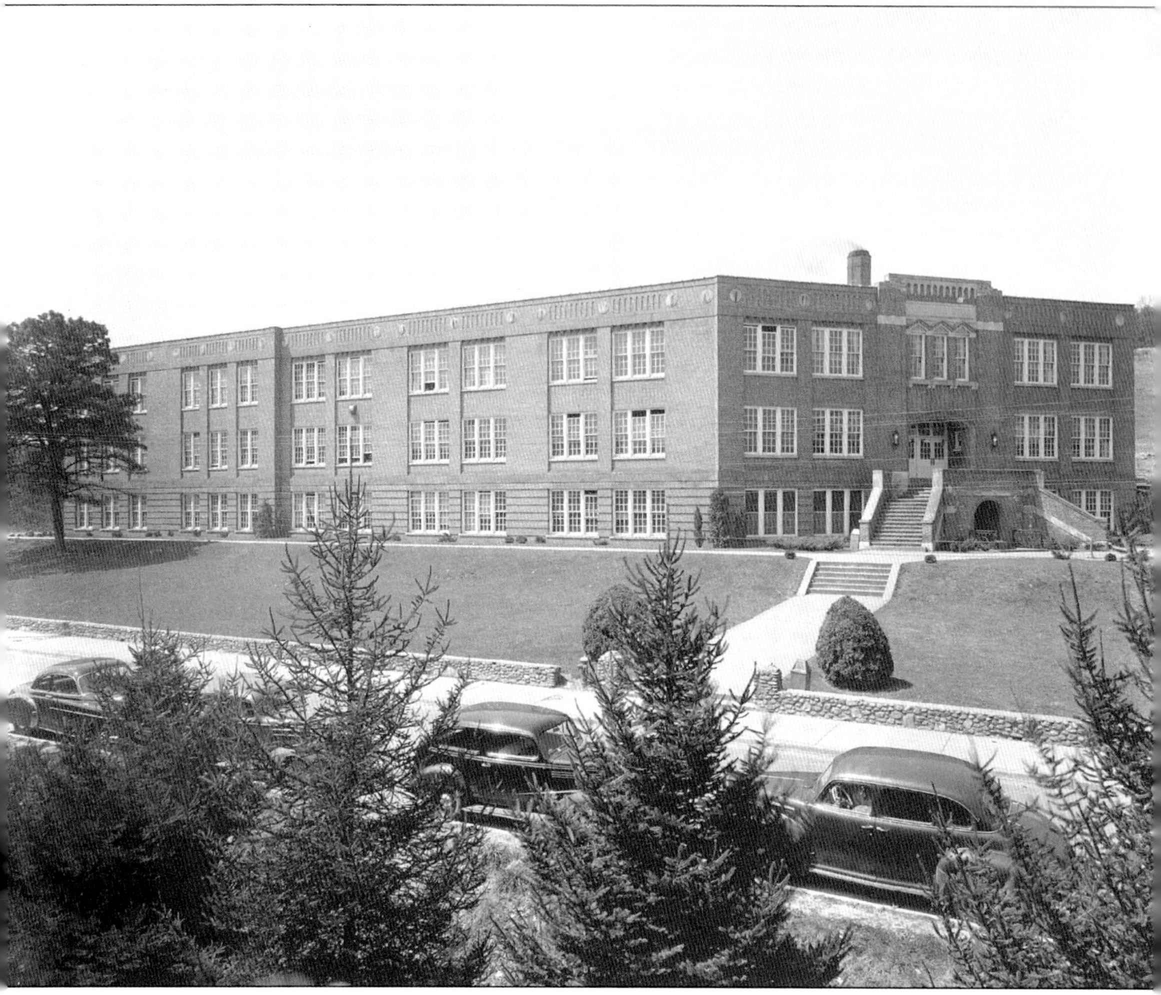

CANTON HIGH SCHOOL. In 1931, Canton High School opened to accommodate upper-level students who had previously been attending Canton Graded School, across town. Around 1960, a junior high school building was added to the property. By 1967, further consolidation moved high school students to Pisgah High School, and the old Canton High School became a facility for middle grades. (Courtesy of the Canton Historical Museum.)

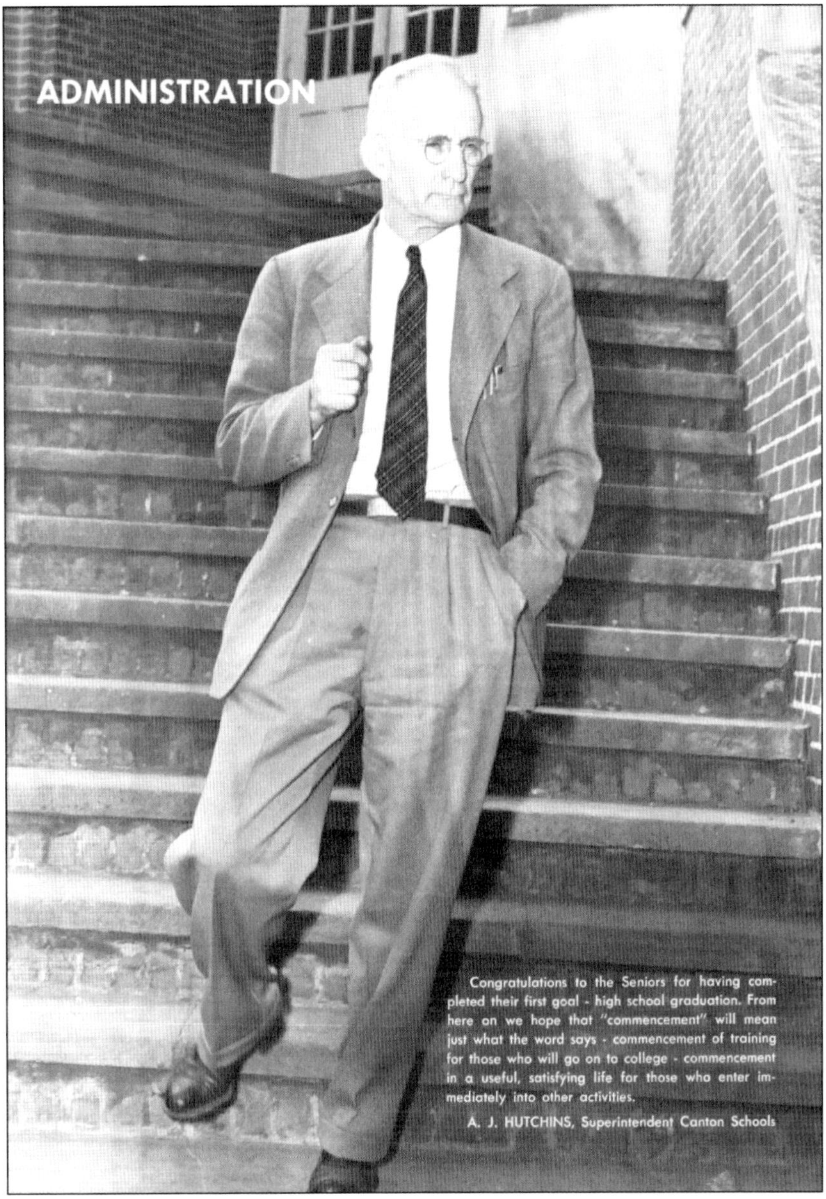

SUPERINTENDENT. When Andrew John Manning Hutchins became the superintendent of Canton city schools in 1924, the schools had almost no library books, no cafeterias, and no vocational programs. By the end of his first year, Canton High School had become the first school west of Asheville with full accreditation. A graduate of Wake Forest College and Columbia University and a former principal of Asheville High School, Hutchins brought high standards to Canton and oversaw major changes to its schools. By the end of his career in 1953, the number of teachers tripled, the schools had libraries, vocational training and academic courses flourished, and sports facilities were upgraded. Hutchins often used his own money to help teachers pay for school supplies, and even paid for some students' college tuition. He hauled rock and helped with the construction of the Canton football stadium and drove icy roads on winter mornings to make sure they were safe for school buses. Hutchins was the first Haywood County educator named to the North Carolina Educators Hall of Fame. (Courtesy of the Canton Historical Museum.)

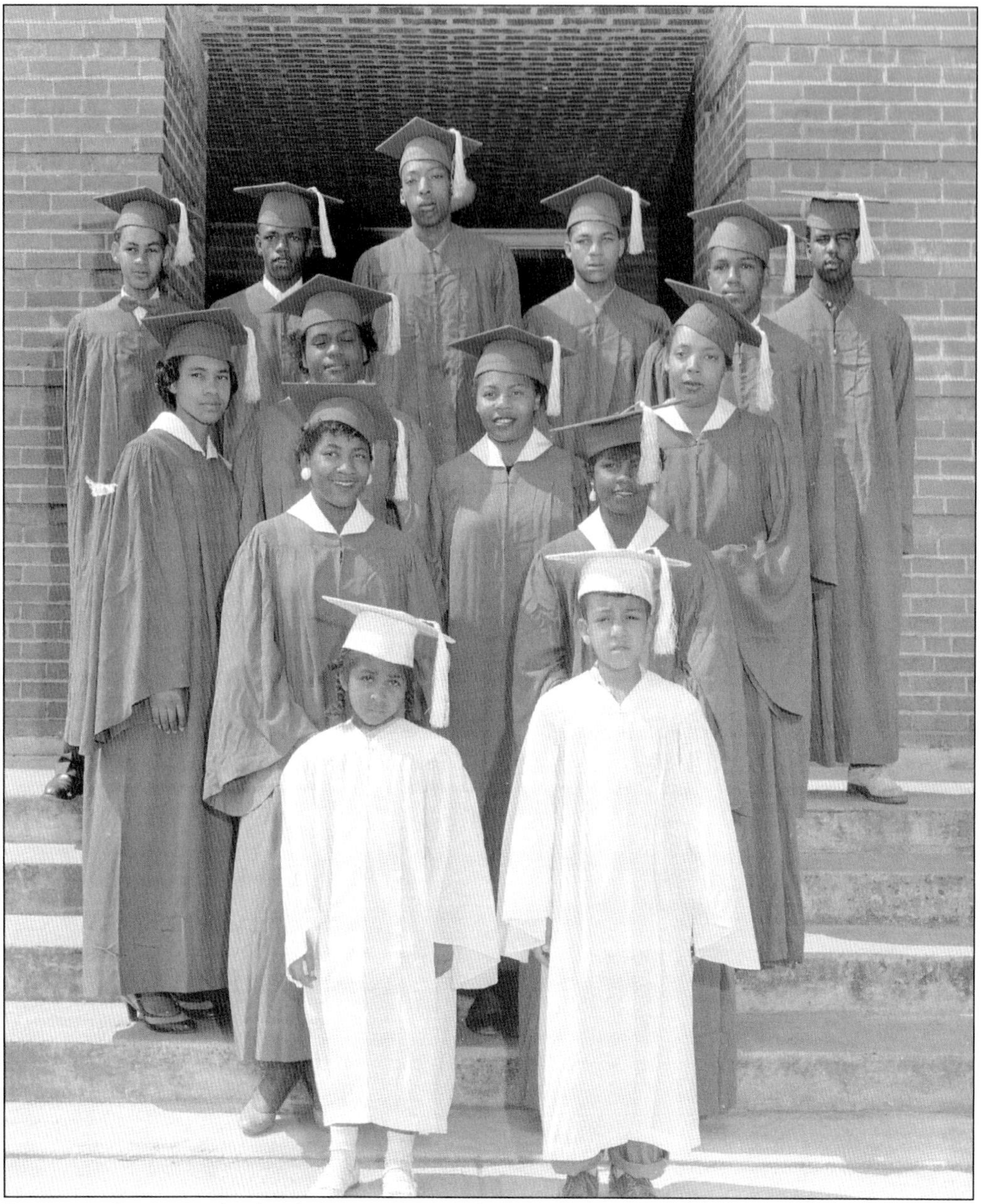

Reynolds School. The first known Canton school for African American students was the Frog Level School, located where the Champion Savings and Loan later operated. By 1918, enrollment had increased and students were moved to a Methodist church in downtown Canton. From there, the school relocated to Baptist Hill. By 1924, the Reynolds School, a two-room wooden building, was built near the Will Oats property. A larger Reynolds School, located in the Gibson Town neighborhood, began on September 27, 1948, and was open to all black high school students in the county. Dr. Ralph Davis served as the school's first and only principal. The brick building included eight classrooms, a library, a gymnasium/auditorium, a lunchroom, and a shop for vocational training. This photograph shows the graduating class of 1955 at Reynolds. The school graduated 16 classes before shutting its doors as part of the county's high school integration and consolidation in 1966. (Courtesy of the Canton Historical Museum.)

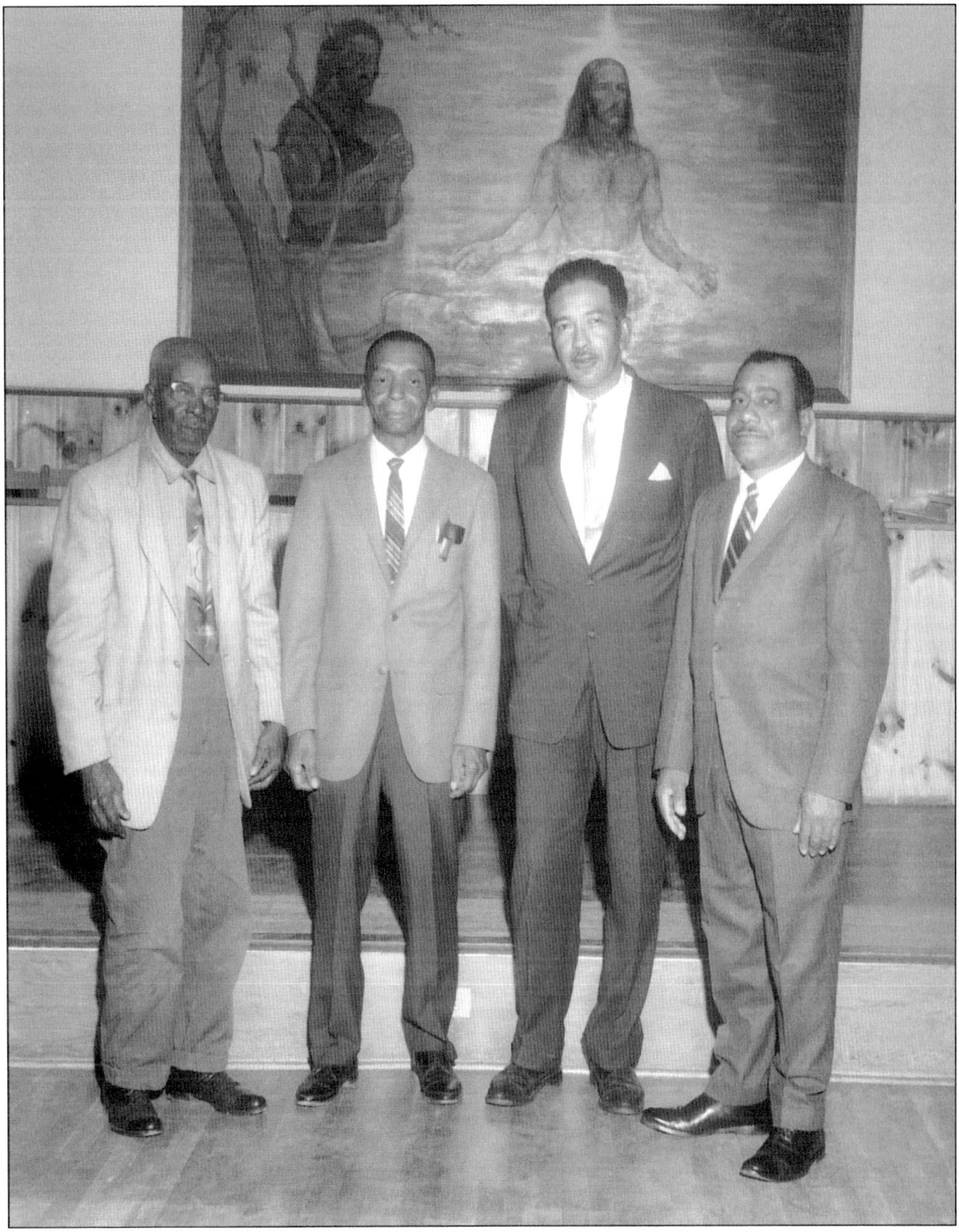

HIGH STANDARDS. Reynolds High School teachers such as Wilbur Eggleston (far right) often taught multiple grade levels and multiple subjects, including math and industrial arts. In 1949, Eggleston came to Reynolds to coach the first all-black football team in western North Carolina west of Asheville. Two years later, the Reynolds Tigers joined the Piedmont Athletic Conference, with Eggleston continuing to teach while also becoming the school's athletic director. After integration came to Haywood County in 1966, Eggleston went on to teach at Pisgah High School. (Courtesy of the Canton Historical Museum.)

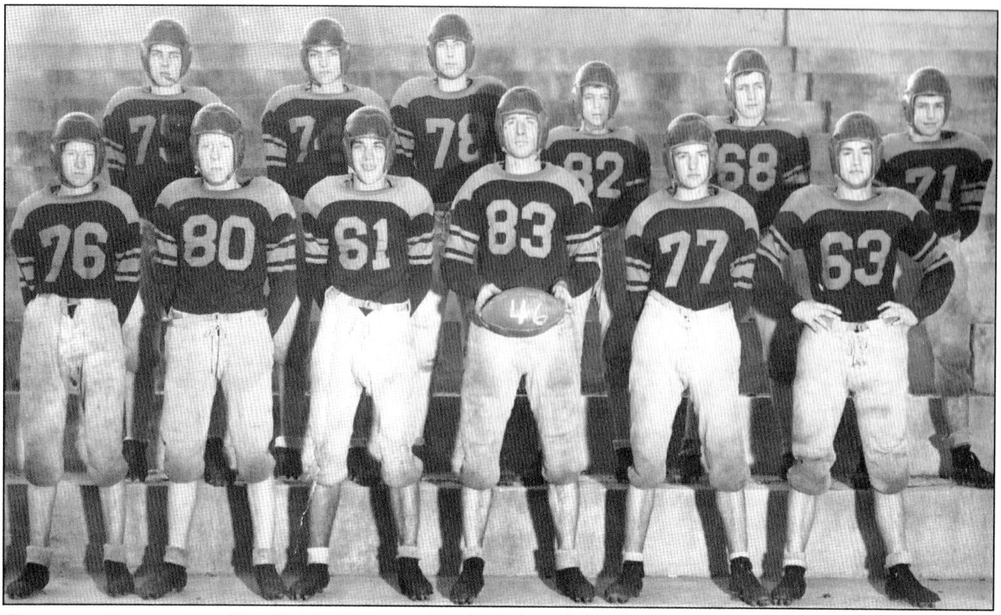

CANTON FOOTBALL. By 1946, Canton High School football teams had become perennial powerhouses, amassing an 11-year record of 89-29-6. Coached by C.C. Poindexter and led by center Getter O'Diear, who was chosen as team captain for three straight years—a school record at the time—Canton High School's football squad won the Blue Ridge Conference title in 1946. (Courtesy of Gerry Kelly.)

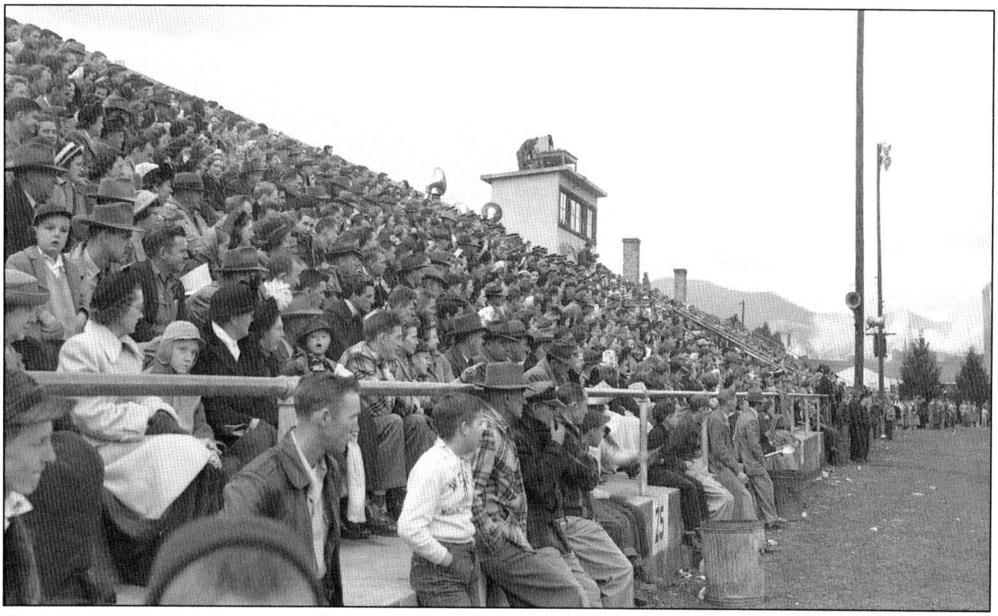

CANTON FOOTBALL STADIUM. Known today as Pisgah Memorial Stadium, the hallowed home of six state championship teams was memorialized to honor former Canton High School students who served and died in World War II. Today, fans pack the stadium by the thousands, especially for the cross-county rivalry with Tuscola High School (formerly Waynesville Township High School). *USA Today* recently tabbed the matchup as the most intense football high school rivalry in the state. (Courtesy of the Canton Historical Museum.)

STATE CHAMPIONS. In 1956, Canton High School fielded one of its best teams in football, outscoring its opponents 413-64 on its way to an undefeated season, a Blue Ridge Conference title, and its first state AA championship. Coached by Boyd Allen, the Canton Bears beat Washington High School 33-6 in the state finals on a cold night at Canton Memorial Stadium. From left to right are Canton's all-conference selections that season: Bill Stamey, David Birch, Jack Conard, and Dale Branson. Stamey and Conard were cocaptains of the team. (Courtesy of the Canton Historical Museum.)

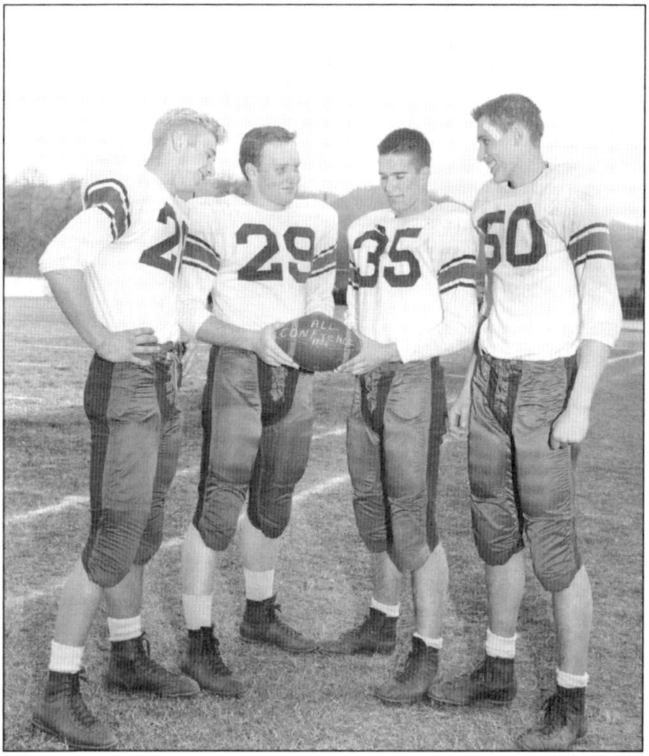

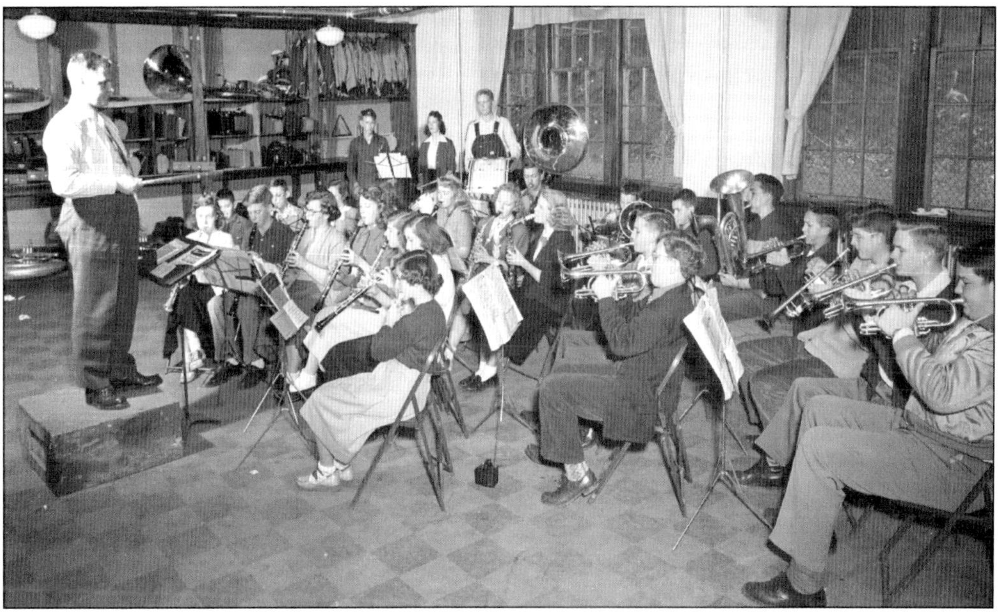

CANTON BAND. Canton High School developed a strong music program. Once during the 1964 football season, the school's marching band, cheerleaders, and hundreds of local fans boarded a passenger train to cheer on its football team for a game in Murphy. The following season, the Canton contingent rode a train once more to Andrews. In both games, Canton won in shutouts. Civic groups and Canton-area business leaders organized these railroad specials. (Courtesy of the Canton Historical Museum.)

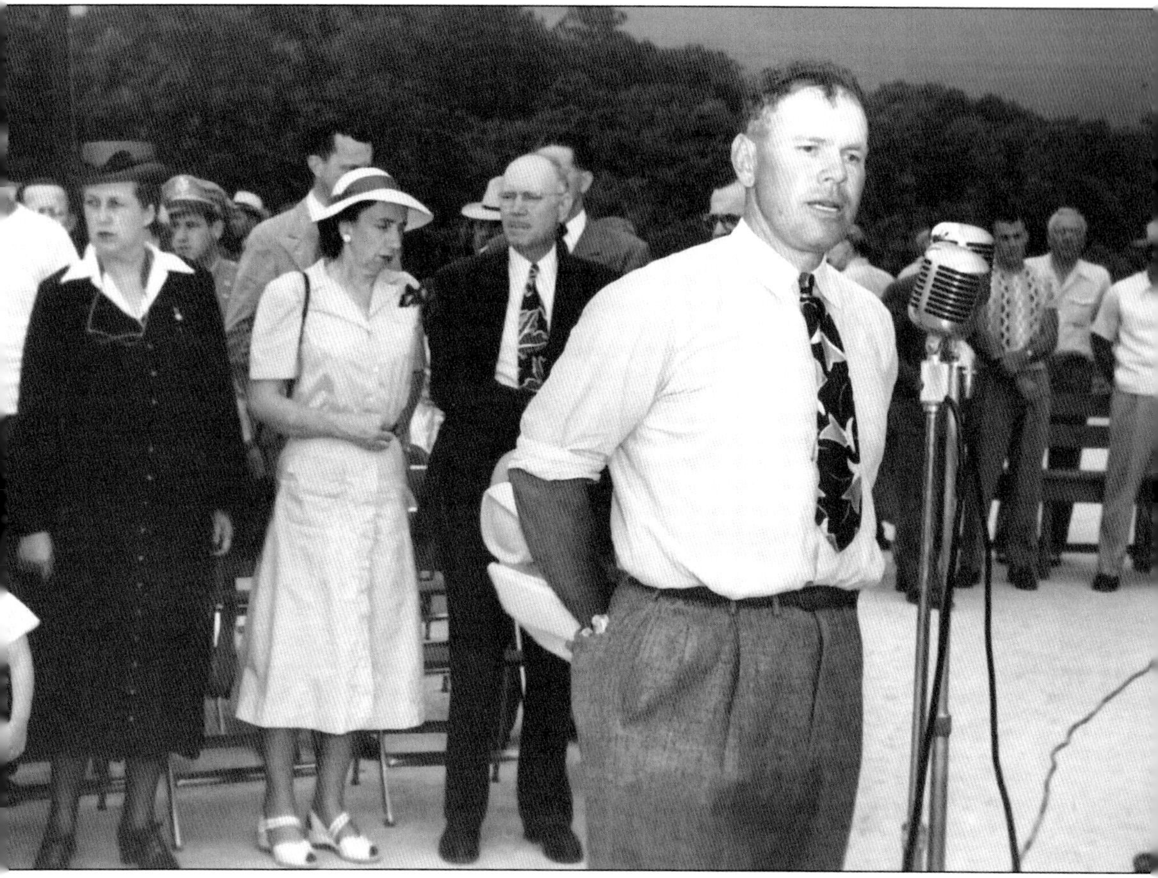

COACH C.C. POINDEXTER. In its earliest days, Canton High School became a formidable sports powerhouse because of tough-minded coaches like C.C. Poindexter, who taught physical education and coached a variety of sports, including football and basketball. His teams won conference titles regularly. After the United States entered World War II, Poindexter made sure his young students were fit for military service. At the completion of one class in May 1943, he ran, jogged, and walked with 13 Canton High School students from Canton to Asheville—25 miles. The students left school at 7:00 a.m., followed Newfound Road east to Asheville, and arrived there before noon. Poindexter served as athletic director and principal at Canton High School and principal at Bethel High School. (Courtesy of the Canton Historical Museum.)

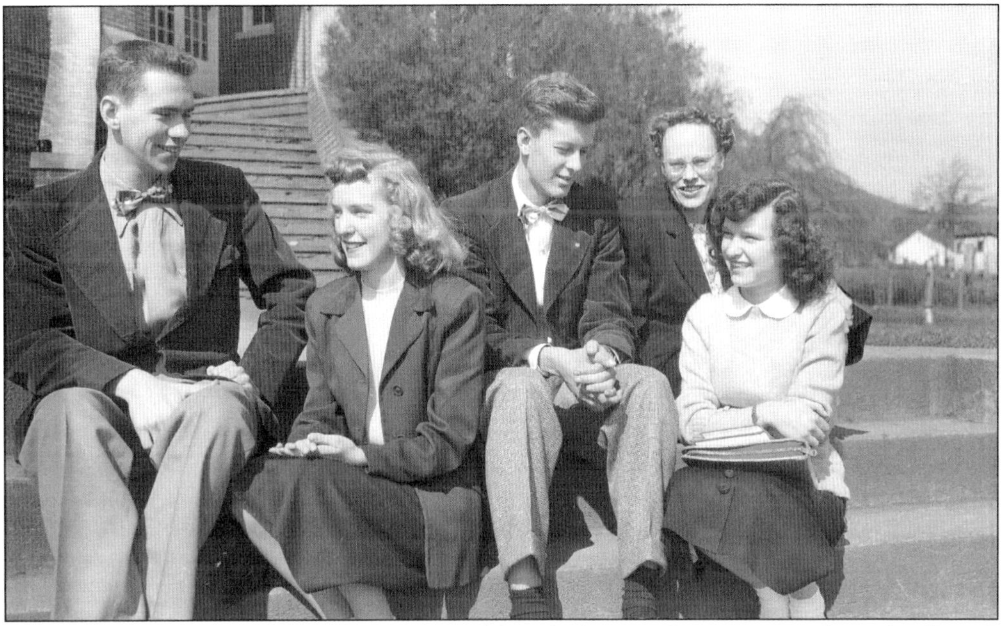

CANTON HIGH SCHOOL STUDENT COUNCIL. Although these students appear calm and collected, elections were hotly contested at Canton High School in the spring of 1950. A runoff election was held for vice president and secretary of the student council. Pictured, from left to right, are council members Mack Barrett, the rising president and president of the North Carolina state High School Student Council; Patsy Ruth Clark, secretary; David Kirkpatrick, vice president; Mel Clontz, student council advisor; and Rose Ann Duckett, treasurer. (Courtesy of the Canton Historical Museum.)

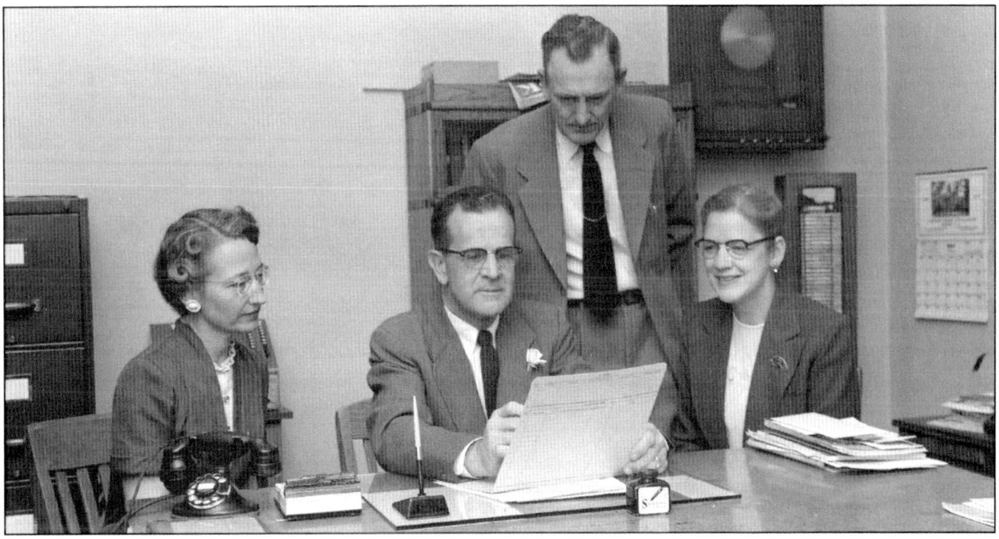

CANTON EDUCATORS. Canton's teachers and administrators maintained high expectations, producing generations of business leaders, doctors, lawyers, military generals, teachers, farmers, mill workers, and a host of other occupations. These Canton High School faculty members are, from left to right, English teacher Mary Gillis, principal William L. Rikard, science teacher J. Boyd Smathers, and math teacher and guidance counselor Martha Matthews. (Courtesy of the Canton Historical Museum.)

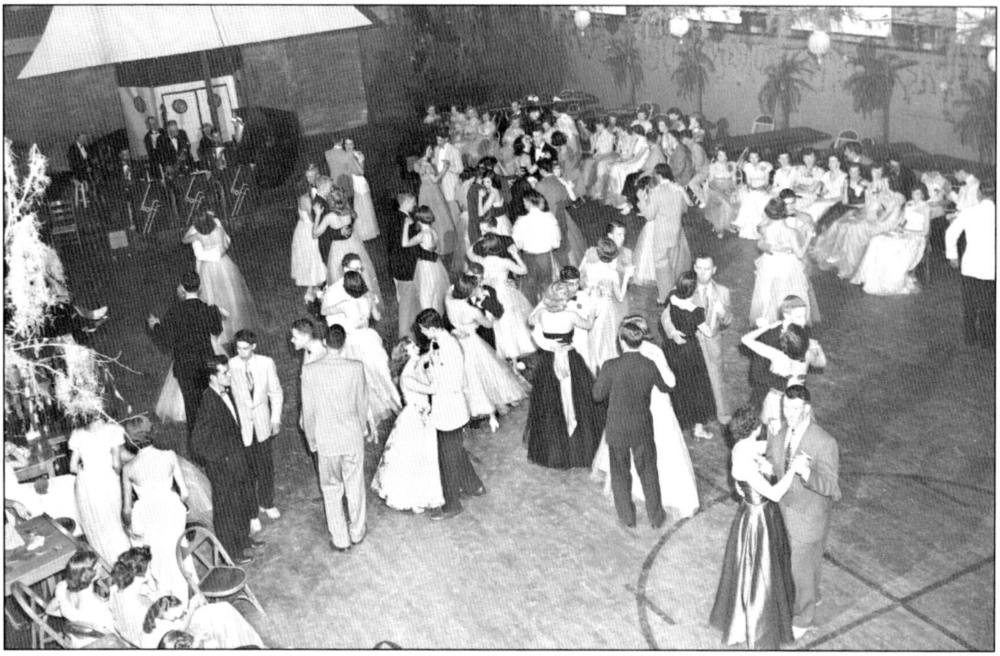

Canton High School Prom. The pinnacle of high school for some, a coming-of-age social event for others, the prom was a date to remember for these students in 1953. They dressed up and danced the night away in the school's gym, which was traditionally decorated by the junior class and then "given" to the seniors. Each year had a particular design theme. (Courtesy of the Canton Historical Museum.)

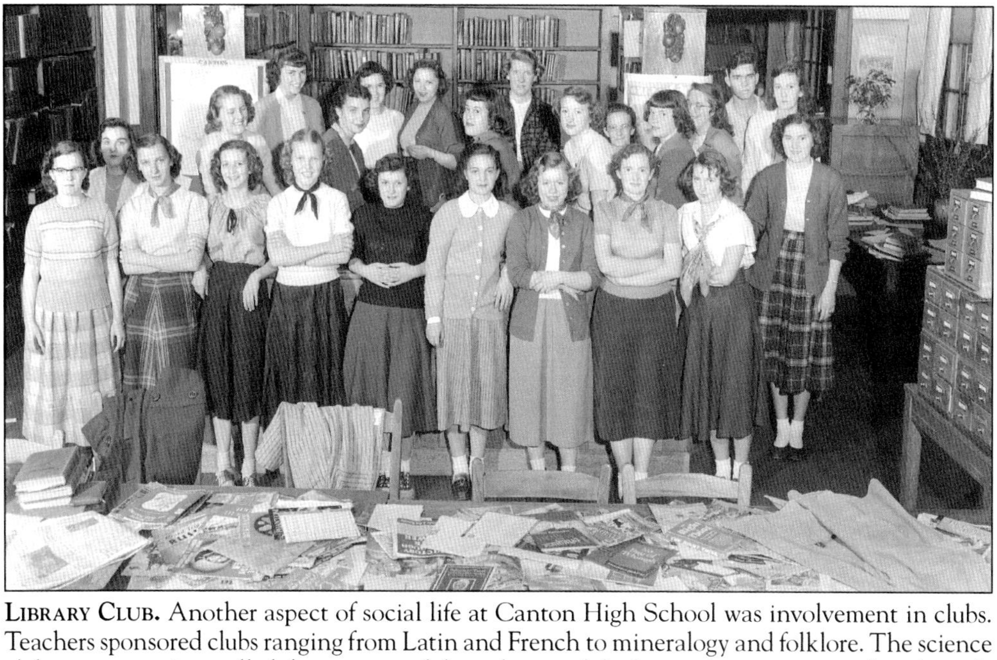

Library Club. Another aspect of social life at Canton High School was involvement in clubs. Teachers sponsored clubs ranging from Latin and French to mineralogy and folklore. The science club was at one time called the museum club, and some clubs featured career-oriented goals, such as Future Farmers of America and Future Homemakers of America. This library club is pictured in the 1950s. (Courtesy of the Canton Historical Museum.)

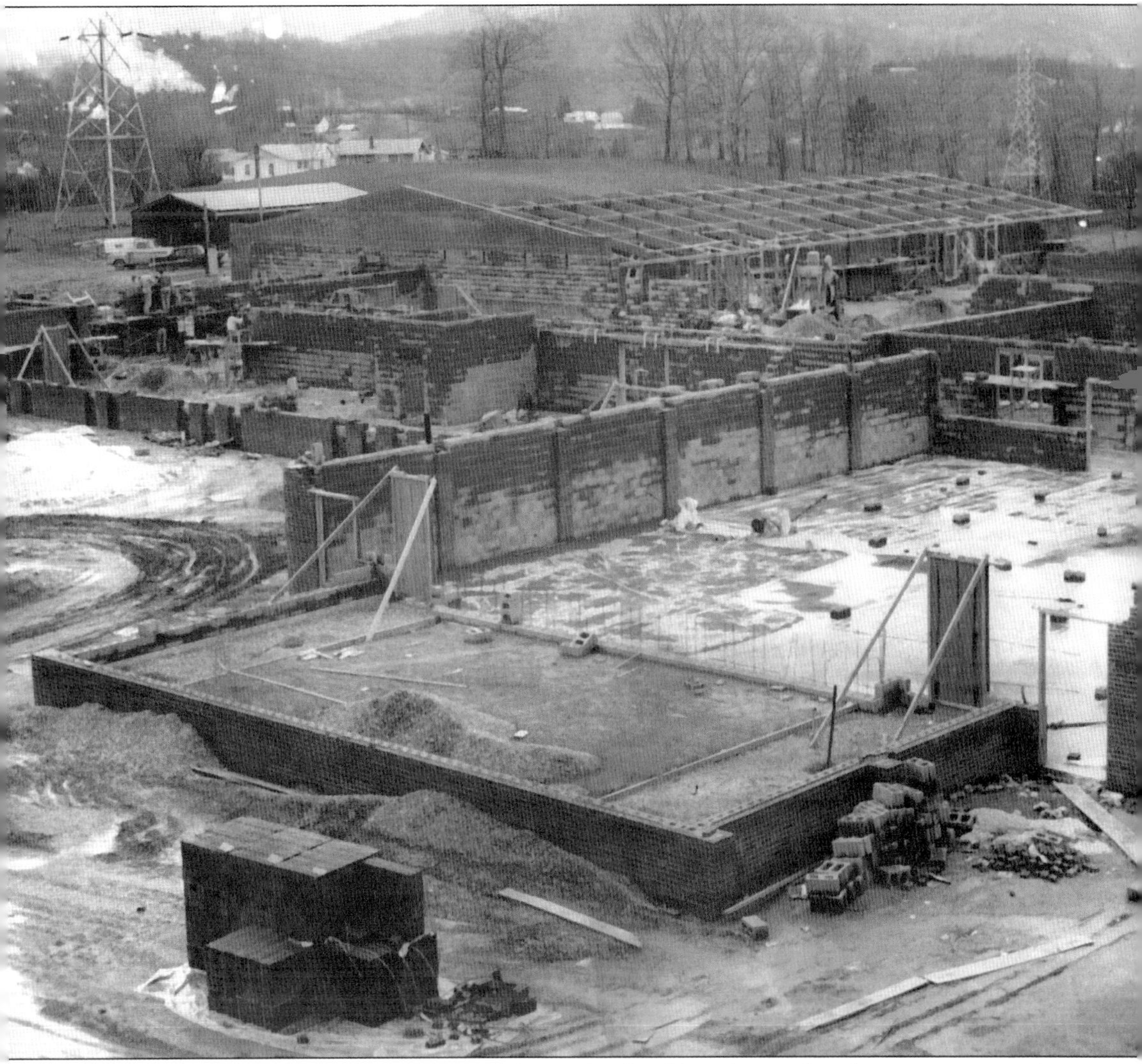

Pisgah Construction. In 1965, Haywood County's school board agreed to the integration and consolidation of its white and black schools. Students and teachers from Bethel, Clyde, Canton, and Reynolds schools merged into one new facility. The construction of Pisgah High School was finished in time for the start of the 1966–1967 school year. The school's name refers to Pisgah Mountain, on the southern edge of Haywood County, as well as the Biblical mountain that Moses stood upon to glimpse the Promised Land. In the school's first year, the Pisgah Bears enjoyed stellar sports seasons. Both the girls' and boys' basketball teams won Blue Ridge Conference titles, and the football team won the state championship in Burlington, defeating Graham High School. That same year, Jan Johnson was chosen as the consolidation night (homecoming) queen, and the senior class voted Carl Stamey and Judy Westmoreland most likely to succeed. B.F. Maree served as the school's first principal. (Courtesy of the Canton Historical Museum.)

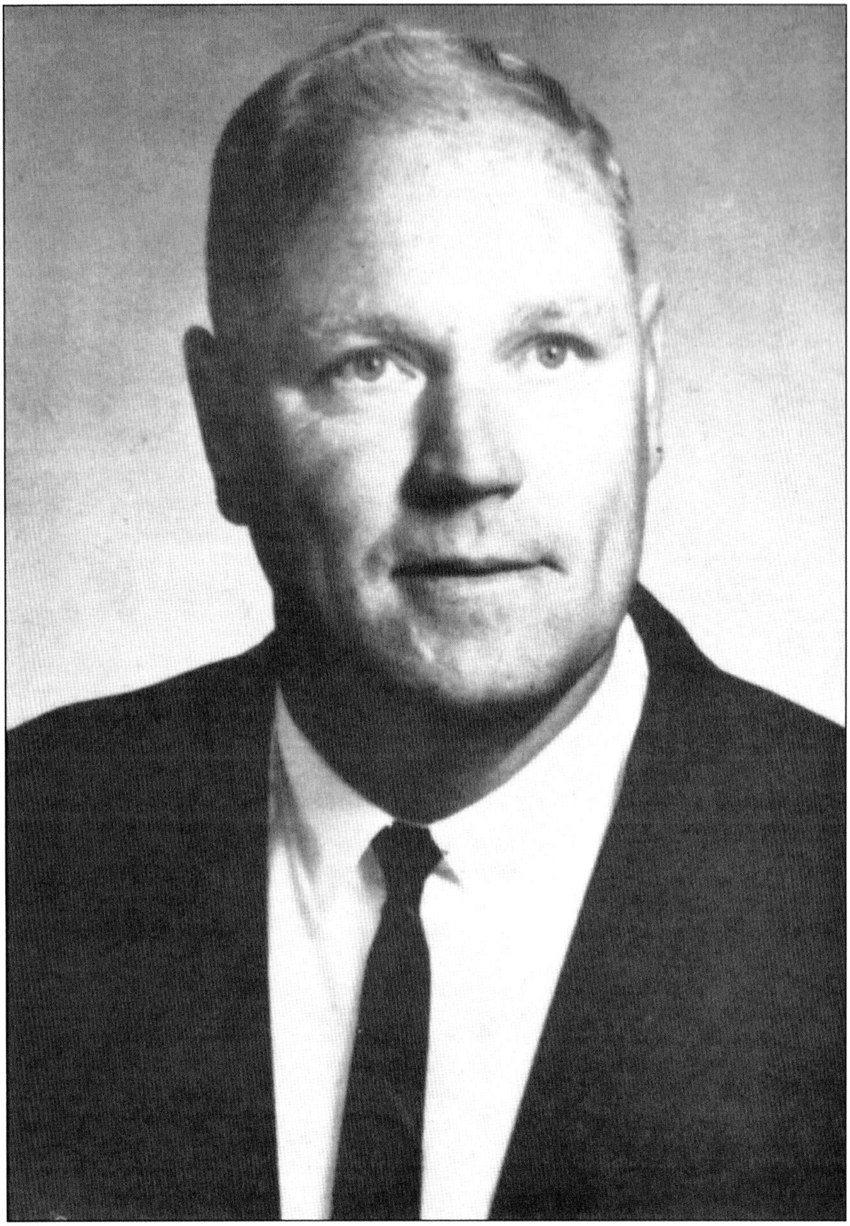

Boyd Allen. A legendary football coach at Canton High School and Pisgah High School, Boyd Allen compiled an impressive 133-31-3 record, with three state championships and seven conference titles. A native of Shelby, North Carolina, he went on to play at Wake Forest College. He was hired at Canton High School as an assistant coach in 1950 and was promoted to head football coach in 1954. He coached the western region team in the 1958 east-west all-star game. On October 17, 1969, at Weatherby Stadium in Waynesville, he was coaching against cross-county rival Tuscola High School on his 46th birthday when he suffered a heart attack shortly before halftime and died. Pisgah won the game, 18-8. On the Monday after, Pisgah observed a day of mourning in his honor. The following year, friends, family, fellow coaches, and former football players dedicated the Boyd B. Allen Field House at Pisgah High School. (Courtesy of Ernest Stines.)

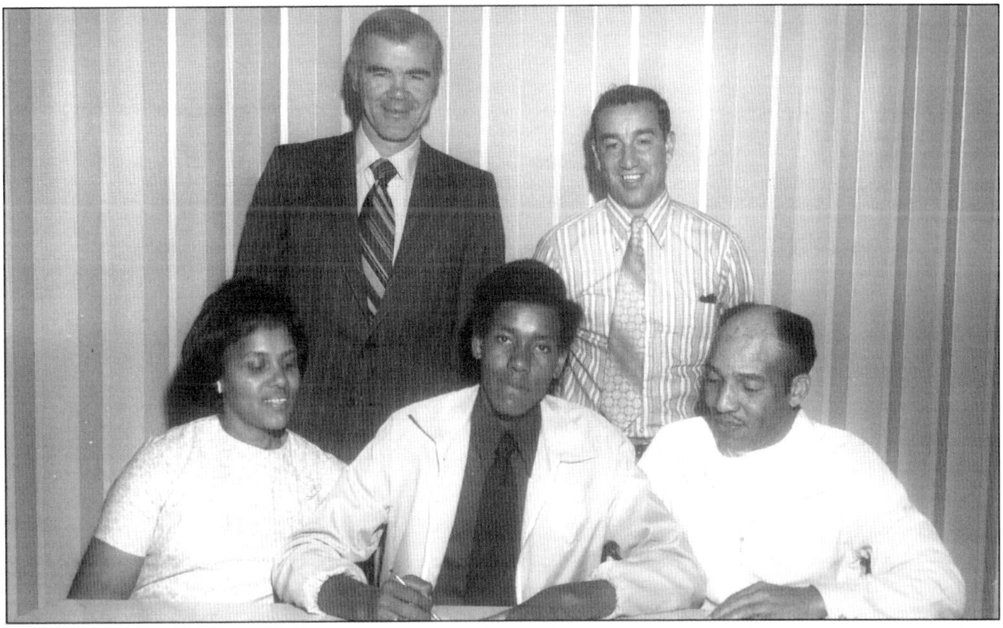

SIGNING. Pisgah and Canton high schools produced dozens of athletes who garnered scholarships to major colleges. In the 1970–1971 school year, Pisgah star basketball player Mike Parrish (center) signed a letter of commitment to Wake Forest University, with his parents on either side of him, Wake Forest basketball coach Jack McCloskey (standing, left) and Pisgah basketball coach Scott Conner (standing, right). In his final full-court campaign at Pisgah, Parrish led the Bears to a 19-1 record and a fourth-place finish in the state playoffs. (Courtesy of the Canton Historical Museum.)

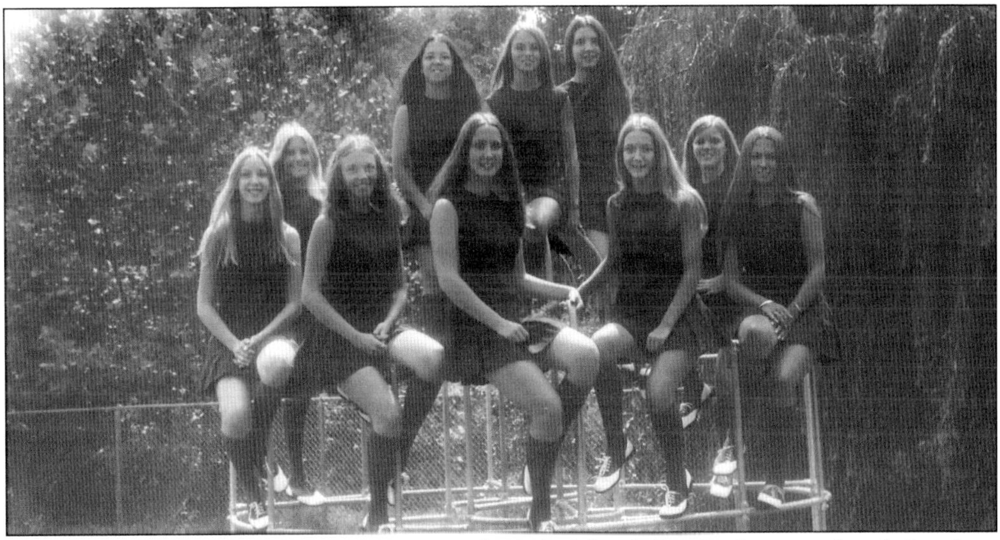

PISGAH CHEERLEADERS. The 1973–1974 Pisgah High School cheerleading squad includes, from left to right, (first row) Debbie Mease, Jan Wells, Mary Ann Watts, Wanda McDowell, and Debbie Blaylock; (second row) Sue Patterson, Cathy Yates, Debbie Clark, Gina Minzenmayer, and Terry Savage. Today, Pisgah's cheerleading teams compete in annual statewide competitions, and they took home top honors in 2012 at the North Carolina State Invitational cheerleading championships in Raleigh. (Courtesy of the Canton Historical Museum.)

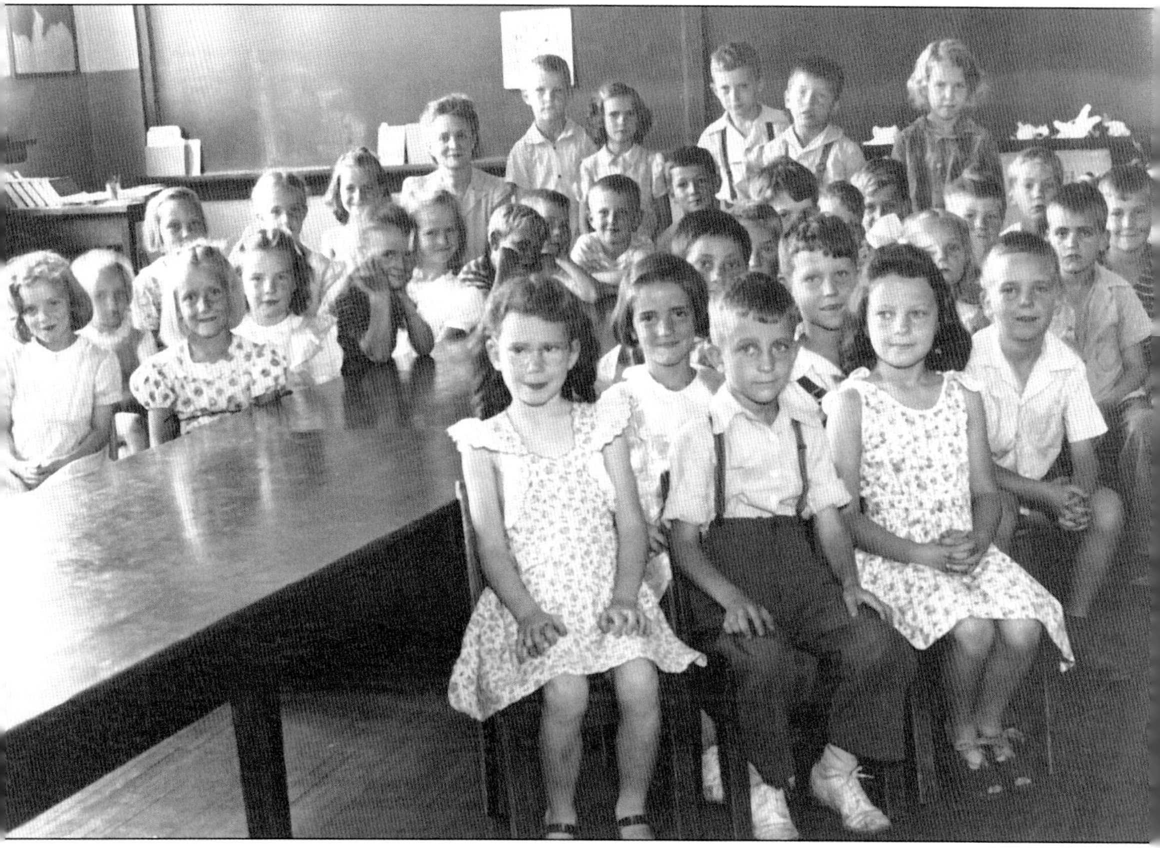

COMMUNITY SCHOOL. In its earliest days, the Canton community had a dozen or so small schoolhouses and church-affiliated academies for students. Schools in the communities of Thickety, Beaverdam, Dutch Cove, Long Branch, Red Hill, and North Hominy, as well as Austin's Chapel and Noah's Chapel, eventually closed to consolidate with larger schools. However, bigger schools did not always mean finer accommodations. When the Pennsylvania Avenue School opened in 1923, the facility did not have its own cafeteria, so some students were offered lunches of soup, crackers, and milk at a home across the street. The school enjoyed its own traditions, such as an annual pet day each spring. Horses, pigs, dogs, snakes, gerbils, and other assorted creatures were brought to the school for students to learn about animals through hands-on activities. This group of students from Thelma Collins's first-grade class at Pennsylvania Avenue School is from the 1944–1945 school year. By 1986, local voters approved a county bond to combine Pennsylvania Avenue and Morning Star Schools into Meadowbrook Elementary School. The old Pennsylvania Avenue School closed its doors. Two incidents of arson destroyed the building, which was torn down and replaced by the present-day Canton Public Library. (Courtesy of Bonnie Stamey.)

Five

BUSINESS

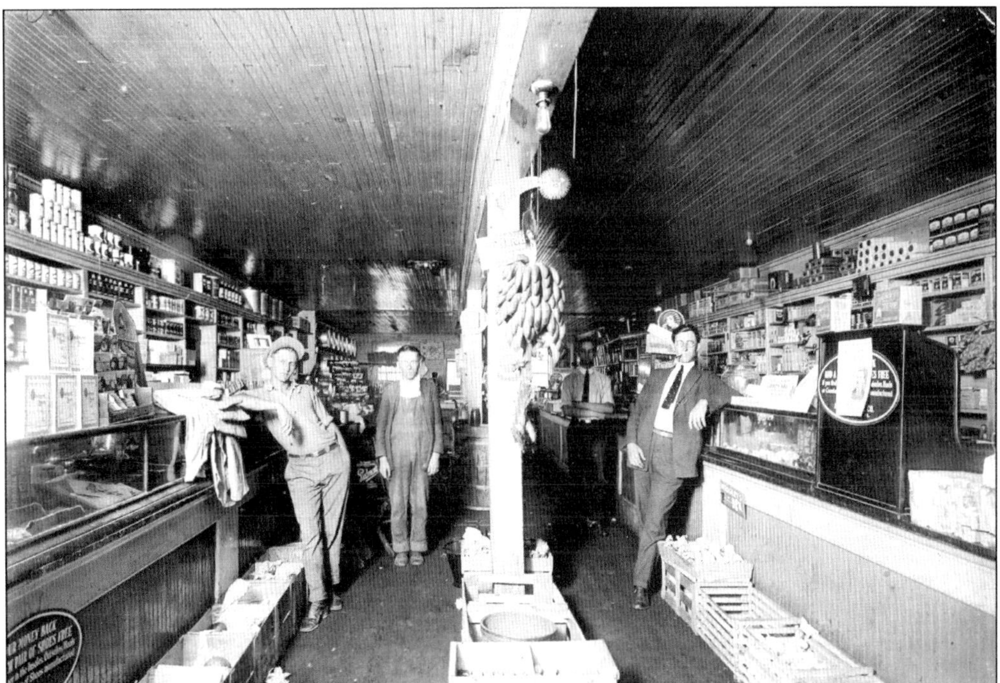

HAYWOOD RESTAURANT. This Park Street eatery, established in the early 1900s, was one of many that sprouted up after the railroad lines came to town. An influx of families, merchants, and salesmen, known as drummers, came looking to find new opportunities. More people generated more businesses. (Courtesy of the Canton Historical Museum.)

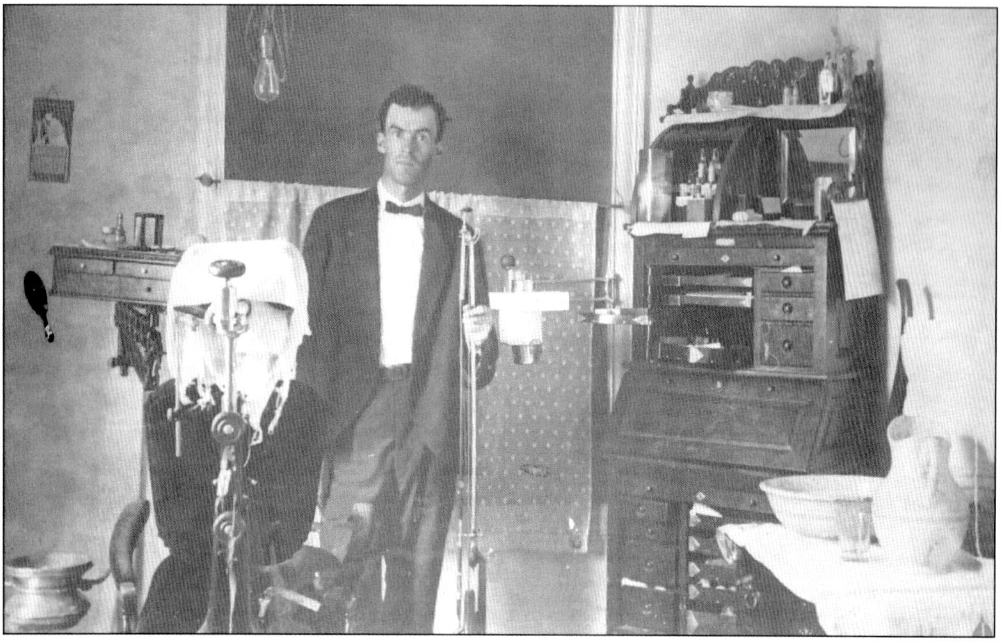

Dr. Theodore A.C. Hargrove. One of Canton's earliest dentists, Hargrove (1877–1926) grew up in a house where Immaculate Conception Catholic Church now stands. After graduating from Southern Dental College in Atlanta, he set up a practice on Main Street. He is seen here in his dental office. Hargrove later recruited dentists Nick Medford and James N. Sturdivant to Haywood County. Hargrove's son Foster also became a dentist. (Courtesy of the Canton Historical Museum.)

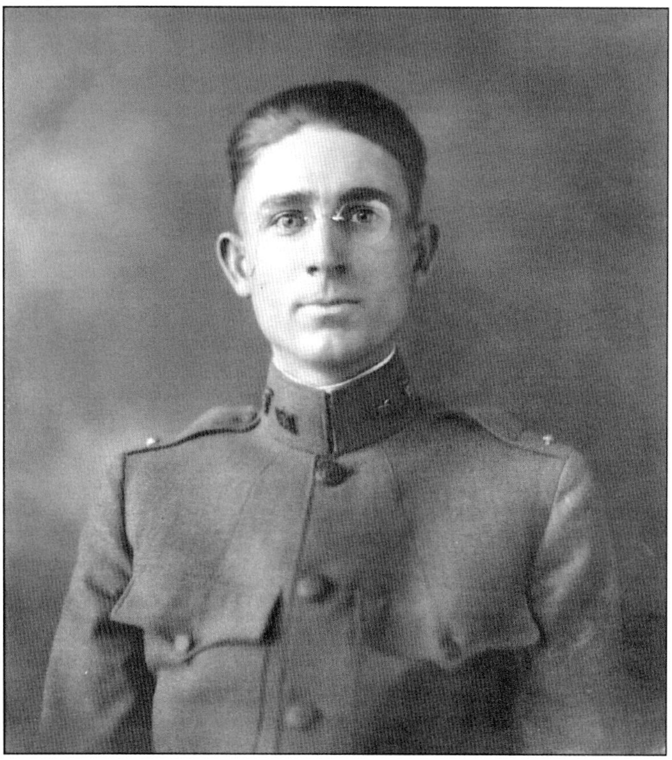

Dr. James Sturdivant. Born in Marshville, North Carolina, in 1892, James N. Sturdivant completed his degree in dentistry in 1915 at Southern Dental College in Atlanta. He came to Dr. Theodore Hargrove's practice in Canton soon afterwards. However, when the United States entered World War I, Sturdivant left his practice to serve in the armed forces. He returned to Canton after the war, but was killed in a car accident just 10 days before Christmas in 1918. He was 36 years old. (Courtesy of the Canton Historical Museum.)

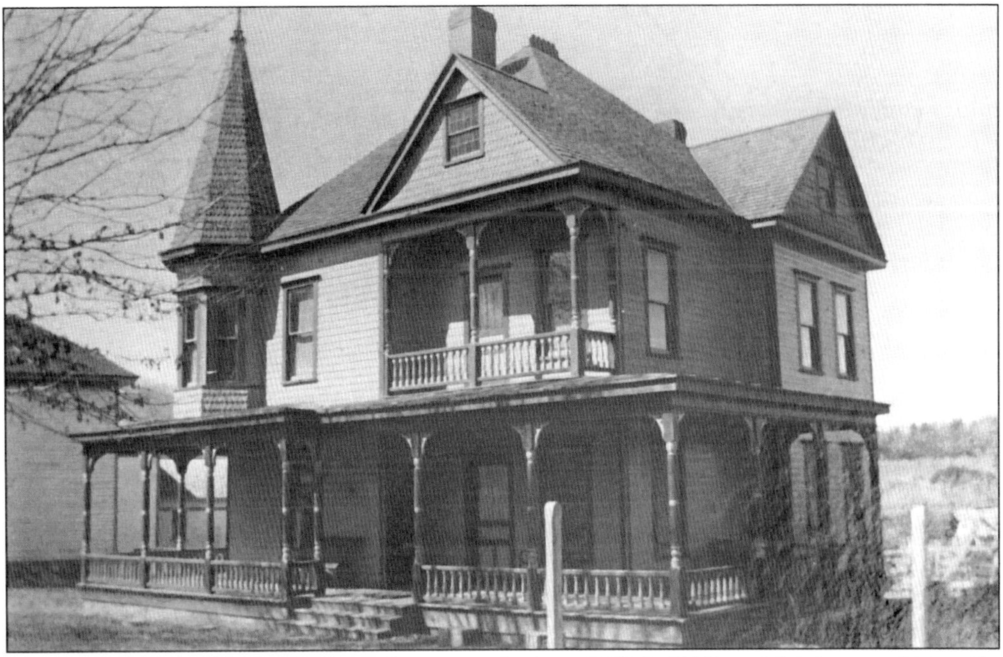

Imperial Hotel. This Queen Anne house was built in 1876 for William H. Moore and his wife, Rhoda. It was purchased in 1910 by businessman W.T. Sharp, who added a four-story tower on the left side and converted the building into a hotel. He also added a commercial building on the hotel's western side. When Edward and Mae Geir of New York took over the management of the hotel, they renamed it the Imperial. With the best amenities in town and a $2 nightly rate, it became the choice reservation for visiting salesmen and executives working with the Champion mill. More rooms were added in the 1930s, and the front was walled up with a facade to give it a more modern look. However, after Interstate 40 was constructed in the 1960s and hotels were built along the highway, the Imperial fell from favor. A recent renovation has restored it to its stately design, and the building is now home to Sid's on Main, a popular restaurant, and also features rooms for businesses. (Above, courtesy of the Canton Historical Museum; below, courtesy of Henry Foy.)

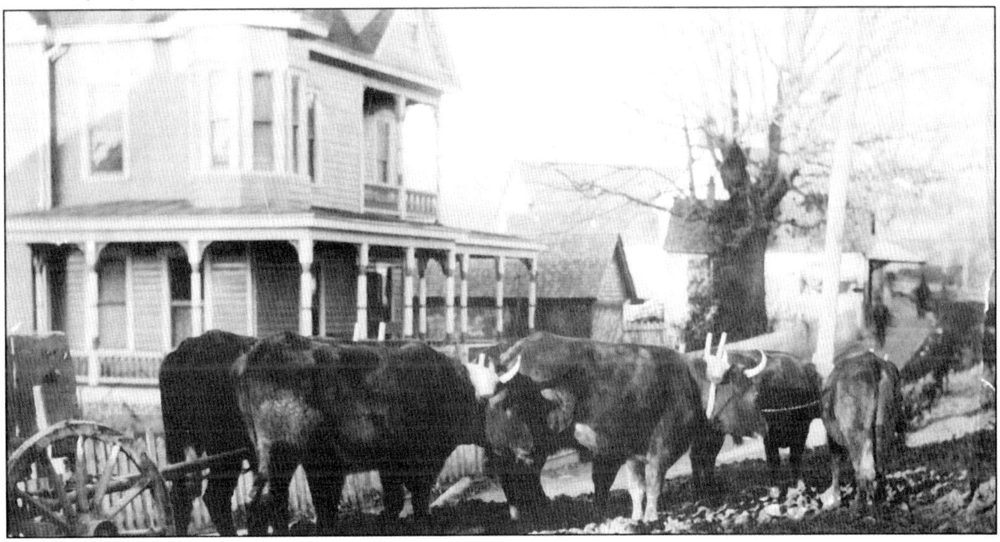

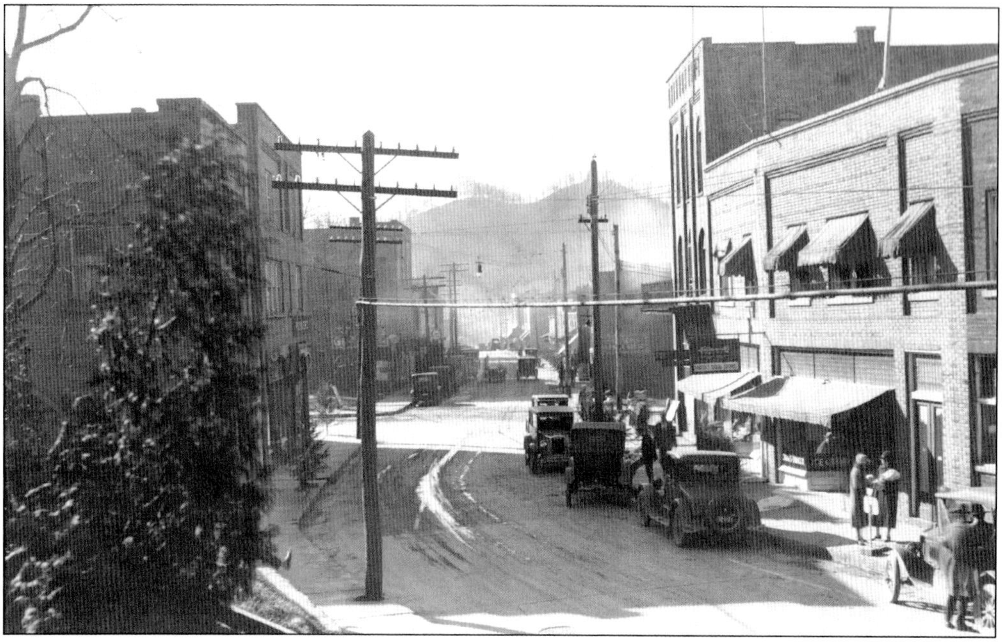

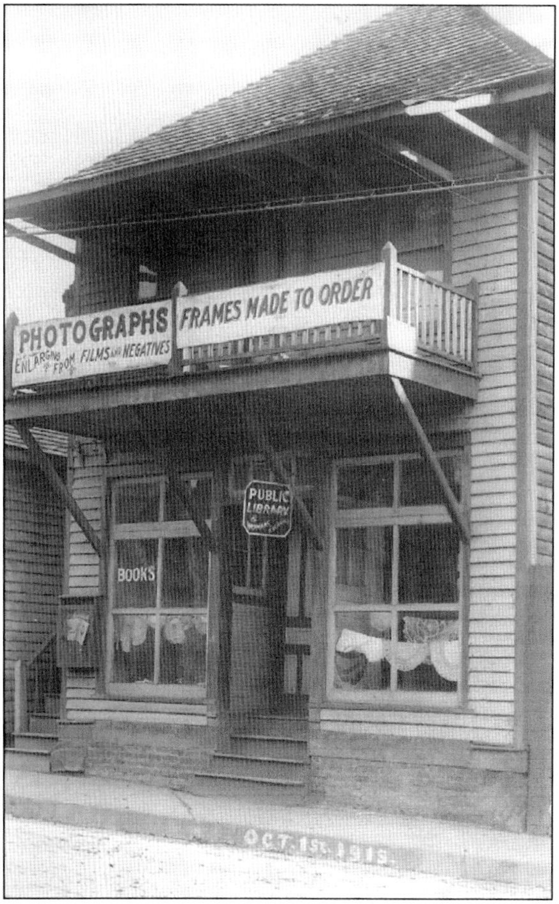

EARLY DOWNTOWN. This photograph from 1926 shows how far Canton grew in just 20 years after the Champion mill came to Canton—from a few general stores and houses to whole neighborhoods and a Main Street flanked by commercial buildings. Automobiles also transformed the town, as dirt roads once navigated by horse and wagon gave way to paved streets. (Courtesy of the Pack Memorial Library, North Carolina Collection.)

ECKENROD PHOTOGRAPHY STUDIO. For many years, this building on the south end of Main Street was the best place in town to get a photograph taken, by Silas Eckenrod. The first story of the building served as the town's public library. Female librarians also sold hand-crocheted doilies, as seen in the front windows. The second story of the building housed the photography studio and Eckenrod's apartment. Various painted scenes on sliding panels or curtains were used as backdrops for his photographs. (Courtesy of the Canton Historical Museum.)

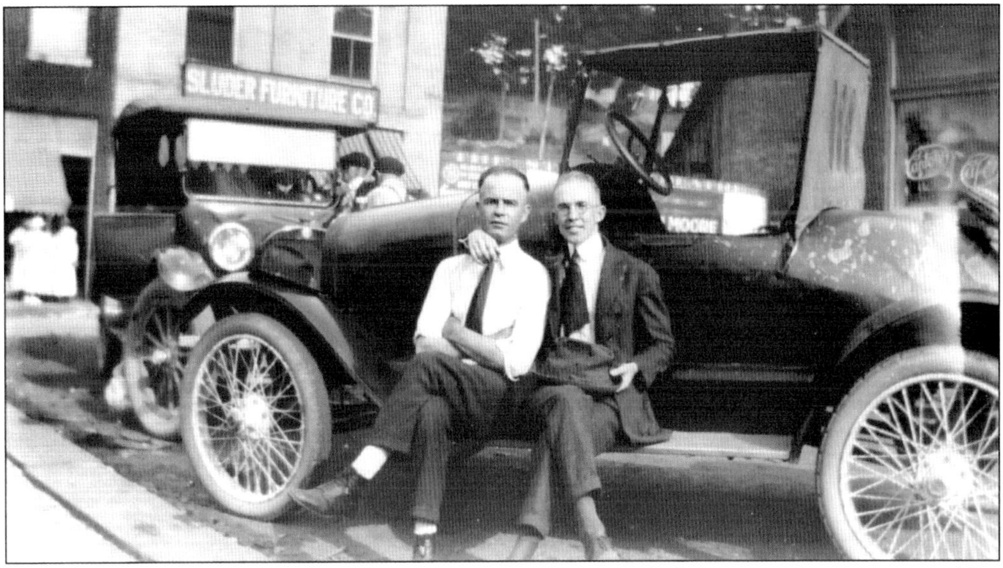

SLUDER FURNITURE. Clyde Freel (left), a founding partner in Sluder Furniture Company, and Dr. Carey Wells Sr., a dentist, share a friendly pose in this 1922 photograph in downtown Canton. Sluder was one of the biggest businesses in town in its heyday, until a fire destroyed the building. The store utilized some attention-grabbing advertising gimmicks, including hypnotizing people and letting them rest for hours on mattresses in its storefront windows. (Courtesy of the Canton Historical Museum.)

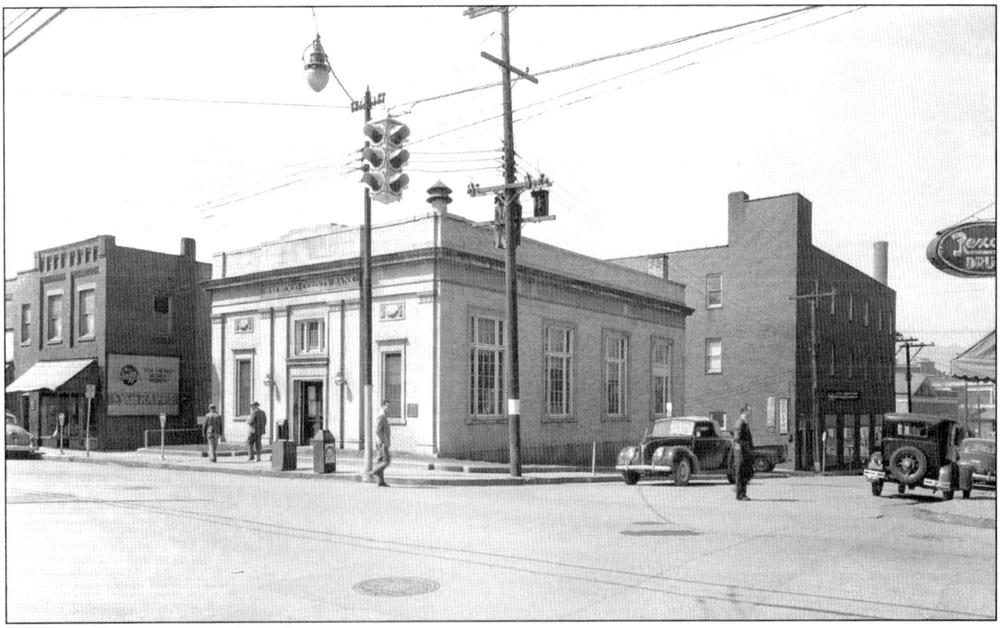

HAYWOOD COUNTY BANK. Around 1890, Col. G.W. Hampton moved to Canton from Leicester and built a two-story house on Main Street. After the property was sold to the Haywood County Bank in 1925, it was torn down to build this Neoclassical, flat-roofed building five years later. For years, it was Canton's only bank. Because of subsequent acquisitions, the bank has changed names, from First Union National Bank to SunTrust, and most recently houses the Champion Credit Union's mortgage offices. (Courtesy of the Canton Historical Museum.)

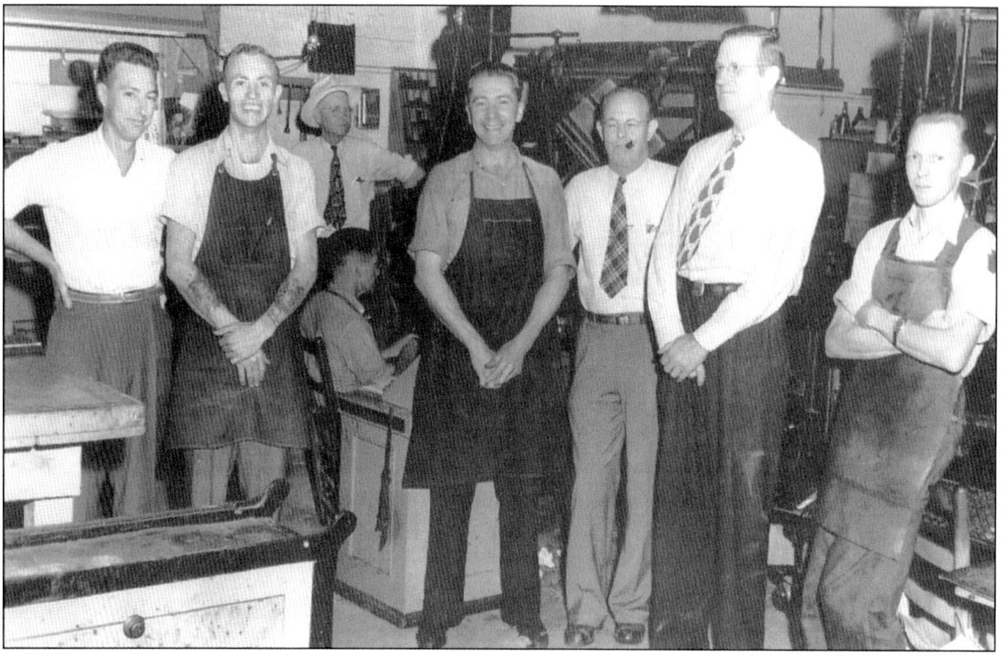

CANTON *ENTERPRISE*. J.H. Hargrove started the *Canton Enterprise* as a one-page letter around 1900. It was printed in Asheville for several years before a handpress was installed in 1906 at its Canton office, located on Main Street above the Bank of Canton. In its earliest days, a yearly subscription cost 50¢. Around 1912, the newspaper moved to the basement of the Imperial Hotel. By 1933, the weekly newspaper cost 5¢ per copy and the front-page masthead proclaimed Canton "The South's Greatest Pulp and Paper Town." In addition to reporting local, state, and national news, the *Enterprise* railed against the dangers of alcohol, shared local history, and lauded community charities. Over the years, the paper changed owners, locations, and names. It was known for a time as the *Vindicator* and then as the *Observer*. Employees of the newspaper are seen above with Harley F. Wright Sr. (third from left, in hat), the owner and editor. (Both, courtesy of the Canton Historical Museum.)

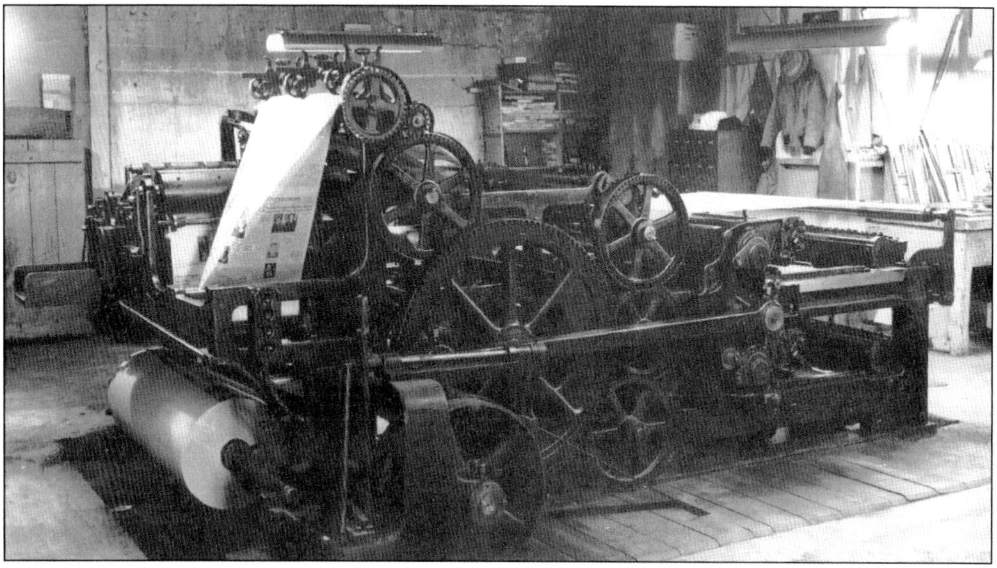

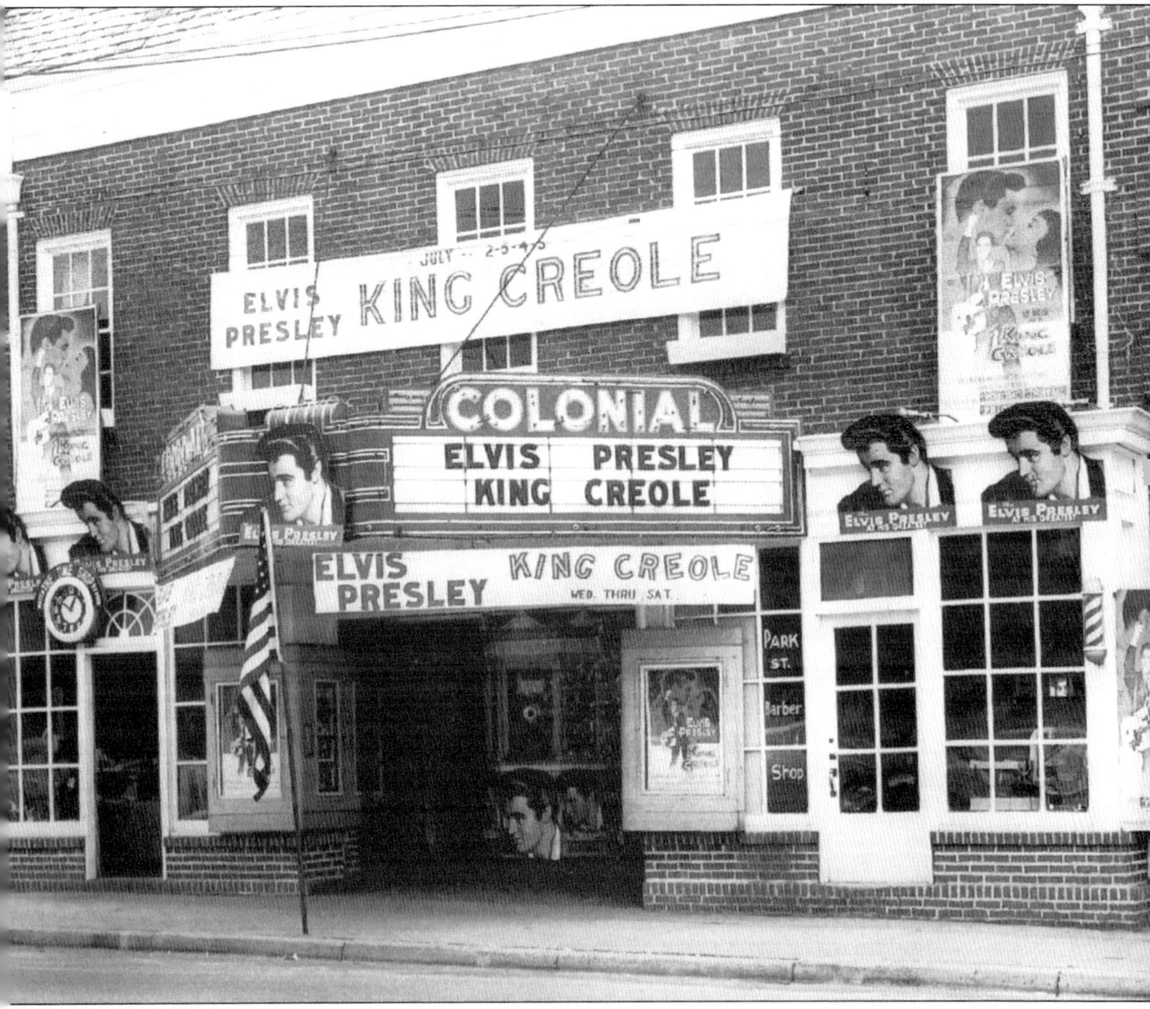

Colonial Theatre. One of Canton's grand theaters, the Colonial first opened on June 6, 1932, under the ownership of Marion Sprinkle and W.H. Odum. For years, it served as a hot spot for young people, families, and dating couples eager to see the latest movies. The big screen, upholstered seats, and balcony made it one of the best theaters in the county. An annex offered additional space for businesses, including a café, a bus terminal, a taxi station, and a liquor store. By the late 1960s, the Colonial had fallen into disrepair, but a concerted effort was made to renovate the building. Despite extensive flood damage in 2004, it was restored into a jewel of downtown life once again, offering stage performances, lectures, movies, and meetings. (Courtesy of the Canton Historical Museum.)

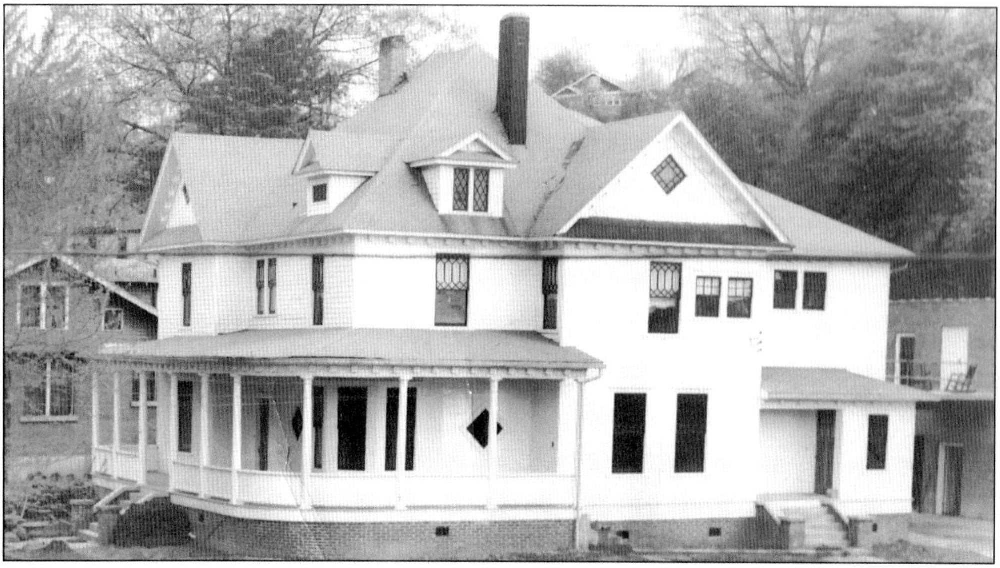

Wells Funeral Home. C.T. Wells Sr. founded Wells Funeral Home in 1888 as Canton's first undertaking business. Today, it is the oldest continuously running business in Haywood County. After Wells had already started a mercantile store in downtown Canton, he operated the funeral home on Main Street until the family moved to another site (pictured), where it operated from 1937 to 1963. Today, it is located on Old Asheville Road and is run by the fourth and fifth generations of the family. (Courtesy of Wells Funeral Home.)

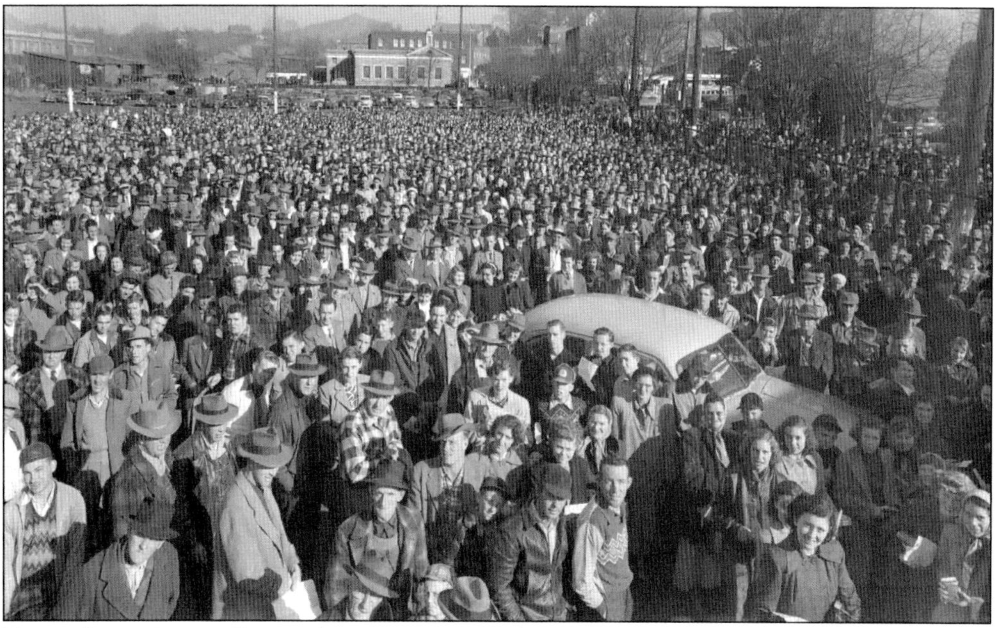

Trade Show. In an effort to draw customers to downtown businesses, the Canton Merchants Association offered tickets to win prizes, including a new car. For every dollar of merchandise purchased, the customer received a ticket. The tickets and prizes were doled out in the weeks leading up to Christmas, with the grand prize drawing for the car, seen here, held on the last Saturday before Christmas. This crowd is gathered on the softball field, at the site of the current town hall. (Courtesy of the Canton Historical Museum.)

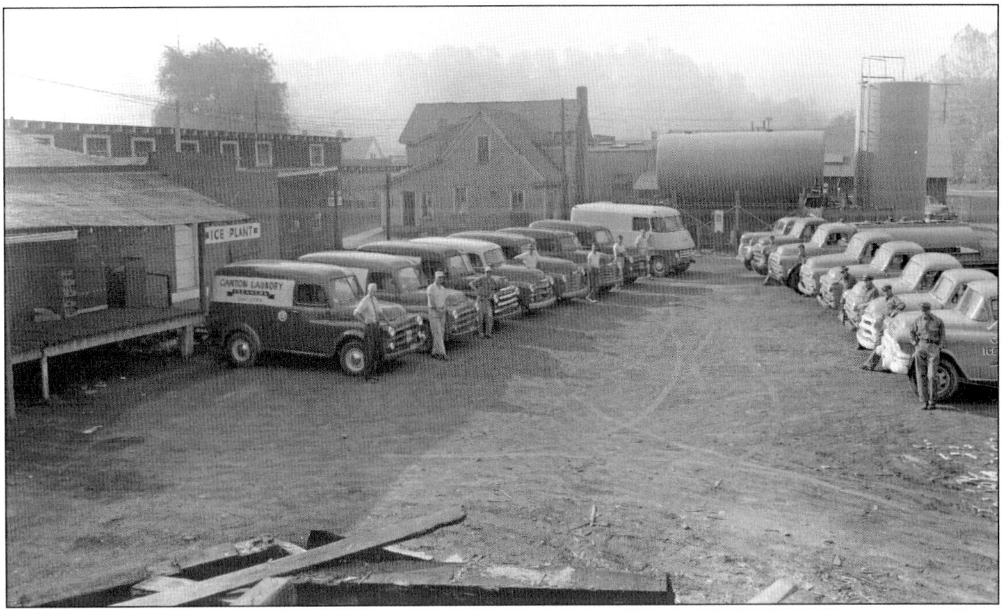

CANTON LAUNDRY. In 1910, R.H. Sorrells and S.H. McNeilly established a one-story ice plant on Main Street that grew to provide three or four tons of ice to local customers in town. A year later, a second story was added for a steam laundry business. The following year, bottling and cold storage was added. By 1920, the building had been demolished and replaced by a three-story brick building. Canton Laundry later became Plus Laundry, which is still in operation today. (Courtesy of the Canton Historical Museum.)

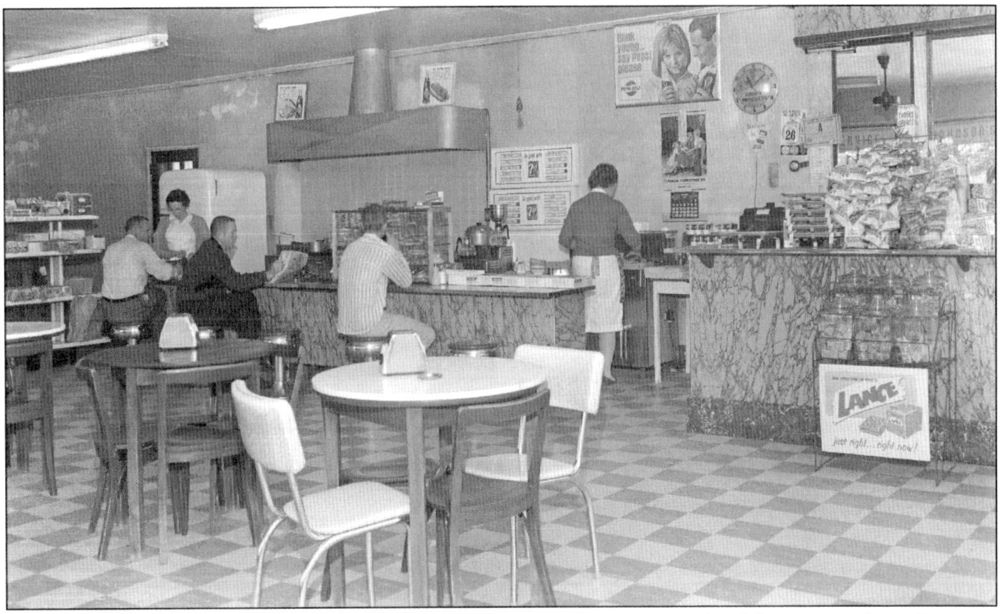

JOHNSON'S DRIVE-IN. In the 1960s, an eager entrepreneur set out to build a racetrack in Canton, but local residents rebuffed the plan, citing the noise it would create in a residential neighborhood. So, rather than a racetrack, the businessman started up a drive-in on the corner of Johnson and Pisgah Drives. The venture only lasted a few years, but the building is now home to the Pisgah Laundromat. (Courtesy of the Canton Historical Museum.)

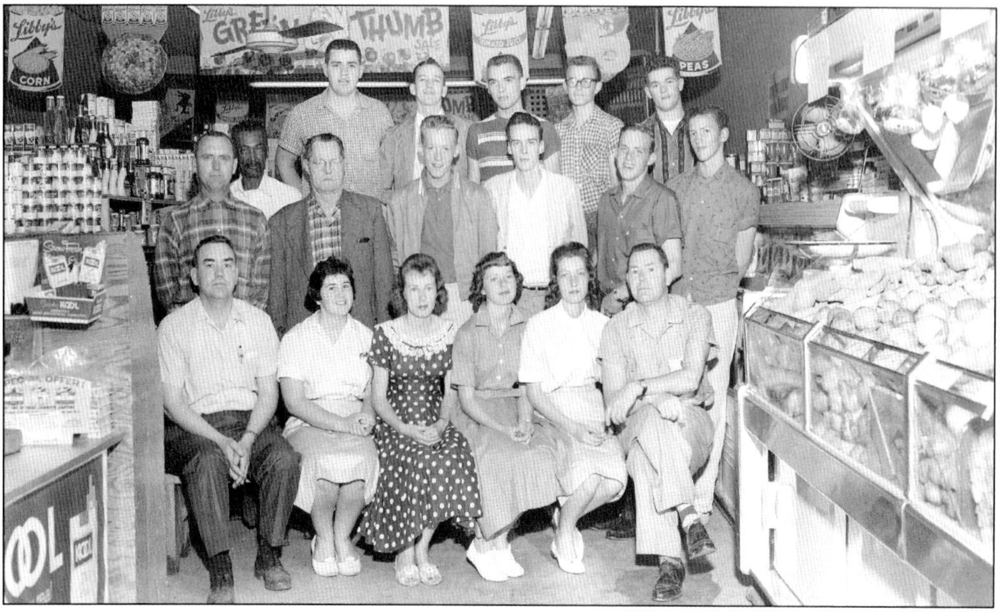

SMATHERS MARKET. After working for a number of years at the Champion company store, Lorenzo Smathers and his brother Underwood ran a downtown grocery store during the 1960s. Smathers Market sold produce, fresh meats, and household items. The store eventually closed and was replaced with a set of retail shops, restaurants, a parking lot, and attorneys' offices. Today, Smathers Square is where Lorenzo's son Pat Smathers, a former mayor of Canton and onetime candidate for lieutenant governor, runs a law office with his son Zeb. (Courtesy of the Canton Historical Museum.)

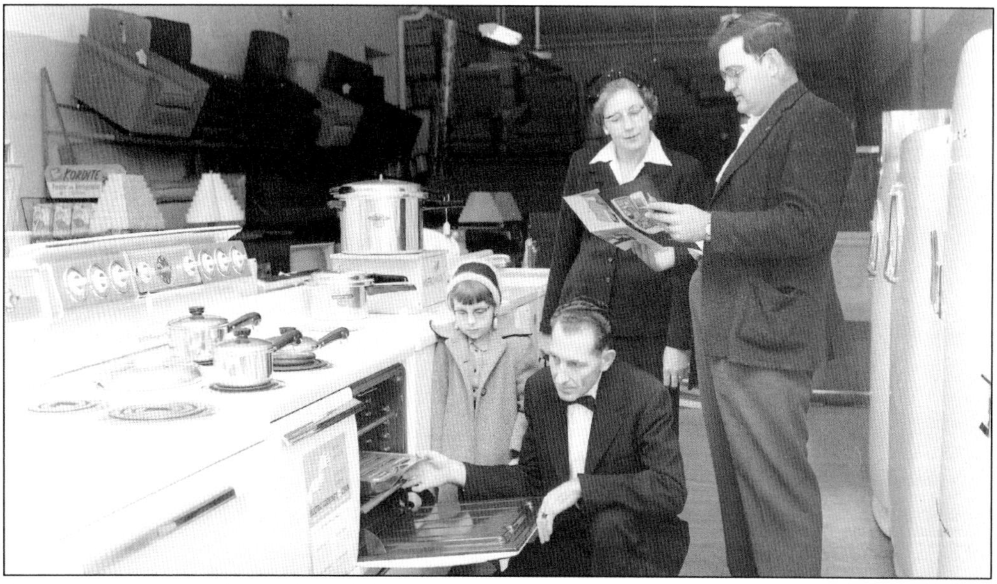

STOVE SHOPPING. Sid Watts (far right) owned and operated a furniture and appliance store on Main Street. Here, he shows Harold Whitted, his wife, Katherine, and their daughter Jane a new stove. Whitted, a World War II veteran, had served in the Army Air Corps and repaired planes while stationed in North Africa. When he returned to Canton, he worked for Champion and helped organize the Haywood County Rescue Squad. (Courtesy of the Canton Historical Museum.)

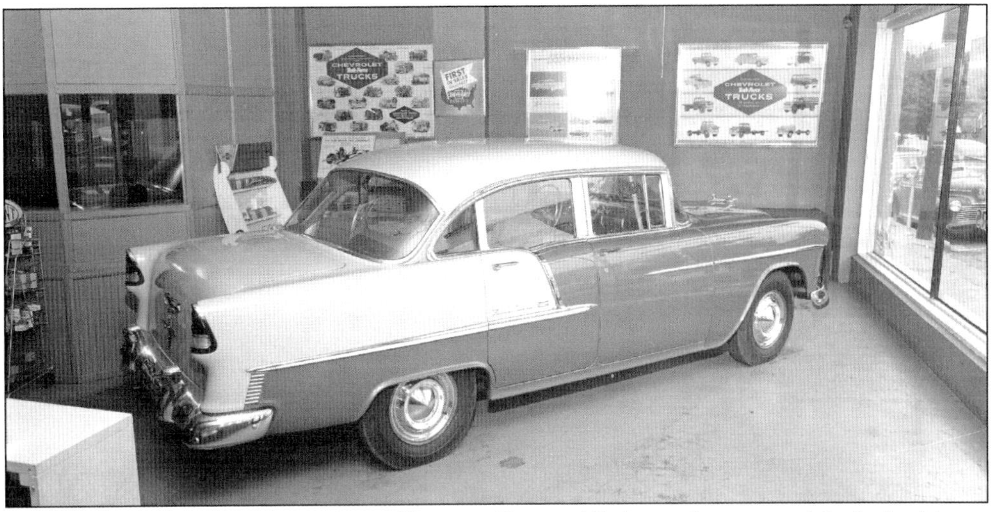

MURPHY CHEVROLET. Pop Murphy and his sons Don and Bob ran this automobile dealership on Main Street and later moved to where Cold Mountain Hardware operates today. In the 1950s and 1960s, downtown Canton had several car dealerships, all of which eventually closed. By the 1970s, Canton's car dealerships set up closer to Interstate 40 to take advantage of customer traffic from the highway. (Courtesy of the Canton Historical Museum.)

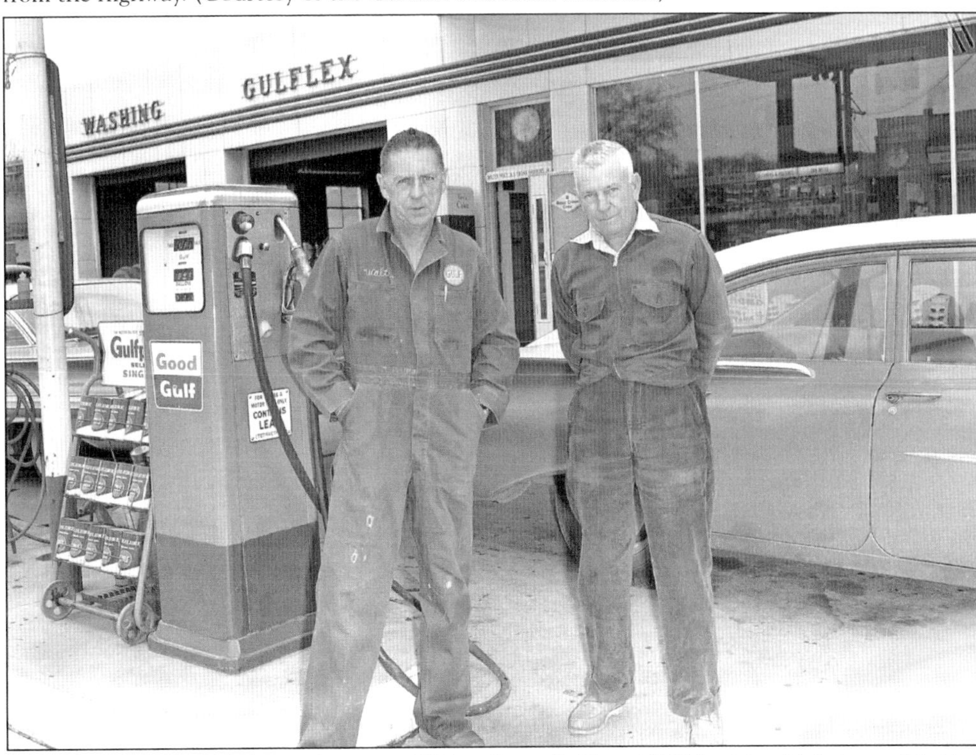

PRICE AND HAWKINS SERVICE STATION. Walter Price (left) and Ed Hawkins (right) ran this Gulf service station, located on the south side of Park Street. It was one of several full-service stations supplying gas, car maintenance, and car washes. However, with the construction of Interstate 40, gas stations also relocated to be closer to highway traffic. This building has since been torn down, and the site is currently a vacant lot. (Courtesy of the Canton Historical Museum.)

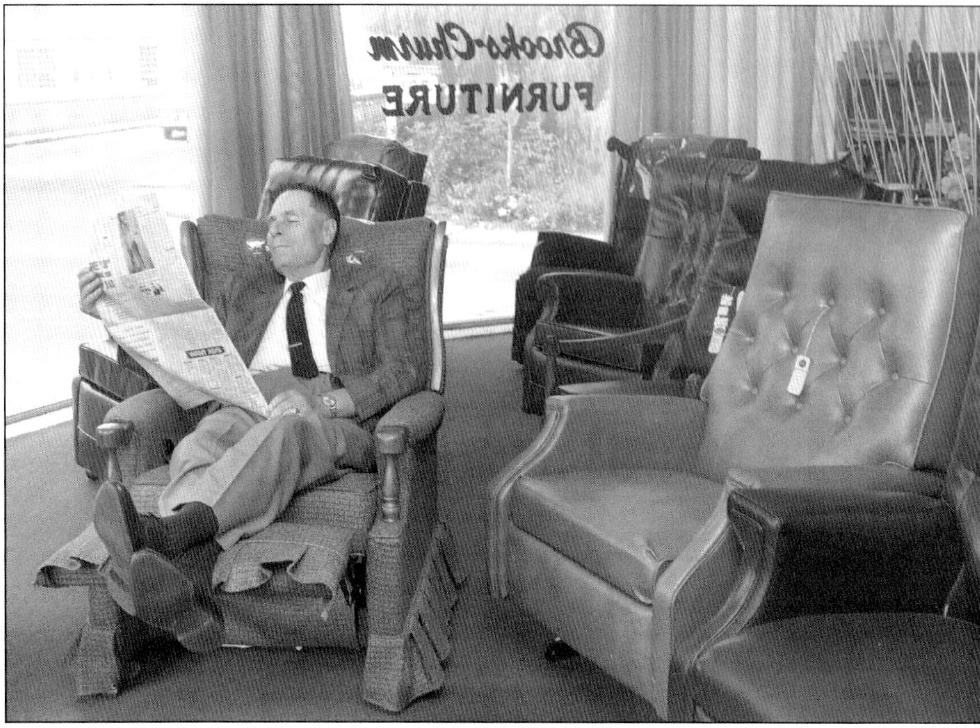

Brooks-Churm Furniture. Maurice Brooks (pictured), his son-in-law Bill Churm, and Neal Duckworth operated this furniture store from 1957 to 1986. Brooks and Churm had worked for Sluder Furniture before that building burned in a fire. The Brooks-Churm business was located on Park Street on what is now a flattened lot in front of the Champion mill. (Courtesy of the Canton Historical Museum.)

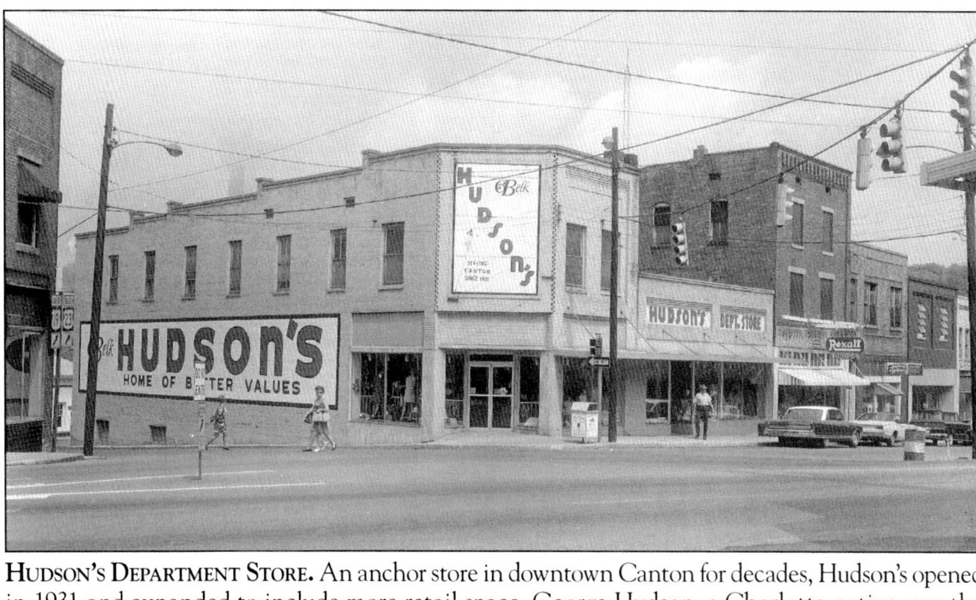

Hudson's Department Store. An anchor store in downtown Canton for decades, Hudson's opened in 1931 and expanded to include more retail space. George Hudson, a Charlotte native, ran the store and remained in Canton after marrying the daughter of Charles Wells, a Canton merchant and the founder of Wells Funeral Home. (Courtesy of the Canton Historical Museum.)

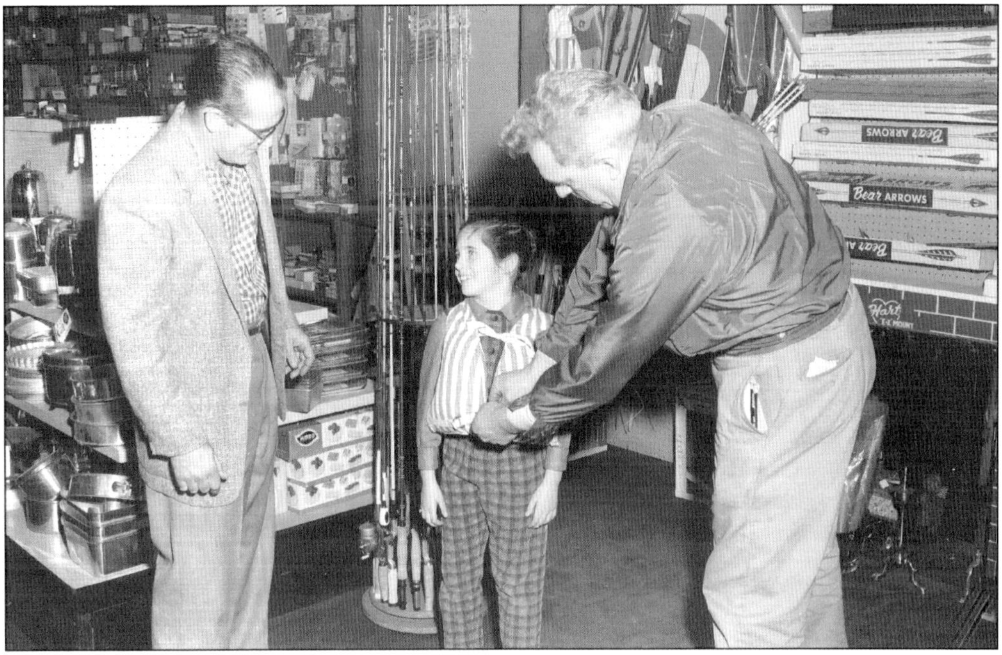

SOESBEE'S HARDWARE STORE. Paul Soesbee (right) ran one of several hardware stores in downtown Canton. Others included Haywood Hardware and the Nantahala Hardware Store. All of the stores sold camping and outdoors equipment. (Courtesy of the Canton Historical Museum.)

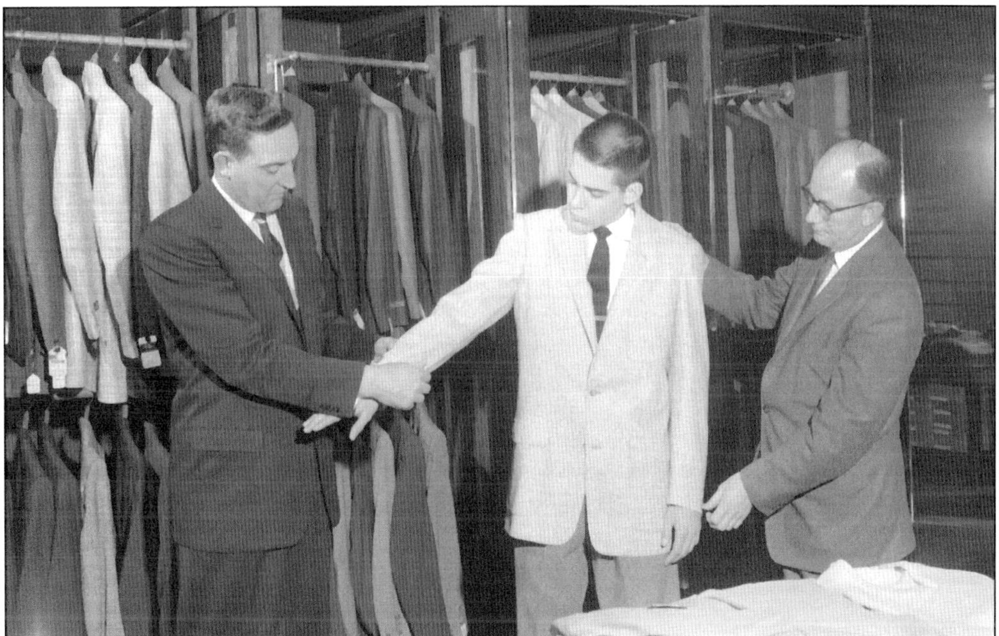

NICHOLLS CLOTHING STORE. Fred Ferguson (left) and store owner C.C. Nicholls (right) help Jay Ferguson (center) into a new blazer at the men's clothing store, located next to what is now Sid's on Main Restaurant. It was one of several fine clothing stores in downtown Canton. Other popular stores included Raiff's, Top of the Line, Winner's, John Graham, and Schulman's Department Store. (Courtesy of the Canton Historical Museum.)

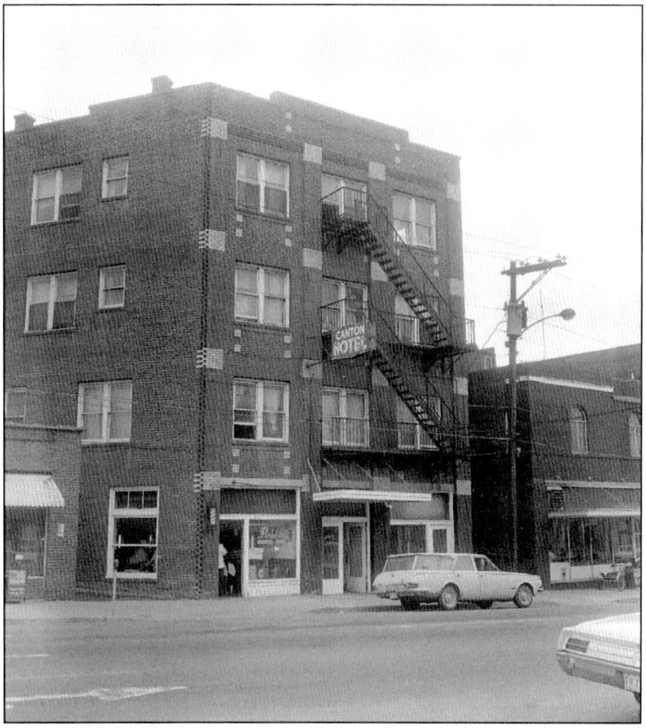

CANTON HOTEL. Built between 1920 and 1925, this four-story brick hotel on Park Street offered rooms to the adjacent Imperial Hotel and was connected to the Imperial Hotel structure. Then, in the early 1940s, it became known as the Canton Hotel. The building provided rooms for a number of businesses, including barbershops and taverns. A sign posted on the west side of the building read, "Stop in for a Red Top." In 1983, a group of Canton businessmen acquired the building to use as apartments for the elderly. (Courtesy of the Canton Historical Museum.)

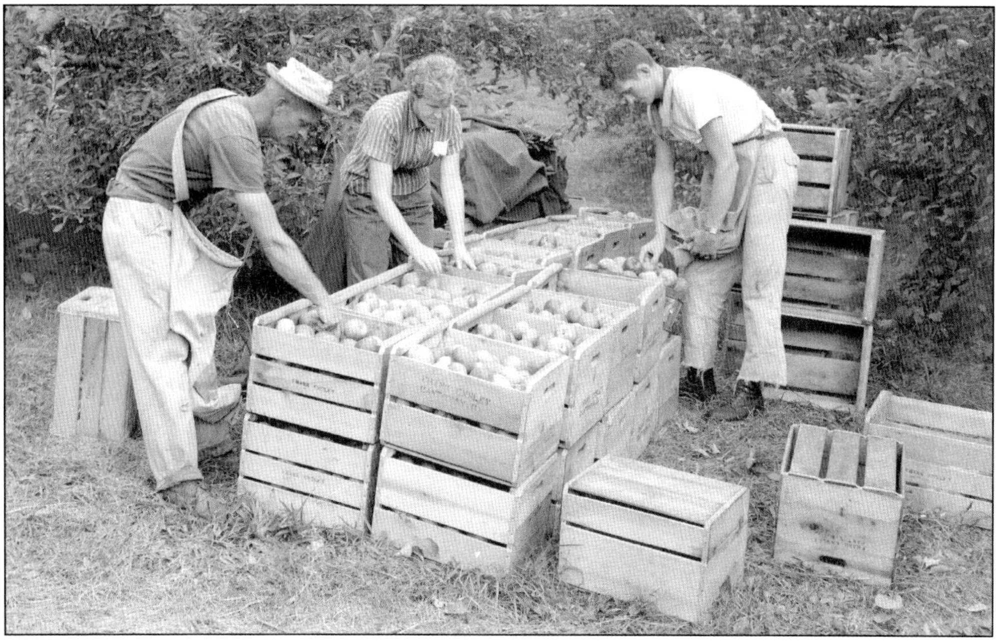

APPLE PICKING. Many of Canton's early businesses were farms that brought local produce to town for sale. Here, workers sort apples at Frank Ensley's farm. One Canton newspaper story in 1919 included a story about a particularly intriguing fruit-bearing tree from the nearby community of Thickety, on the property of C.R. Clark. It was thought to be the county's largest apple tree, measuring 48 feet in height and with a trunk 8 feet in circumference. Its limbs stretched 46 feet on one side and 54 feet on the other. (Courtesy of the Canton Historical Museum.)

Six

ARTS AND SOCIAL LIFE

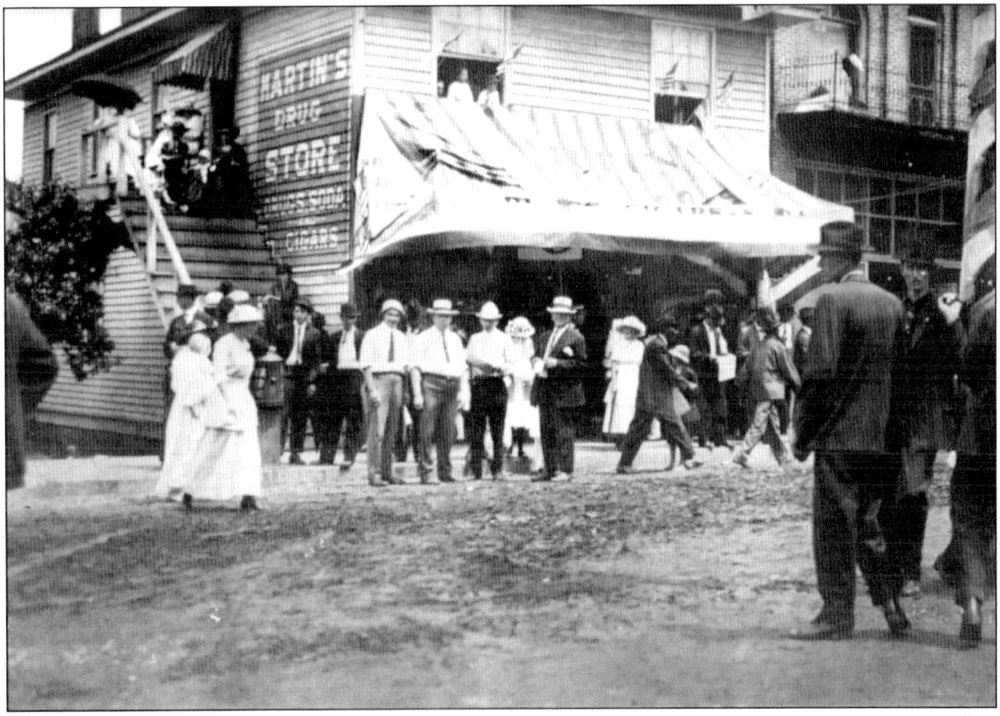

MARTIN'S DRUG STORE. When Dr. Walter S. Martin came to Canton in 1910, he opened this drugstore on Main Street, offering medicines, candy, assorted household items, and a popular soda fountain. This photograph, taken on Independence Day in 1910, shows the building that was torn down in 1917 and replaced with a brick, two-story commercial building. Martin rented space to various businesses, including a jewelry shop, an insurance agency, a barbershop, and a restaurant. (Courtesy of the Canton Historical Museum.)

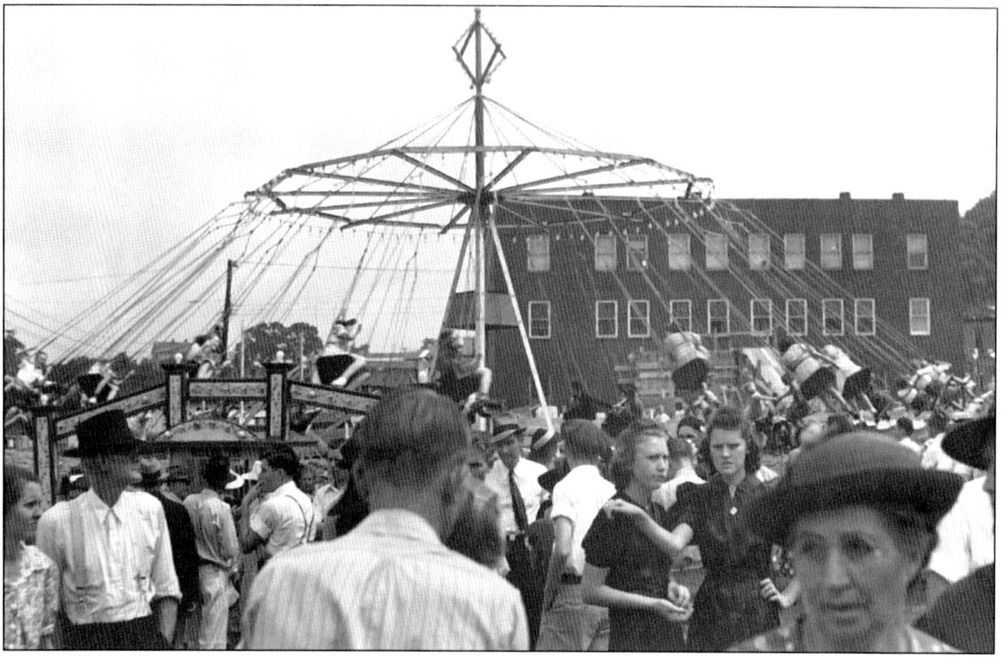

LABOR DAY FESTIVAL. Canton's oldest and most popular cultural event is its annual Labor Day festival, which draws big crowds each year. Begun in 1906, it is thought to be one of the longest-running events of its kind in the nation. In 1935, estimates of the attendance ranged from 12,000 to 15,000 people. In addition to carnival rides, festivalgoers took part in contests and competitions, including singing, square dancing, skeet shooting, football throwing and kicking, track and field, swimming, tennis, softball, bowling, and dog-calling. (Courtesy of the Canton Historical Museum.)

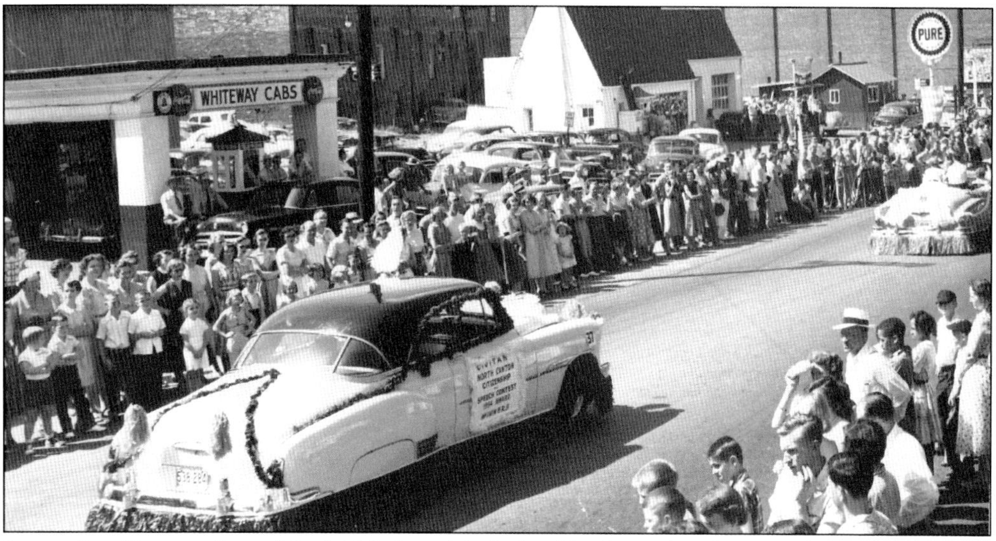

LABOR DAY PARADE. One of the highlights of the Labor Day festival each year is the parade through downtown Canton. Prizes are awarded to the best-decorated car or float in a range of divisions. Occasionally, the parade has been canceled due to inclement weather, but it is traditionally the largest event in the downtown area, with thousands lining the streets. (Courtesy of the Canton Historical Museum.)

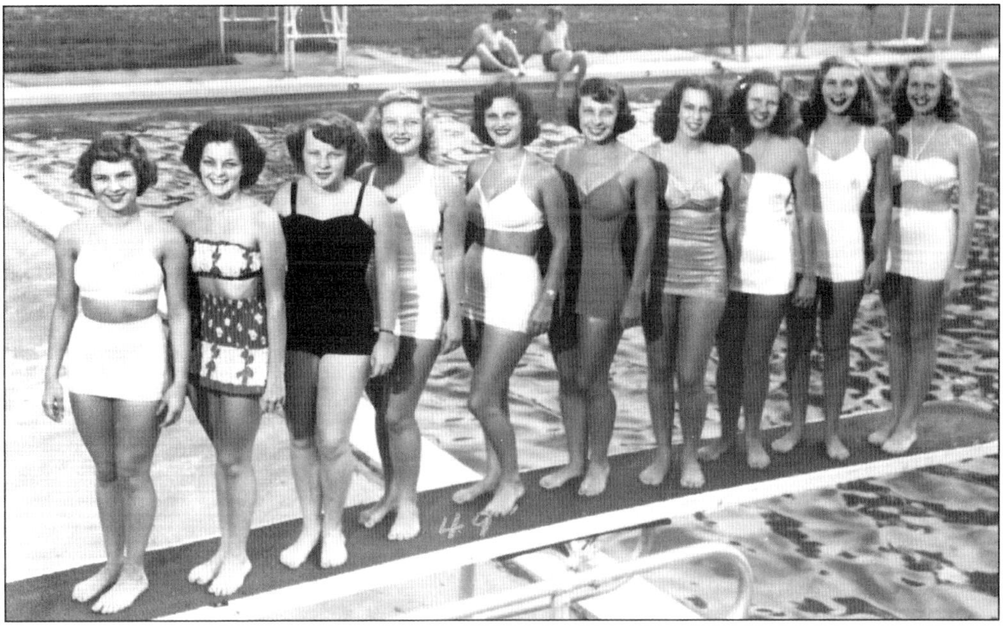

Miss Labor Day Contestants. The Labor Day festival includes the Miss Labor Day pageant, which recognizes beautiful young ladies in the Canton area. Pearl Coman was crowned the first Miss Labor Day in Canton in 1906. In those days, women wore full-length dresses for the competition. A dance was held that first year in the Champion Fibre Company storeroom. These ladies, posing on the diving board at the Canton Recreation Park, competed for the 1949 crown. (Courtesy of Anita Churm.)

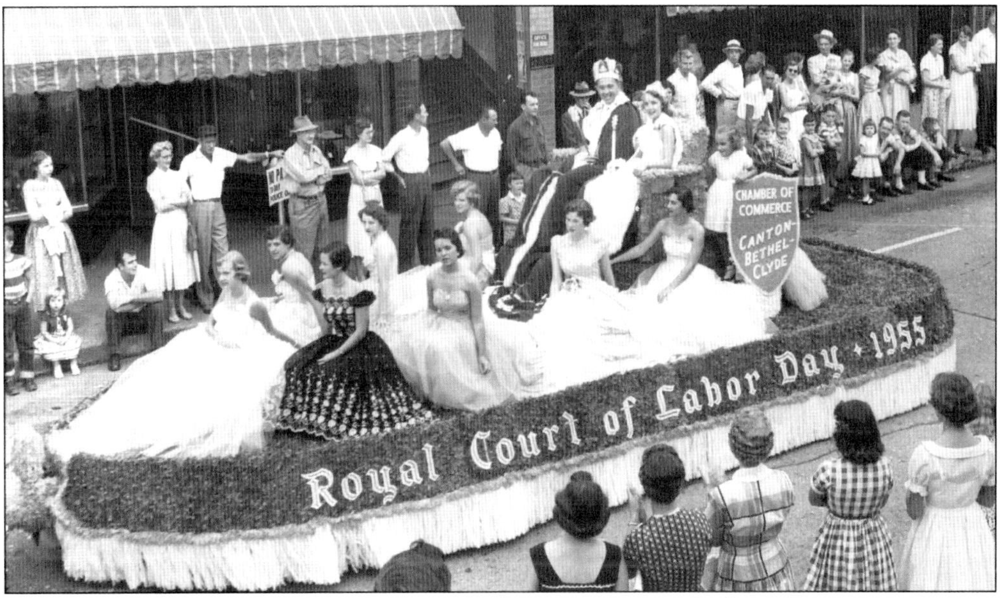

Miss Labor Day Float. Pageant contestants and Miss Labor Day ride through downtown Canton as part of the annual Labor Day parade. The Miss Labor Day pageant was temporarily dropped from the festival in favor of a Miss Haywood County pageant. But it later returned, evolving into a scholastic program requiring contestants to be a senior in high school and involved in community and extracurricular activities. (Courtesy of the Canton Historical Museum.)

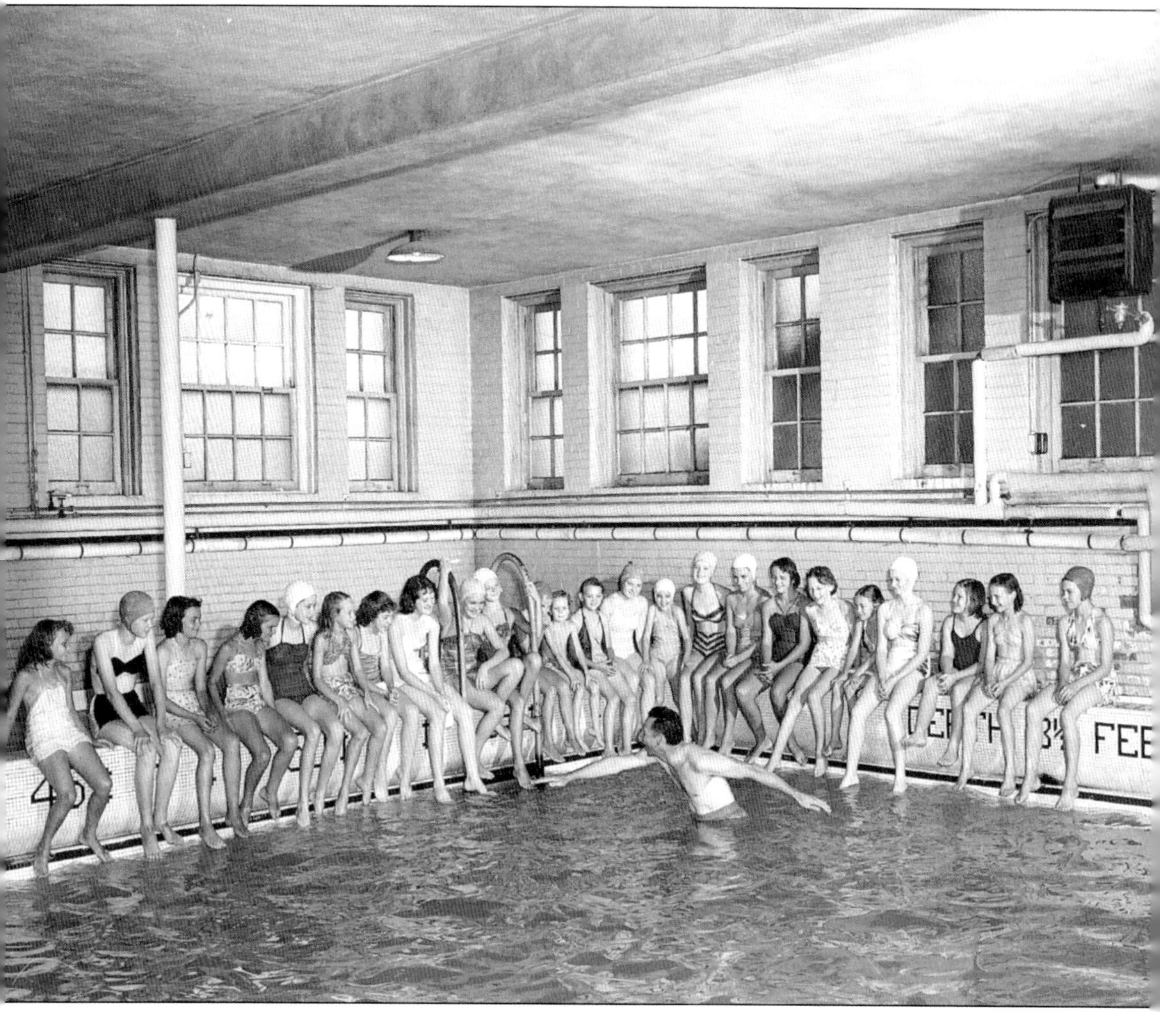

Swimming Lessons. Many Canton residents first learned to swim at the Champion YMCA pool. In the 1950s, a $1.25 membership provided access to all the YMCA had to offer. A swimming instructor was on hand throughout the year to teach swimming and diving classes to boys and girls, as well as adults. On a given evening, the pool may also have been reserved for groups like local Boy Scout troops. Generations of youngsters played in recreational basketball, baseball, softball, and football games affiliated with the YMCA. The gym also served as a site for community meetings, social events, square dancing, and Christmas food drives to help the poor. (Courtesy of the Canton Historical Museum.)

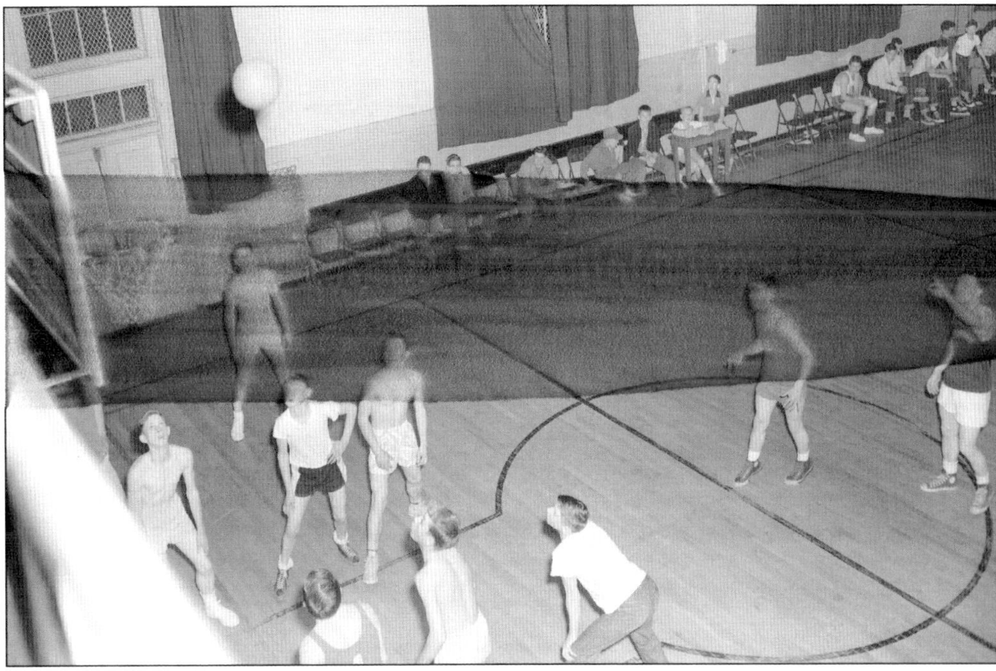

Above the Rim. The Champion YMCA gym echoed with the sounds of squeaking shoes and swishing baskets, as boys' and girls' basketball teams competed on the court for coveted trophies and town pride. The YMCA had a bus for teams to travel in to compete against other YMCA teams in the region, including venues in Asheville and in Sumter, South Carolina. (Courtesy of the Canton Historical Museum.)

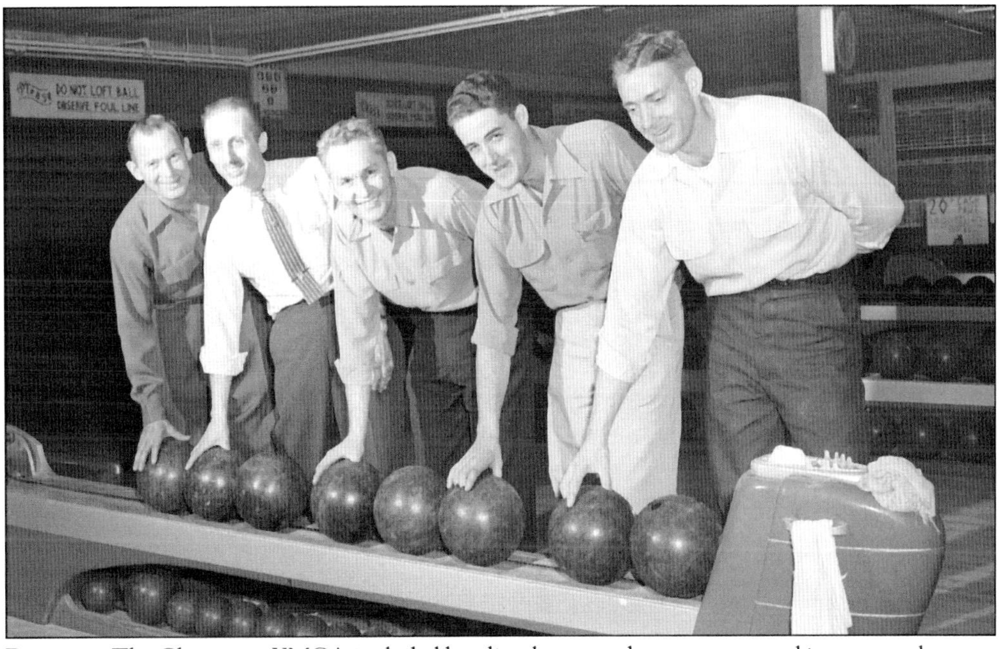

Bowling. The Champion YMCA included bowling lanes, and teams competed in amateur leagues. During World War II, the YMCA had to suspend its bowling league due to the large number of men who left Canton to serve in the military. (Courtesy of the Canton Historical Museum.)

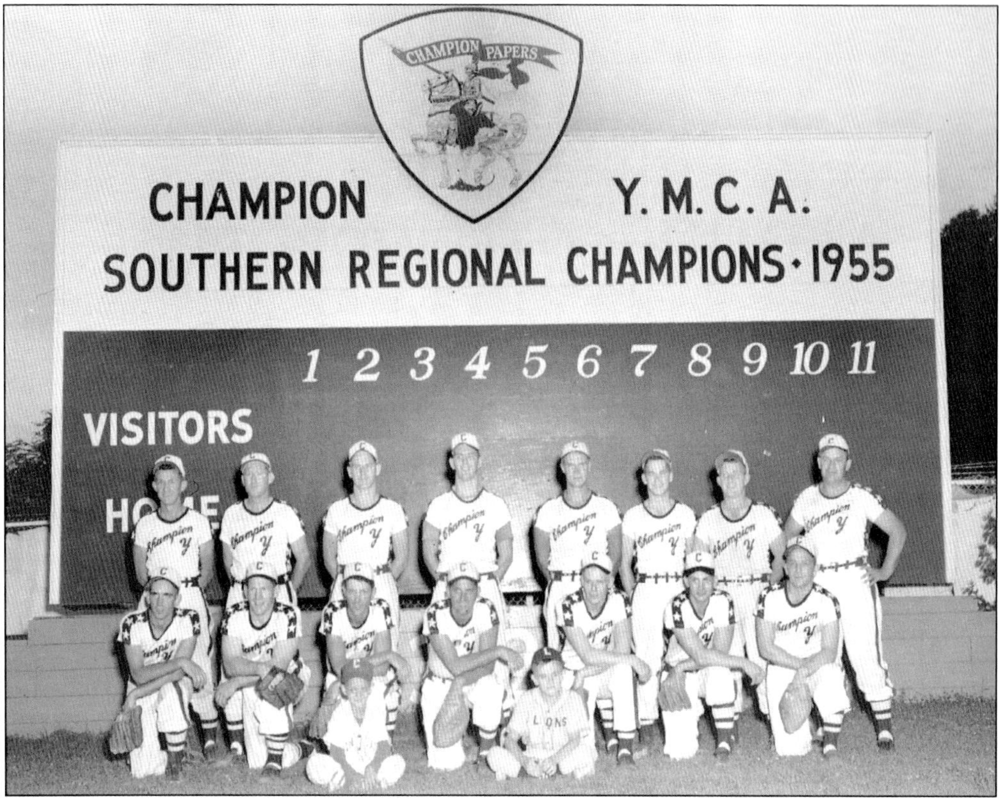

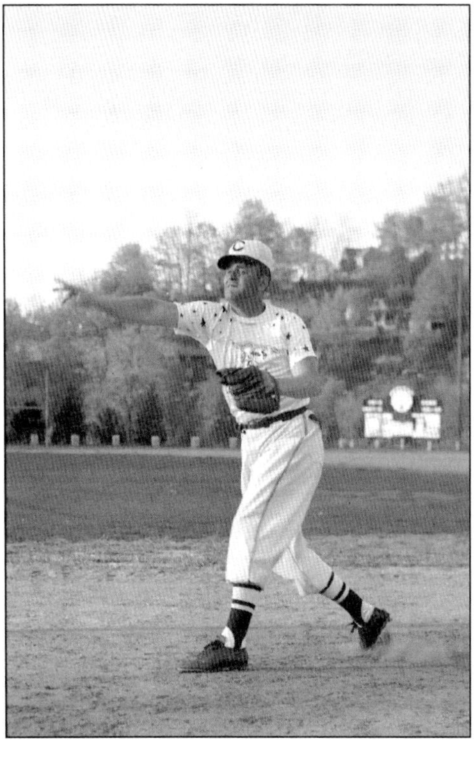

CANTON SOFTBALL. In the 1950s and early 1960s, Canton's Champion YMCA softball teams were nearly invincible. During that stretch, pitcher German "Nazi" Miller (left) led his teams to six North Carolina amateur softball titles, five regional championships, and at least three world championship invitations. Miller later coached and managed Champion YMCA teams and served as the North Carolina commissioner of softball. In 1969, he was honored as the most outstanding commissioner in the nation and was inducted into the Amateur Softball Hall of Fame. Another Hall of Fame pitcher for the Champion YMCA softball teams was Wade Garrett, a Guilford County native who compiled a 358-83 record, with 40 no-hitters and 78 innings of scoreless pitching. A member of all-state or all-south teams 15 times, he appeared in 10 world softball tournaments and made the Guinness Book of World Records for consecutive innings pitched by a single pitcher, with 22. In 2013, he was inducted into the North Carolina Sports Hall of Fame. (Both, courtesy of the Canton Historical Museum.)

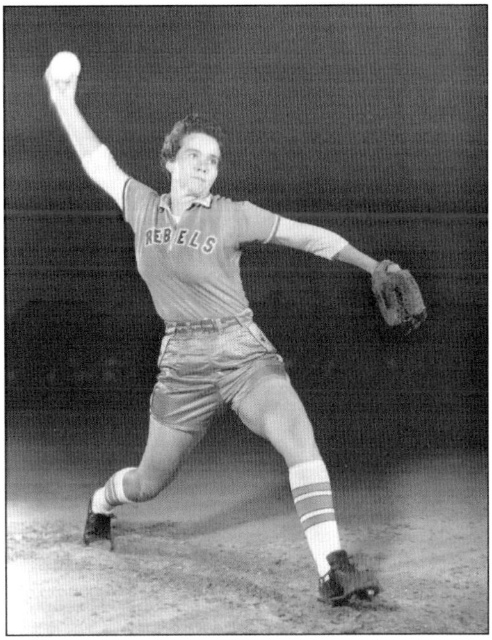

Jean Daves. A Canton native and outstanding softball pitcher, Daves pitched for 20 years with teams in Atlanta, Birmingham, Washington, DC, and Orlando. She taught herself fast-pitch throwing by hurling softballs into a blanket hung over a clothesline. When she retired in 1971, she had compiled a 255-59 record, with 2,944 strikeouts, 197 shutouts, and 41 no-hitters. Every year from 1966 to 1971, she earned a spot on either the first or second All-America team compiled by the Amateur Softball Association, and she was inducted into the National Softball Hall of Fame in 1980. (Courtesy of the Canton Historical Museum.)

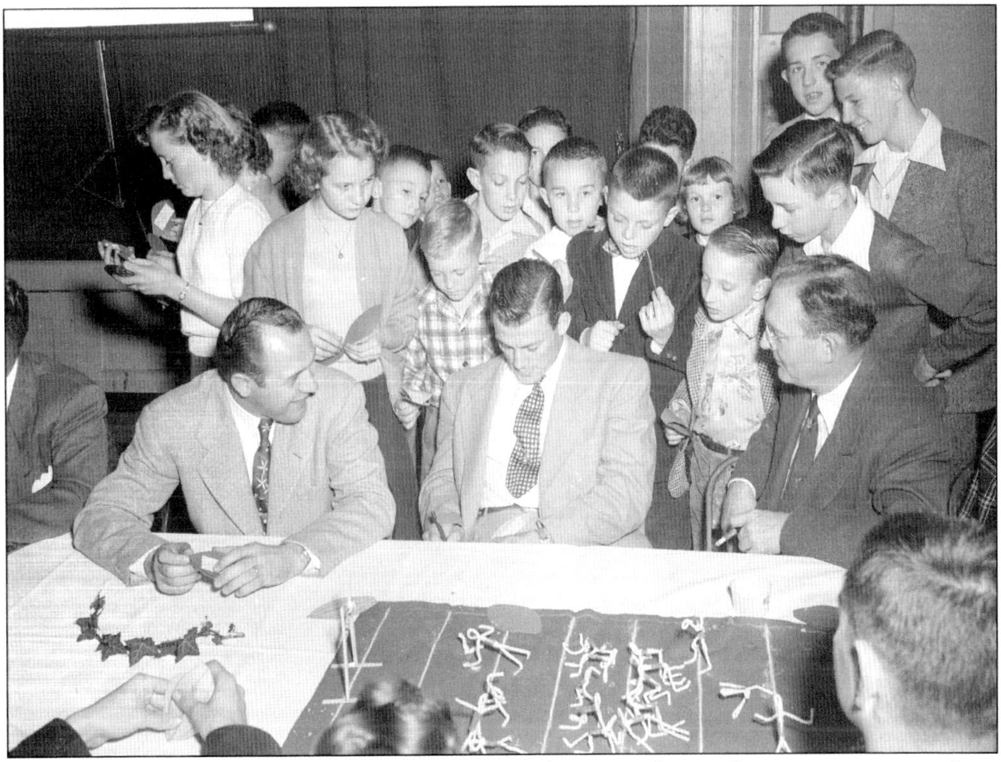

Signing Autographs. Champion YMCA sports banquets featured guest appearances from famous athletes like Charlie "Choo Choo" Justice (center), a legendary Asheville running back and All-America football star at the University of North Carolina at Chapel Hill. His brother Jack (left, front row) served as the director of the Champion YMCA. (Courtesy of the Canton Historical Museum.)

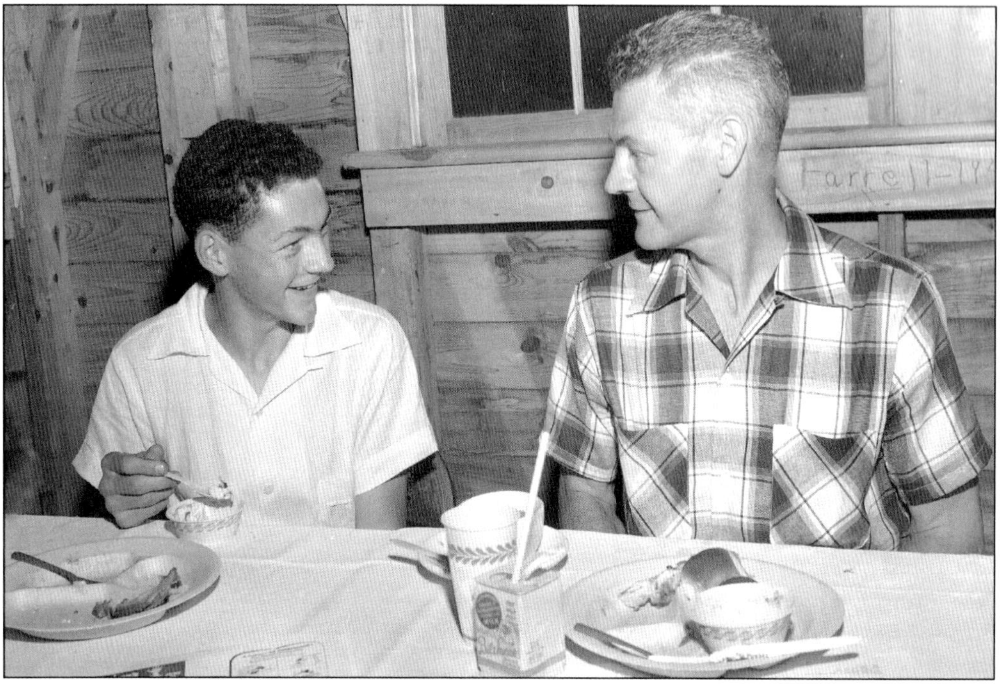

FATHER-SON BANQUET. The Champion YMCA sponsored annual father-son banquets at its Camp Hope lodge, south of Canton. R.E. Osborne and his son Roland are seen here in 1953, sharing a meal at a banquet honoring youth sports accomplishments. Roland played basketball, baseball, and football and won a state championship in basketball with one of his YMCA teams. R.E. was a pipe fitter at the Champion mill and also worked as a logger and a road builder. (Courtesy of the Canton Historical Museum.)

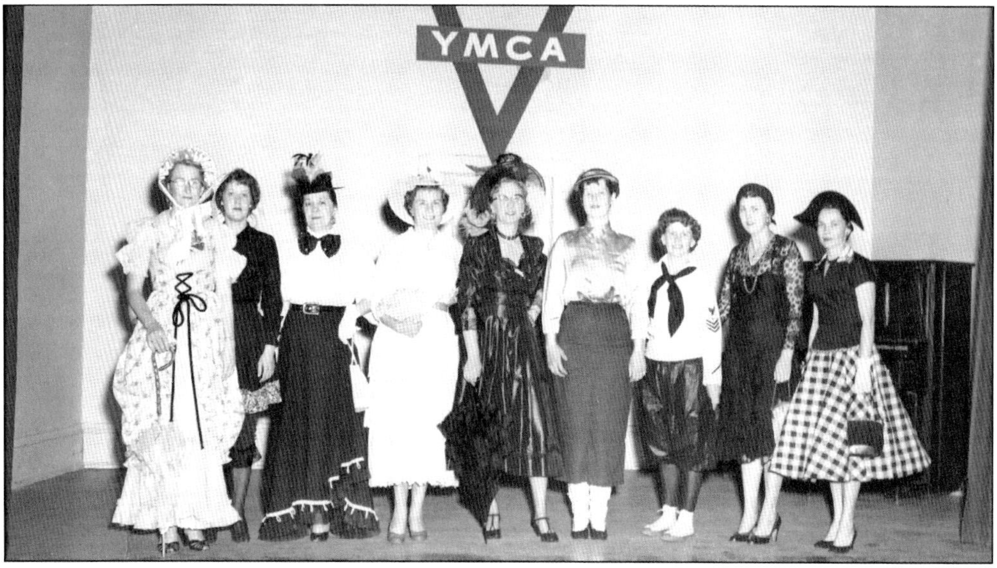

COSTUME PARTY. The Champion YMCA in Canton often hosted holiday events and special occasions for dressing up, like this costume party. Pictured, from left to right, are Bobby Carter, Margaret McDowell, Mary Reeves, Myrtle Miller, Elizabeth Thompson, Toba Grogan, Dorothy Driver, Edna Broyles, and Mary Love Hyatt. (Courtesy of the Canton Historical Museum.)

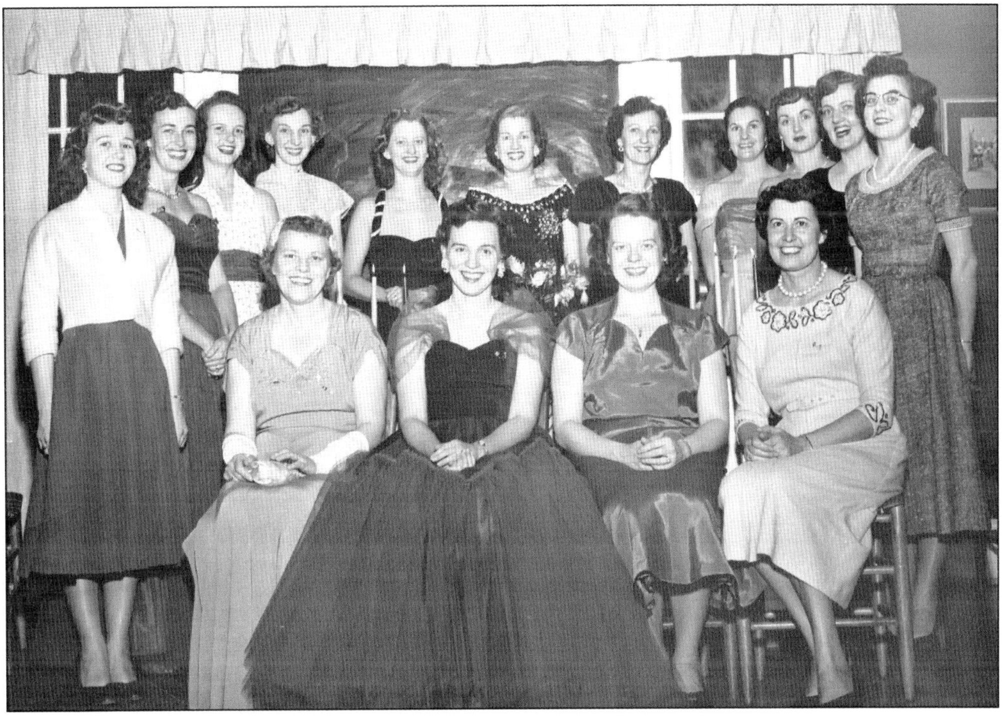

High Society. The Gamma Epsilon Chapter of Beta Sigma Phi in Canton included some of the town's most beautiful ladies. The sorority also had a high school club chapter in which students were selectively chosen and introduced as debutantes. (Courtesy of Anita Churm.)

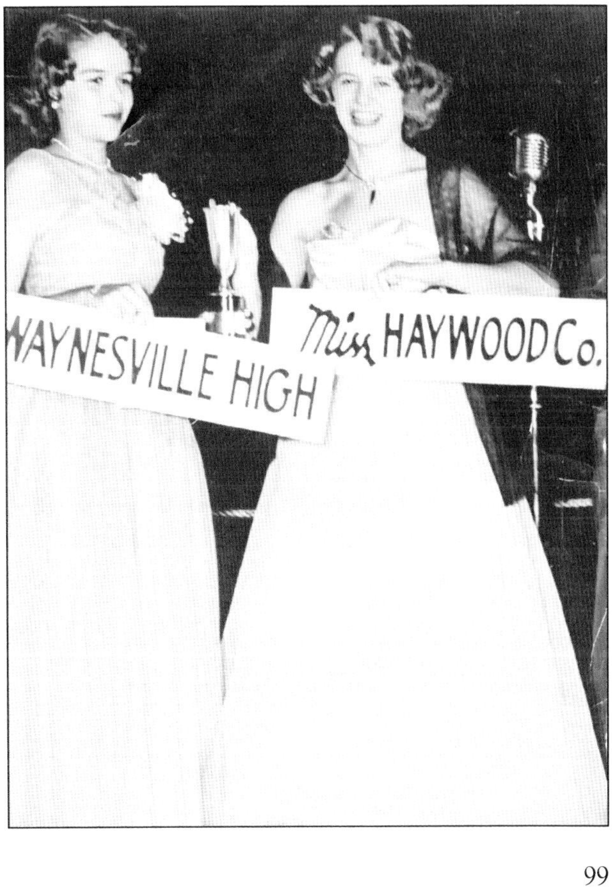

Miss Haywood County. Norma Lou Jones (right), a 17-year-old from the Henson Cove community, south of Canton, won the inaugural title of Miss Haywood County in 1950. Jones also starred for the Bethel High School basketball team and averaged 25 points per game en route to a state basketball championship in 1952. Her fellow players nicknamed her Squirt. (Courtesy of Tammy Ingle)

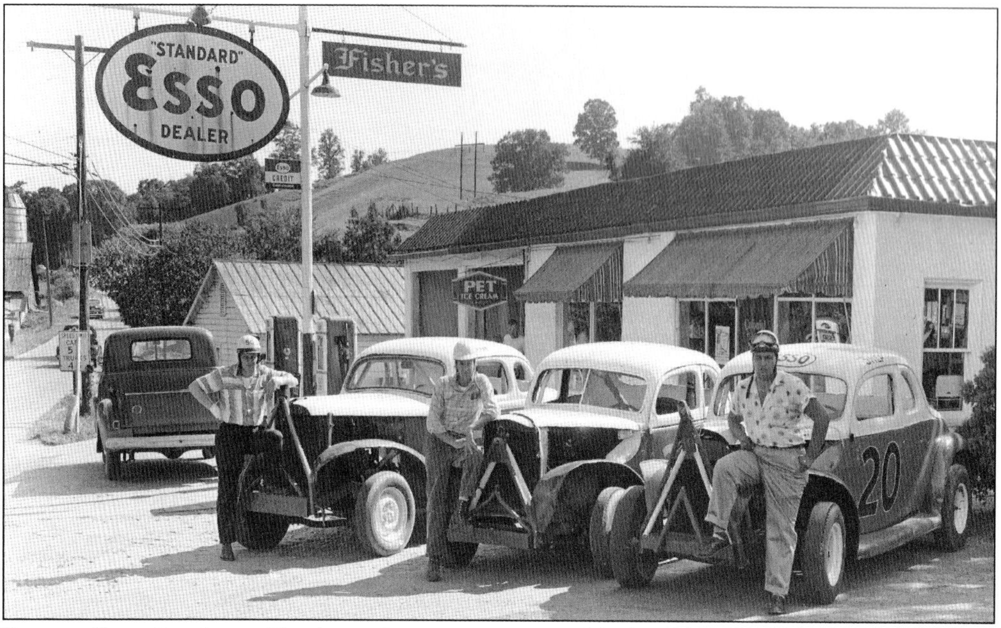

RACING CARS. Stock cars like those above were sponsored by local businesses such as the Esso gas station in Canton, on Highway 110 where the Black Bear Café now stands. Canton racecar drivers, some of whom were Champion mill employees, competed weekly at the quarter-mile oval track at McCormick Field Raceway in Asheville, now the site of the Asheville Tourists' minor-league baseball park. Other racetracks included ovals in Weaverville, North Carolina; Marion, North Carolina; Gaffney, South Carolina; and Newport, Tennessee. The triangular pieces on the fronts of the cars were used for towing and then removed before the race. One of the drivers was Johnny Rhodarmer, a postal employee in Canton who co-owned and drove the No. 40 car below. Other "Haywood Speed Kings" were Bob Browning (41), Jim Long (50), Jim Pace (21), Forest Messer (42), and Homer Hannah (77). (Both, courtesy of the Canton Historical Museum.)

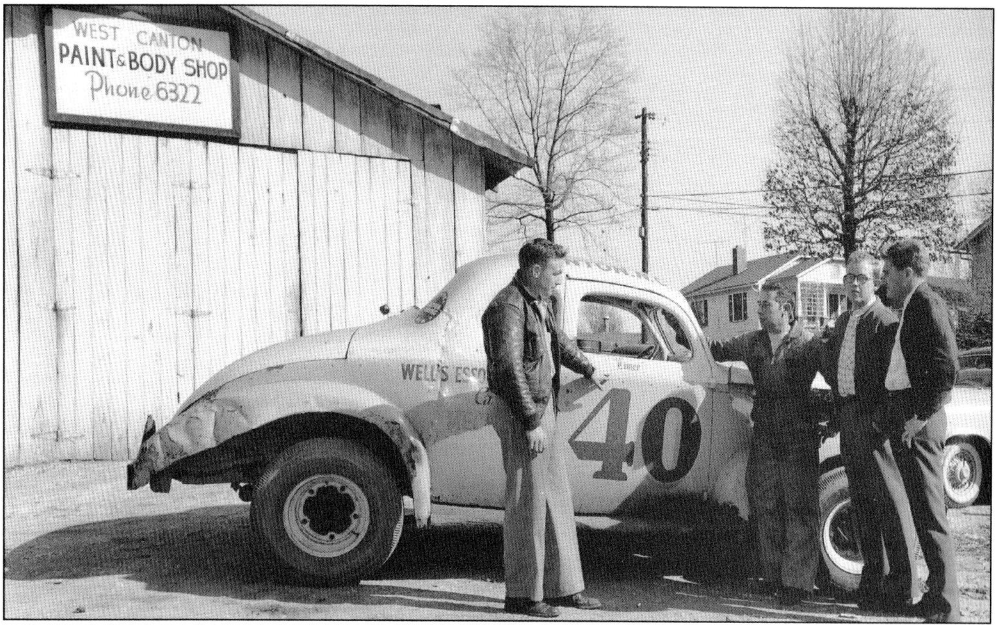

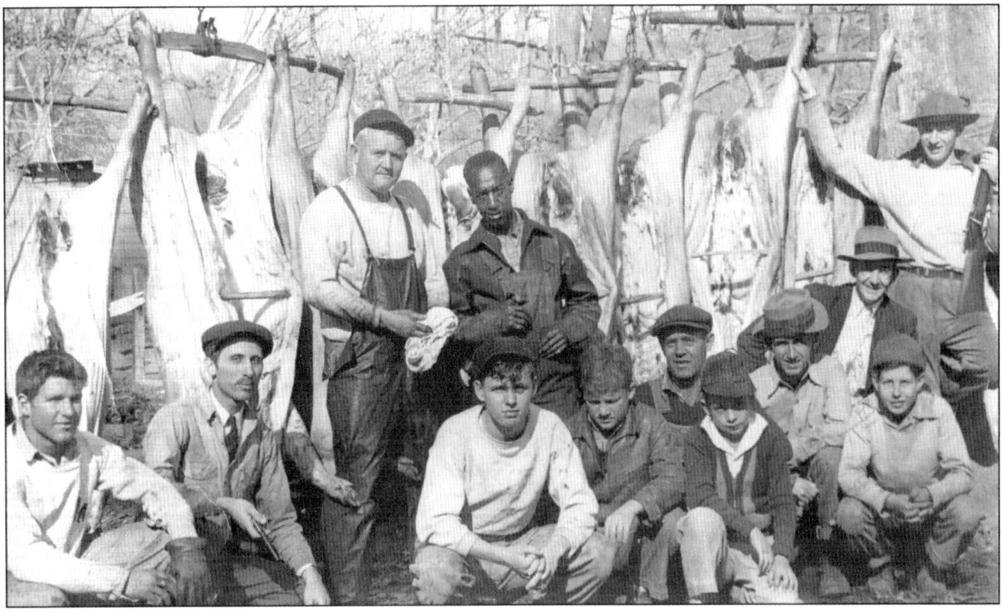

HOG KILLING. Each fall, after the first cold spell, meat needed to be prepared and stored for the winter, and killing a hog was a time-honored tradition for many families. A hog was killed and hung on a pole before being lowered into a vat of scalding hot water in order to scrape off the animal's hair. Next came cutting up the meat and trimming away the excess fat. Meat cured with salt and seasonings made for hearty meals in the winter. This hog-killing took place in the Fibreville community of Canton. (Courtesy of the Canton Historical Museum.)

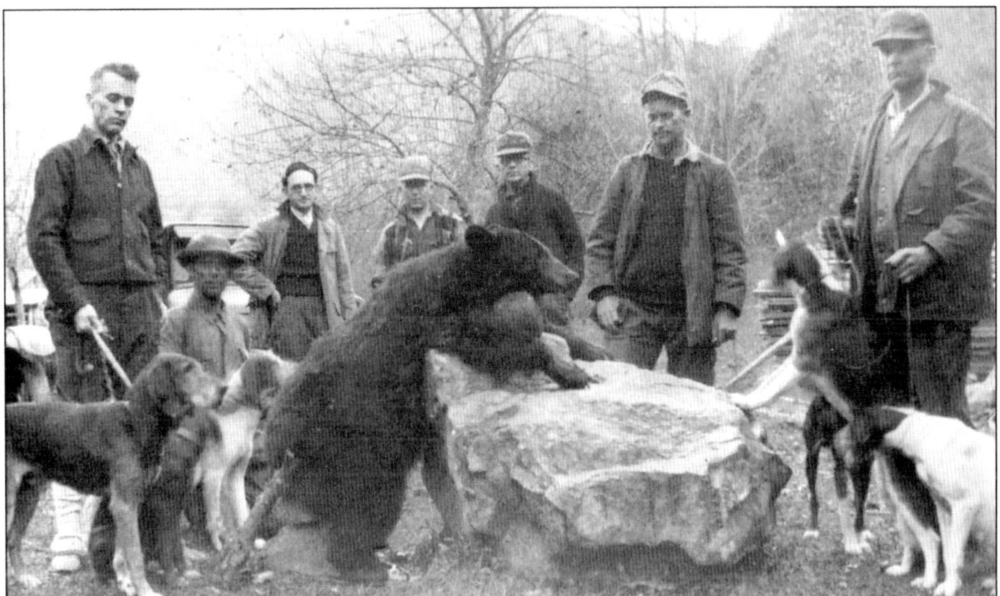

BEAR HUNTING. Bear hunting was a popular pastime for some Canton residents. Joe Hargrove (far right) was a well-known bear hunter and farmer who was born in the Pigeon Valley community in 1874. He married Mary Shook in 1897, and the two were together for 56 years until his death at the age of 79. Waynesville dentist Nick Medford (far left) was a fellow hunter with Hargrove. (Courtesy of Edith Burnette.)

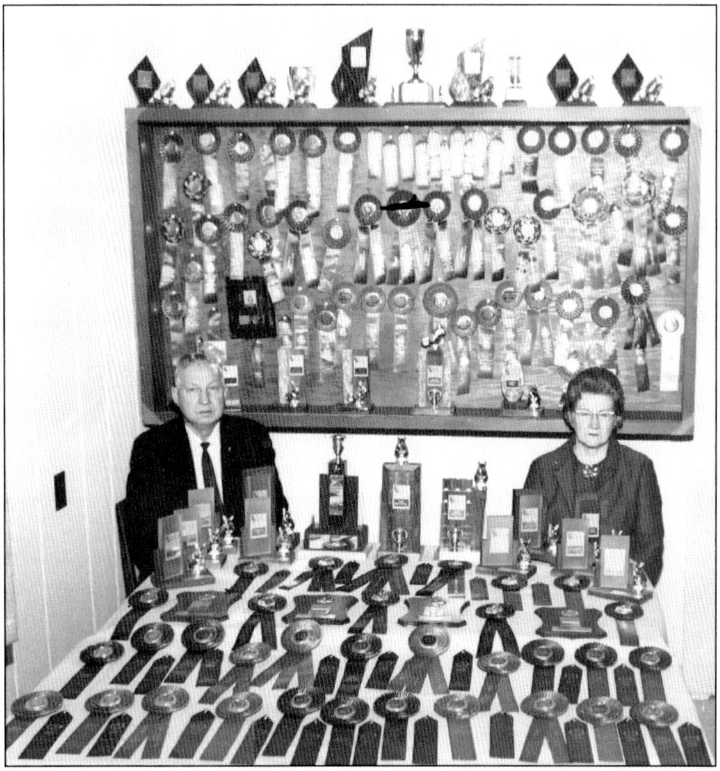

Trophies and Ribbons. Charlie Fullam and his wife Ollie earned many awards for raising prize-winning chinchillas, squirrel-like animals that are native to the Andes Mountains of South America. Fullam worked for many years in Canton delivering and collecting subscriptions for the *Asheville Citizen-Times*, running a stand on the corner of Main and Academy Streets. He was also a huge fan of Champion YMCA sports and traveled extensively to cheer on the softball teams in tournaments. (Courtesy of the Canton Historical Museum.)

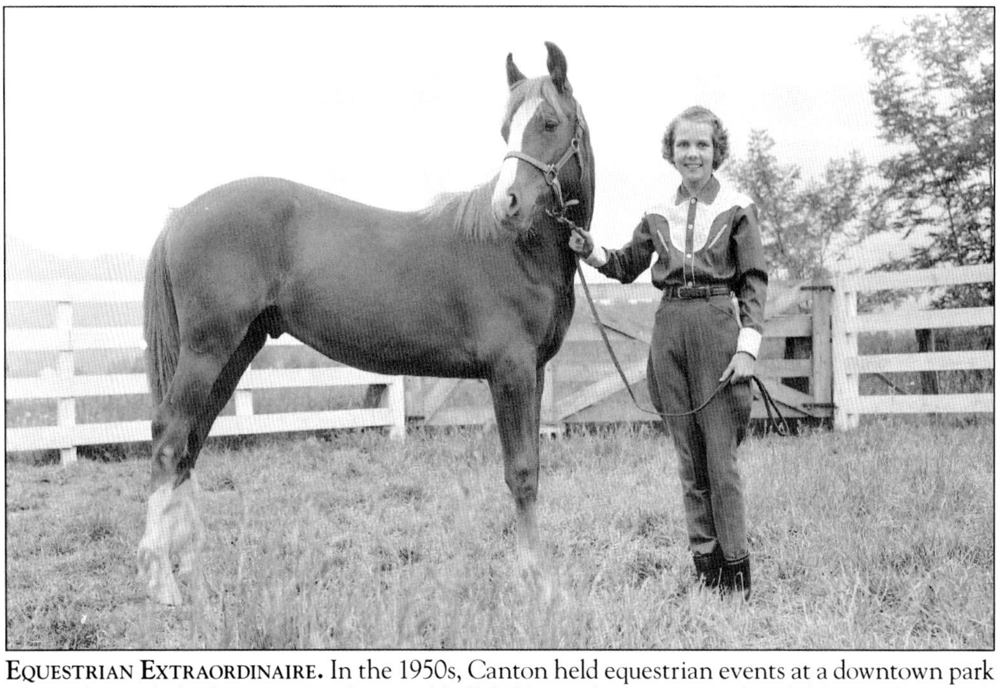

Equestrian Extraordinaire. In the 1950s, Canton held equestrian events at a downtown park where the Bethel Christian Academy softball field is today. Bootsy Bohnsdahl, seen here with her horse, was a frequent competitor. Her father was a board inspector with the Champion mill and her mother was a school librarian. (Courtesy of the Canton Historical Museum.)

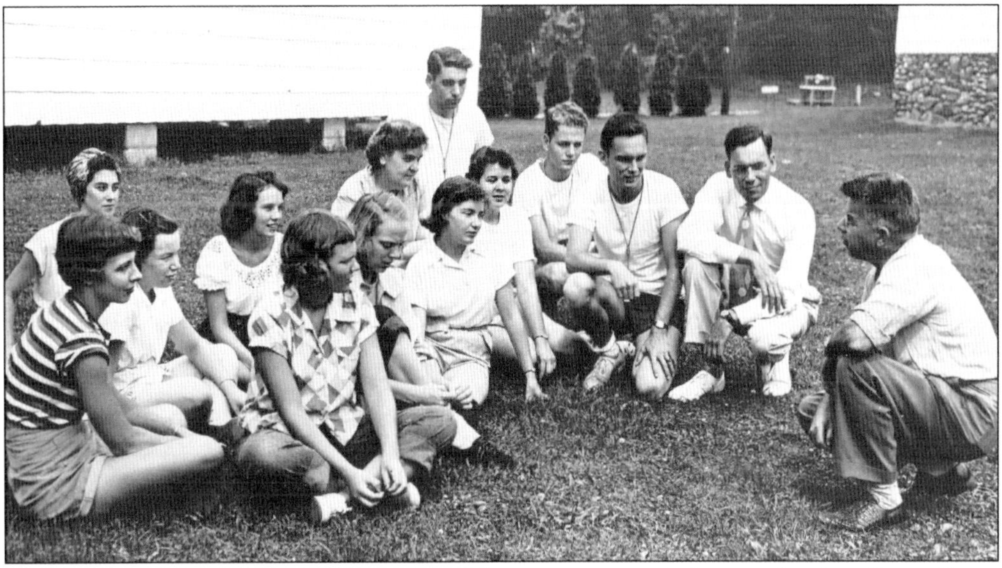

Camp Hope. The Champion YMCA operated summer camps for boys and girls at Camp Hope, at the southern end of Haywood County near what was once the Sunburst logging community. Campers recalled learning and practicing archery, arts and crafts, and various sports. In the 1945-era photograph above, Grover Suttles (above, right), the longtime director of the Champion YMCA, meets with camp counselors at Camp Hope. Suttles oversaw a professional staff and volunteers and helped build the Champion YMCA's programming into a dynamic center of the Canton community. Many of Canton's top athletes began playing sports at the Champion YMCA, and Suttles coached, directed, and oversaw programs for generations of Canton residents. On some occasions, Champion opened Camp Hope for summer events, where families enjoyed free carnival rides (below), potato sack races, and outdoor entertainment. (Both, courtesy of the Canton Historical Museum.)

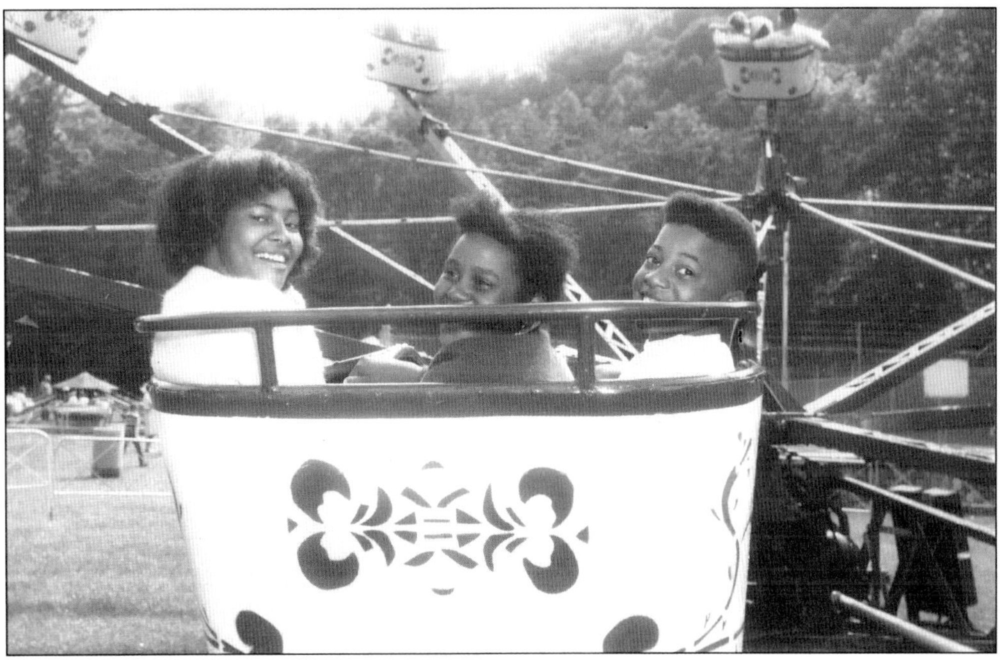

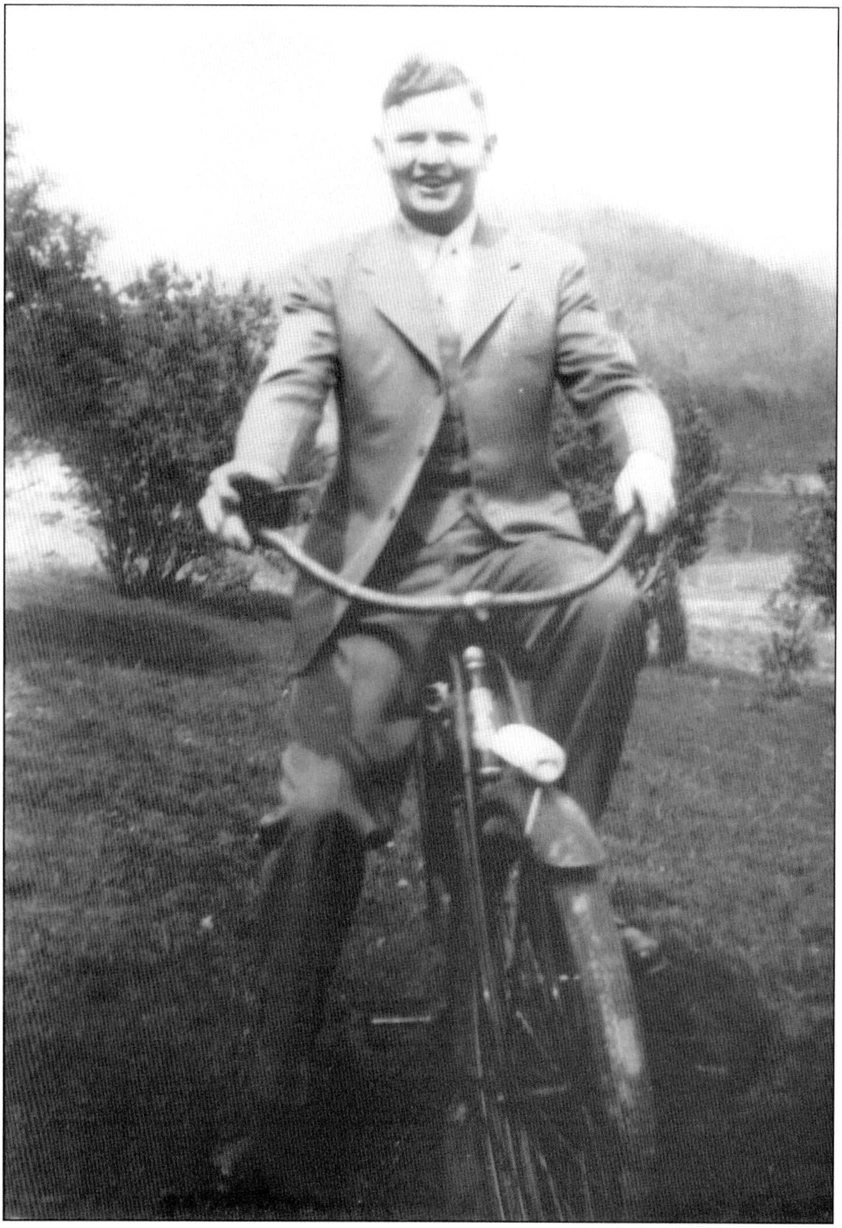

QUAY SMATHERS. In 1919, at the age six, Quay Smathers began attending singing school at Morning Star Methodist Church, learning church hymns using the shape-note singing method. As an adult, he played guitar, sang, and led a family band with his three daughters, performing in folk festivals throughout the Southeast. He taught music workshops at Berea College, Western Carolina University, Mars Hill College, and Warren Wilson College. His students included such notables as Grammy Award–winning storyteller, musician, and singer David Holt and nationally acclaimed folk singer, musician, and storyteller John McCutcheon. Smathers received the prestigious North Carolina Folk Heritage Award in 1991. He was also a master carpenter, building a number of houses and commercial buildings in the Canton area. He died in 1997 and was buried in the cemetery at Morning Star United Methodist Church in Dutch Cove. (Courtesy of June Jolley.)

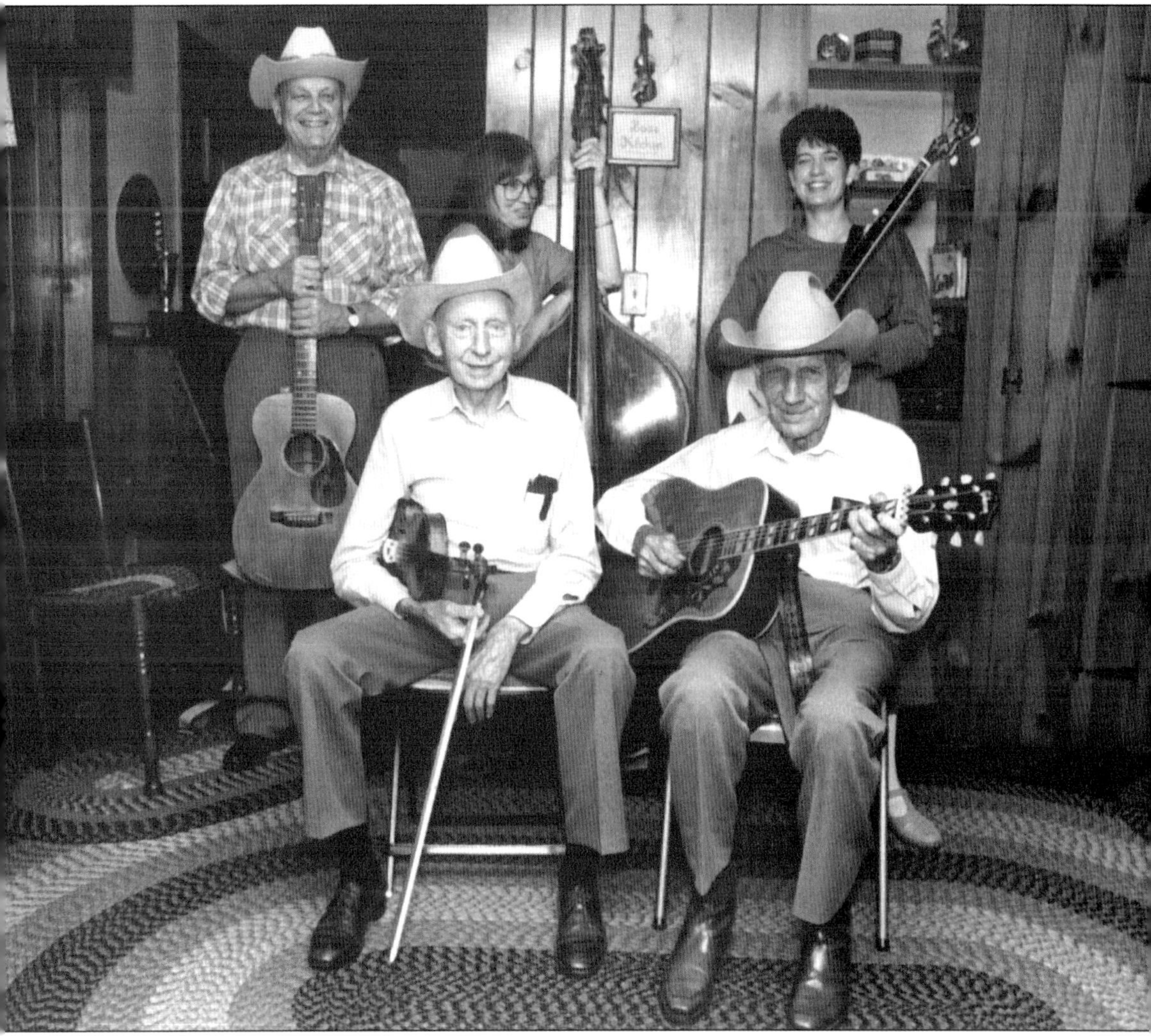

Luke Smathers Band. In the 1920s, the Smathers brothers of Canton—George, Harold, and Luke—learned to play musical instruments they ordered from a Sears, Roebuck & Co. catalog. Luke (seated, left) learned to play the fiddle, while Harold and George played guitar. They formed a popular local band that performed at ice cream socials and developed a unique style they called mountain swing, inspired by old-time mountain tunes and the big band sound of that era. Unfortunately, World War II broke up the band. After they had not played for about 25 years, a folk music revival made their brand of music popular once again. At that time, Luke formed a new family band that included different combinations of musicians, including eventual Grammy Award–winner David Holt. They toured all over the Southeast and the Midwest, recorded albums, and rehearsed in the kitchen of Luke's home. All this was done after Luke lost three of his fingers in a Champion paper mill accident. Both Luke and his brother Harold (seated, right) were awarded the North Carolina Folk Heritage Award. Pictured in the back row are, from left to right, Charles Gidney, Hillary Dirlam, and Laura Boosinger. (Courtesy of Haywood Snapshot Project.)

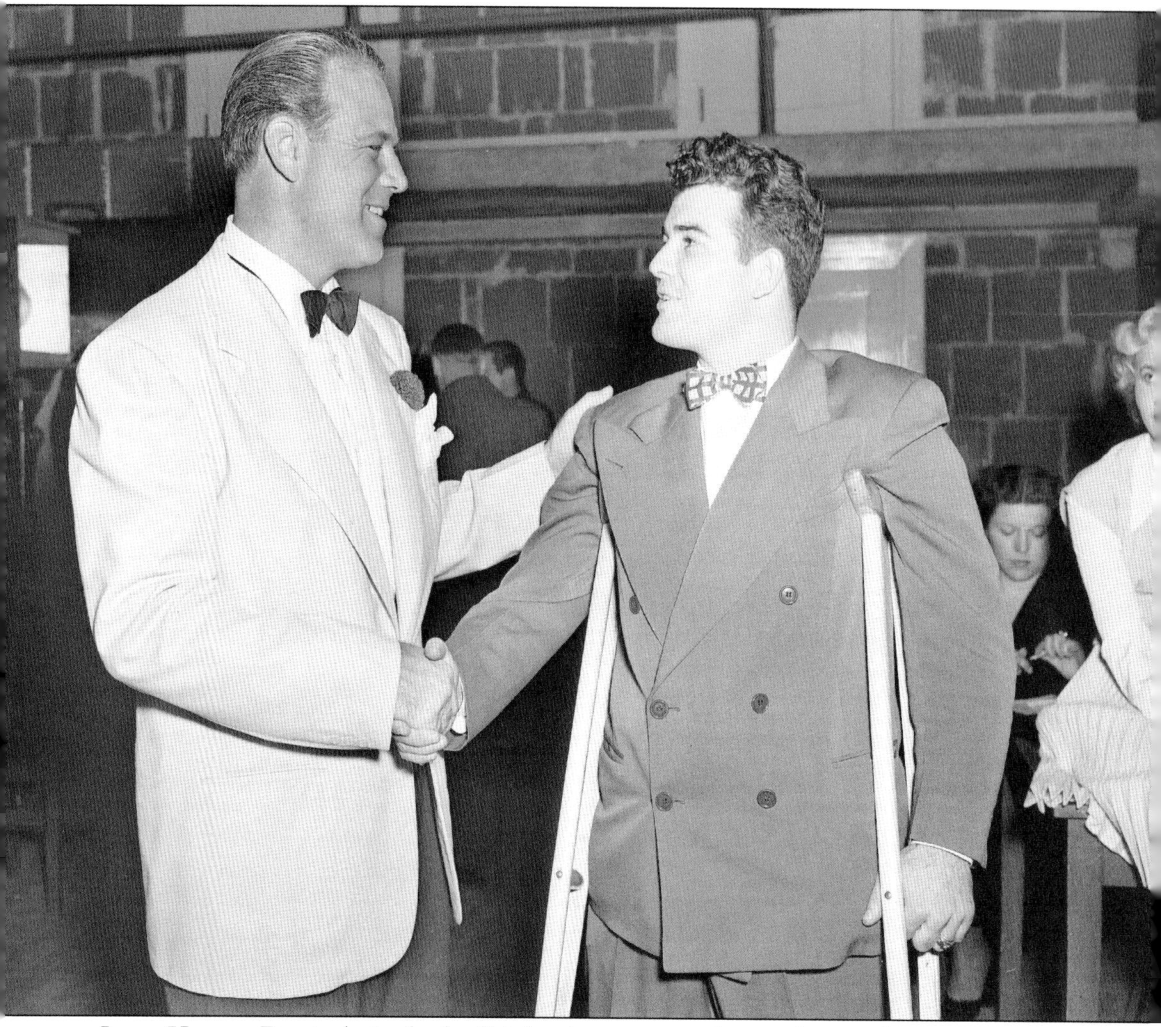

JIMMY HAYNIE. Despite losing both of his legs in a train accident at the age of 16, Haynie went on to perform all over the country as a guitarist and singer. He wrote ballads about Canton notables like Champion executive Reuben B. Robertson and football coach Boyd Allen. Haynie won the top ballad singer prize at the 1952 National Folk Festival and sang alongside country greats like Conway Twitty and Grandpa Jones. Haynie (right) is seen here meeting with Horace Heidt, a popular big band leader and television and radio personality of the 1930s and 1940s. Haynie later became a local radio deejay in the 1960s and 1970s. He thrived as a performer in the 1950s, when Canton held a folk festival at Canton Memorial Stadium, where clogging teams performed and competed at annual competitions in the summer. (Courtesy of the Canton Historical Museum.)

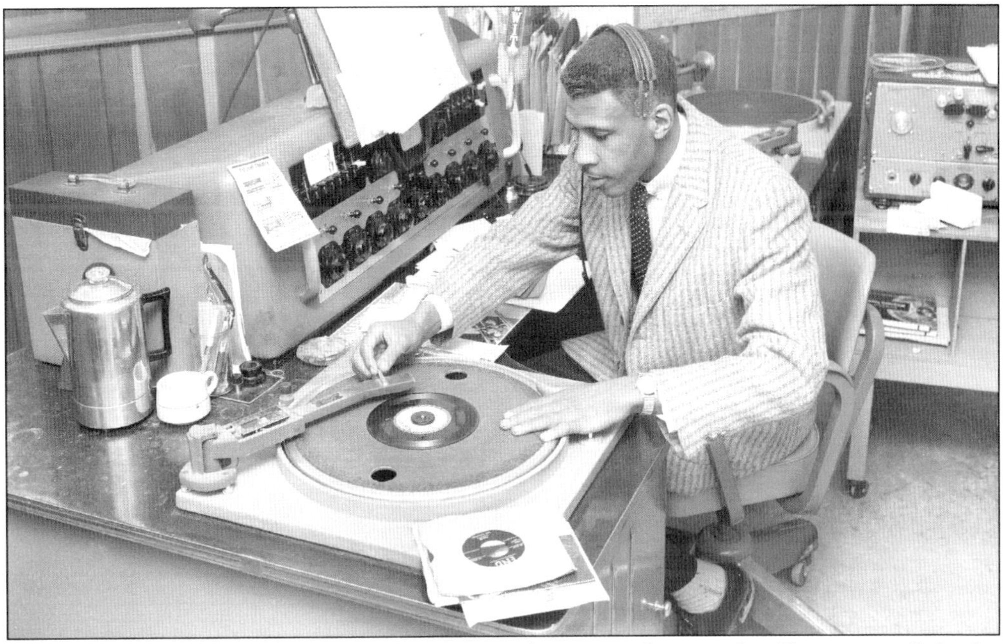

Nat the Cat. By day, Nathaniel Lowery was a mail room employee at the Champion mill. In the evenings, he became Nat the Cat, a smooth-talking radio deejay spinning the hot sounds of the 1950s and early 1960s at WWIT in Canton. "It's five past five and time to jive" was a typical line he started the show with. Lowery earned fan praise from both black and white listeners during the turbulent era of the civil rights movement. (Courtesy of the Canton Historical Museum.)

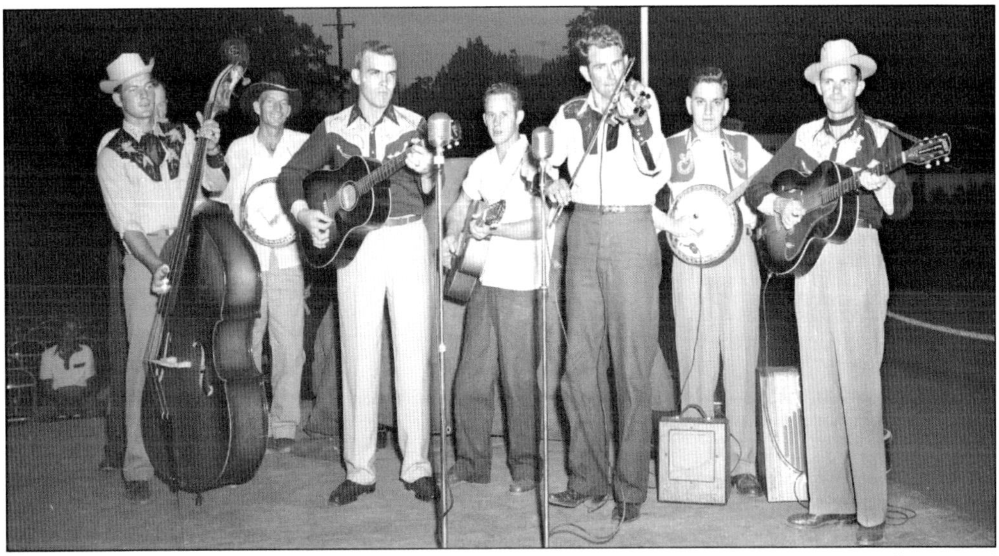

Pickin' in the Park. Bands like this one from the 1954 Veterans of Foreign Wars Folk Festival performed and competed in the summers at Canton's Memorial Stadium. More recently, every Friday night from June through Labor Day, the Canton Recreation Park comes alive with the sounds of bluegrass and old-time mountain music. Local and regional musicians, singers, bands, and clogging teams perform. Hundreds of people come and set up lawn chairs to enjoy the free entertainment. (Courtesy of the Canton Historical Museum.)

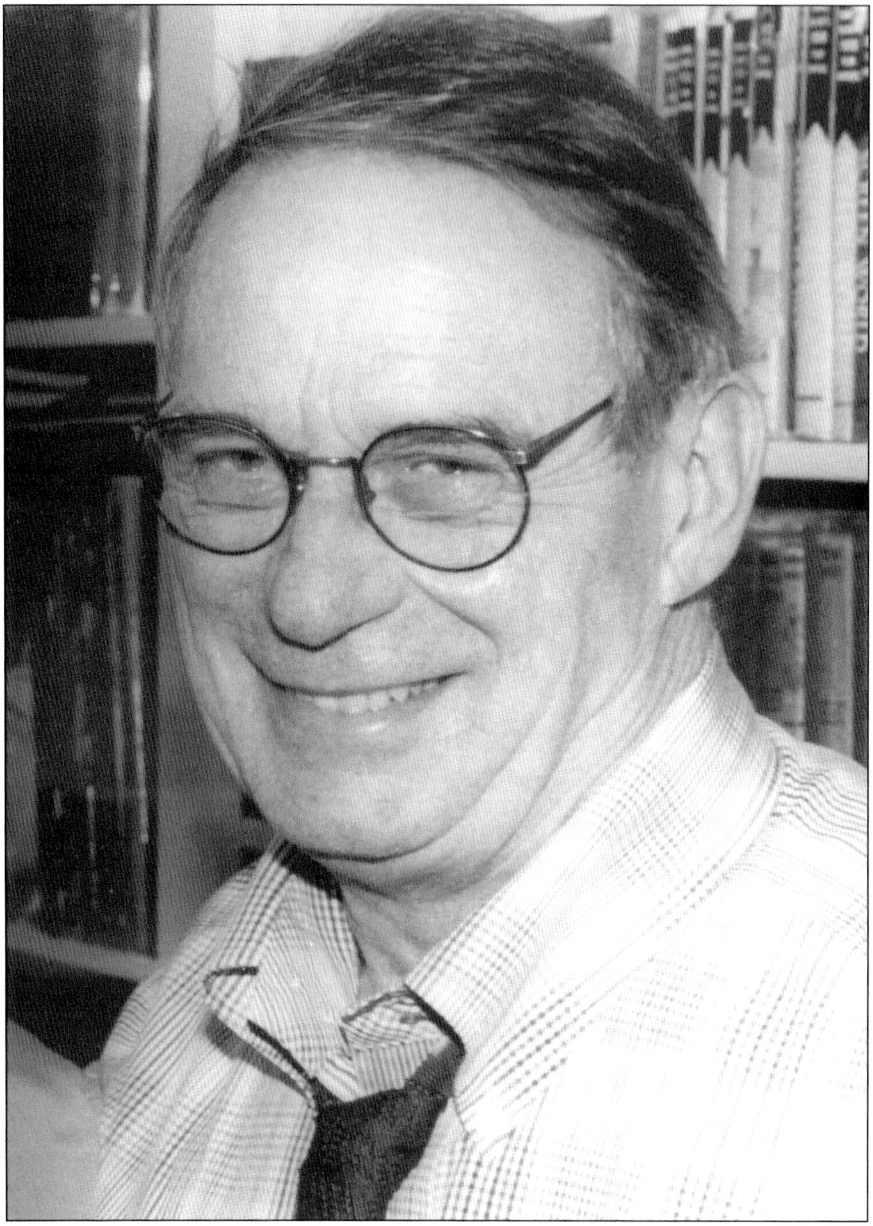

FRED CHAPPELL. A prodigious poet, novelist, short story author, essayist, and critic, Fred Chappell was an English professor at the University of North Carolina at Greensboro for 40 years and has written more than 30 books. Born in 1936 and raised in the Beaverdam community, he fell in love with writing at an early age. His schoolteachers later recalled him dreamily gazing out the window as he imagined new stories and poems. After graduating from Canton High School, he attended Duke University and studied under the legendary professor William Blackburn, who taught other gifted writers such as Anne Tyler, Reynolds Price, and William Styron. Chappell published award-winning novels, short stories, and poetry collections that drew on his childhood experiences growing up in Haywood County. He fictionalized the town of Canton as Tipton, and the Champion paper mill was referred to as Challenger. From 1997 to 2002, Chappell served as North Carolina's poet laureate. (Photograph by Jan G. Hensley.)

Seven

SERVICE

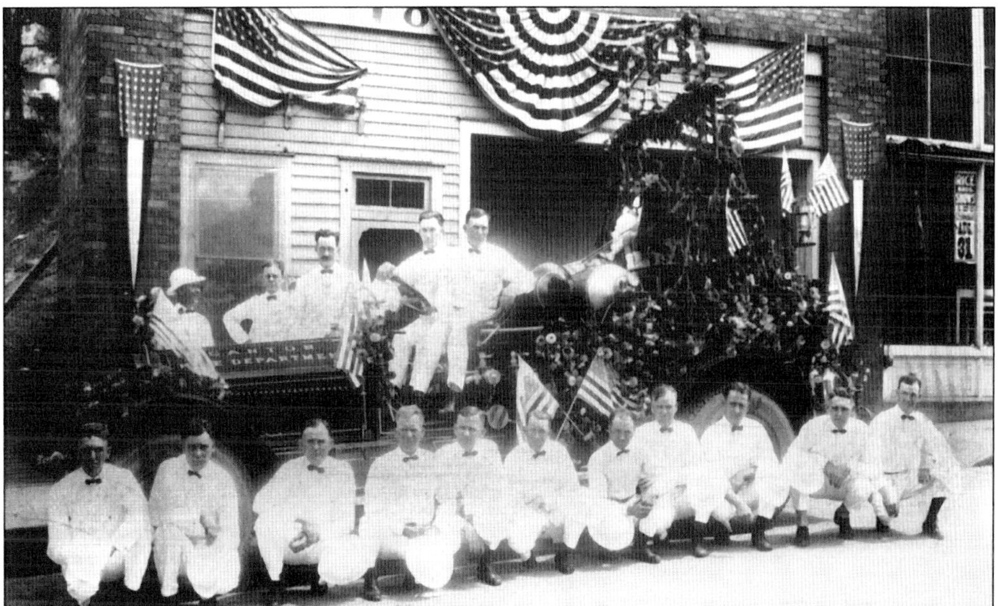

FIRE DEPARTMENT. Canton established its first fire department in 1909 at 155 Main Street. By 1930, the department had a new truck and a new headquarters, at 27 Church Street, and was led by fire chief C.L. Westmoreland. (Courtesy of the Canton Historical Museum.)

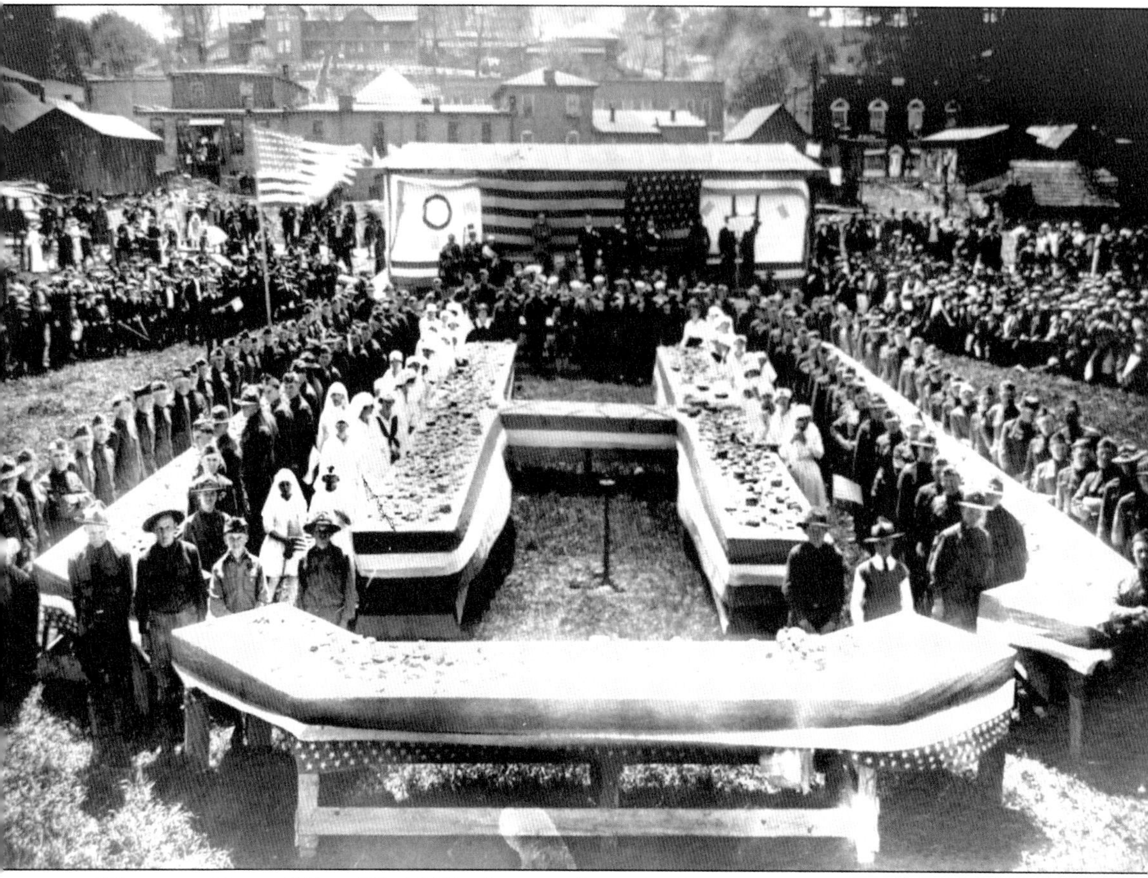

Welcome Home. When World War I troops from the Canton area returned home, they were given a victorious celebration in downtown Canton, at the current site of the town hall. This photograph was taken on Saturday, May 3, 1919. R.E. Hipps, Canton's mayor at the time, wrote the following proclamation for the town's newspaper: "As they sacrificed their vocations and businesses for the call to arms, so should we cheerfully give to them at least a half day of our time to extend them a welcome." North Carolina lieutenant governor Oliver Max Gardner of Shelby gave a speech, and the festivities included a parade, a picnic, and a presentation of certificates to returning veterans and their families. The soldiers and nurses included members of an ambulance corps that served on the front lines and carried wounded soldiers off the battlefields in France during the final assault of Allied forces against Germany. Organized in 1914, this ambulance unit was the first company of its kind in North Carolina. Many of the original members were residents of Canton and Clyde who worked for the Champion mill, which subsidized the ambulance crews. The tables spell out the letters O and *H*, representing Old Hickory, the nickname of the 30th Division that the ambulance corps served with during the war. (Courtesy of the Canton Historical Museum.)

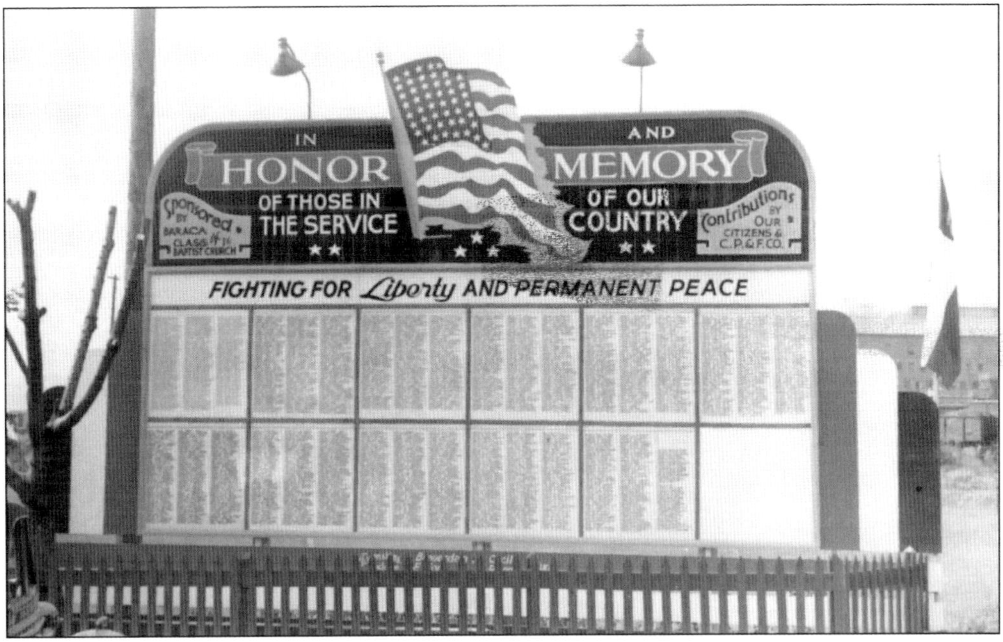

Honoring Service. During World War II, the Champion paper mill in Canton posted this sign, listing all the local men and women who were serving in the armed forces throughout the nation and the world. In the era of Rosie the Riveter, some local women came to work for Champion while the men were away. When veterans returned from the war, their jobs were waiting for them at the mill. (Courtesy of Anita Churm.)

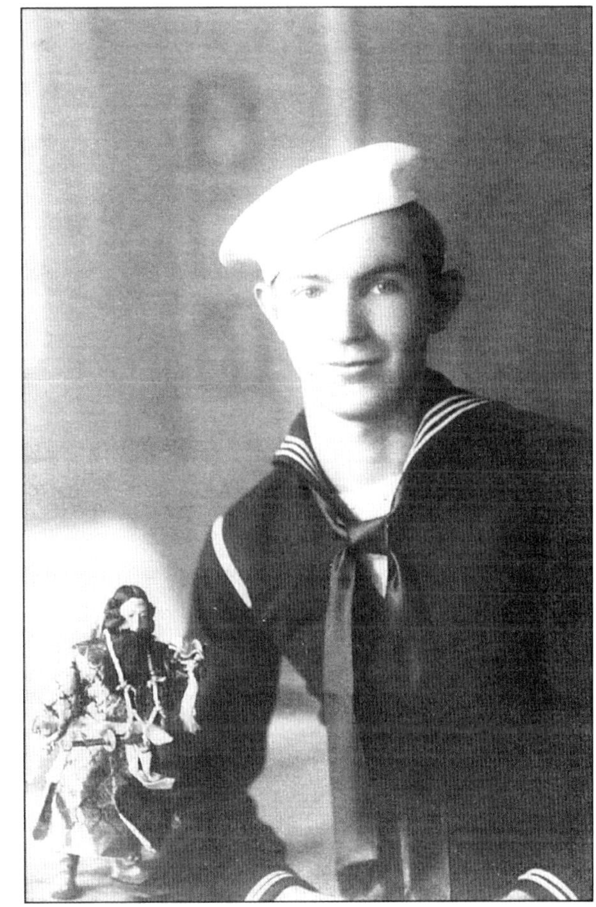

Veteran. Jack Rice was one of three brothers who served in the military. Born in the Beaverdam community in Rice Cove, Jack served in the Navy as a seaman first class during the US occupation of Japan following World War II. His brother William Rice served in the Army from 1942 to 1946 and worked at the Champion mill for 38 years. A third brother, Josh Rice, served in the Air Force from 1951 to 1955, which included the Korean Conflict. (Courtesy of Beaverdam Community Association.)

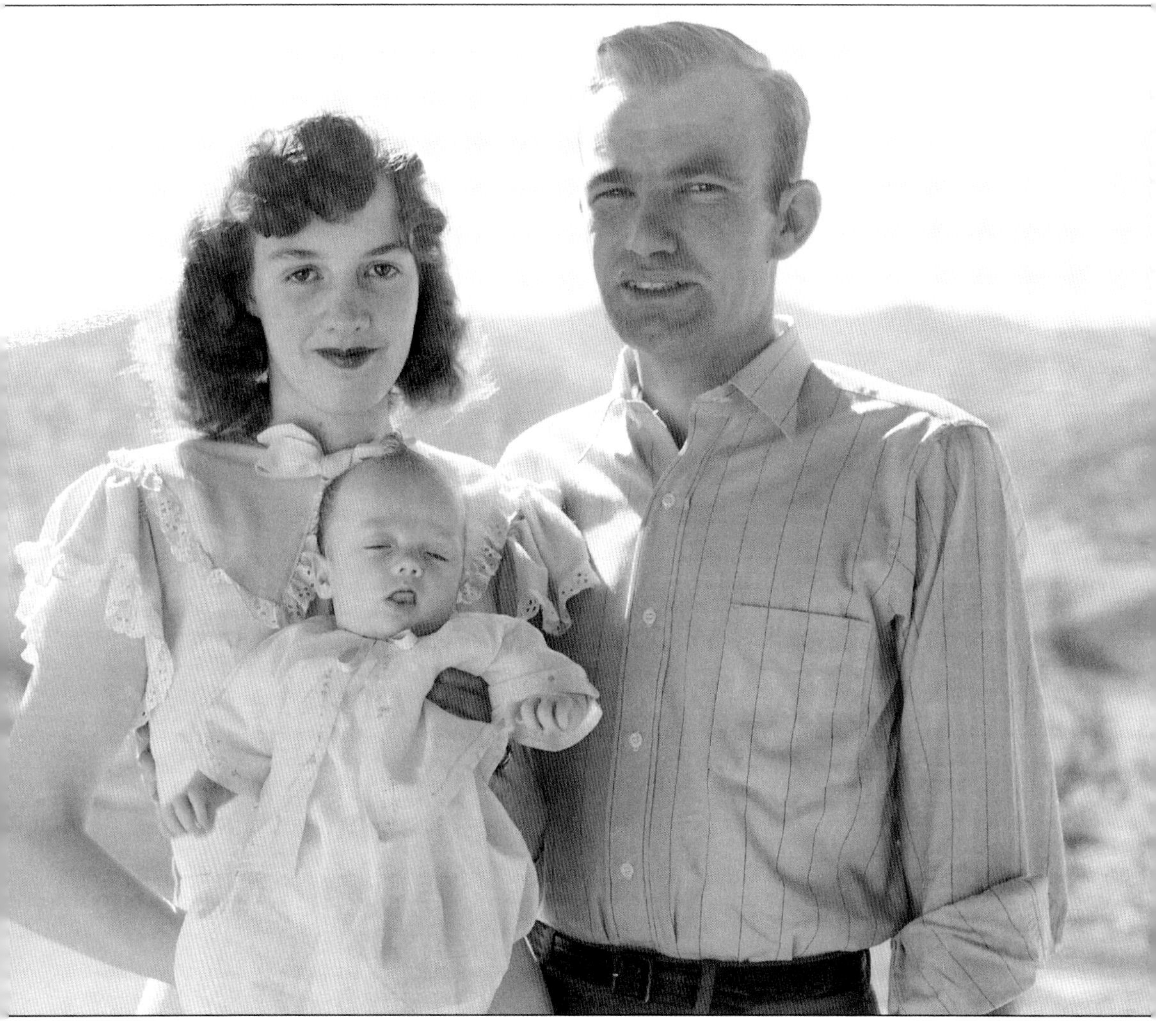

HONORS. Two Canton area men received the prestigious Medal of Honor for their service in World War II—Max Thompson and William Halyburton. Thompson, pictured with his wife, Iris, and their daughter Shirley, was serving as an Army sergeant in Germany when infantry and tanks besieged his company. Using a machine gun, automatic rifle, rocket gun, and grenades, he attacked German installations to help secure a key hill despite taking heavy fire and getting wounded. After the war, he returned to Haywood County and worked for Champion International Paper's inspection department. Halyburton, a native of Canton, was serving as a Marine in Okinawa, Japan, near the end of the war when he ran through a hail of bullets to render first aid to a wounded soldier. Shielding the fellow marine from gunfire, Halyburton was himself wounded and died. The USS *Halyburton*, a guided missile frigate, was named in his honor, as were a naval medical center in Bethesda, Maryland, a naval station quarters in Charleston, South Carolina, and a naval aerospace medical center barracks in Pensacola, Florida. (Courtesy of the Canton Historical Museum.)

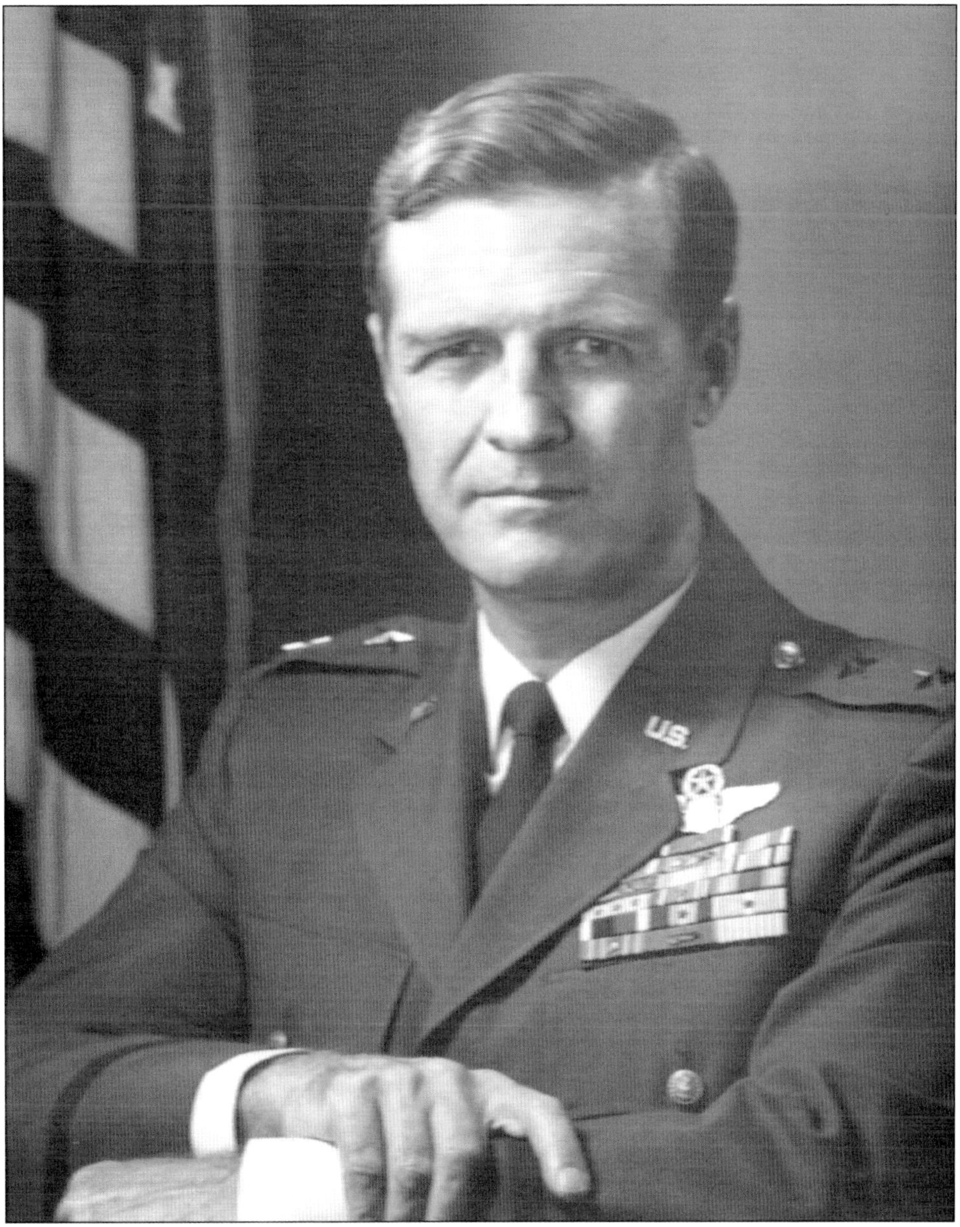

Maj. Gen. Roger K. Rhodarmer. Born in Kims Cove, outside of Canton, in 1922, Roger Rhodarmer graduated from Canton High School in 1940 and joined the Air Force during World War II. He flew bombing missions over Italy, Sicily, and southern France, and later served in the Pacific. After the war, he flew escort missions during the Berlin Airlift, a Cold War crisis in which the United States and other western nations dropped food, fuel, and other supplies into West Berlin during a Soviet blockade of the city. Rhodarmer became an expert in aerial reconnaissance, helping in the research and development of the F-15 fighter jet. He was assigned to Shaw Air Force Base in South Carolina, where he became squadron commander, training crews for the Korean War. By 1970, he assumed command of the Air Force's Tactical Air Reconnaissance Center at Shaw, and, in 1971, he took command of the 9th Air Force at Shaw. He retired in 1973. (Courtesy of the Canton Historical Museum.)

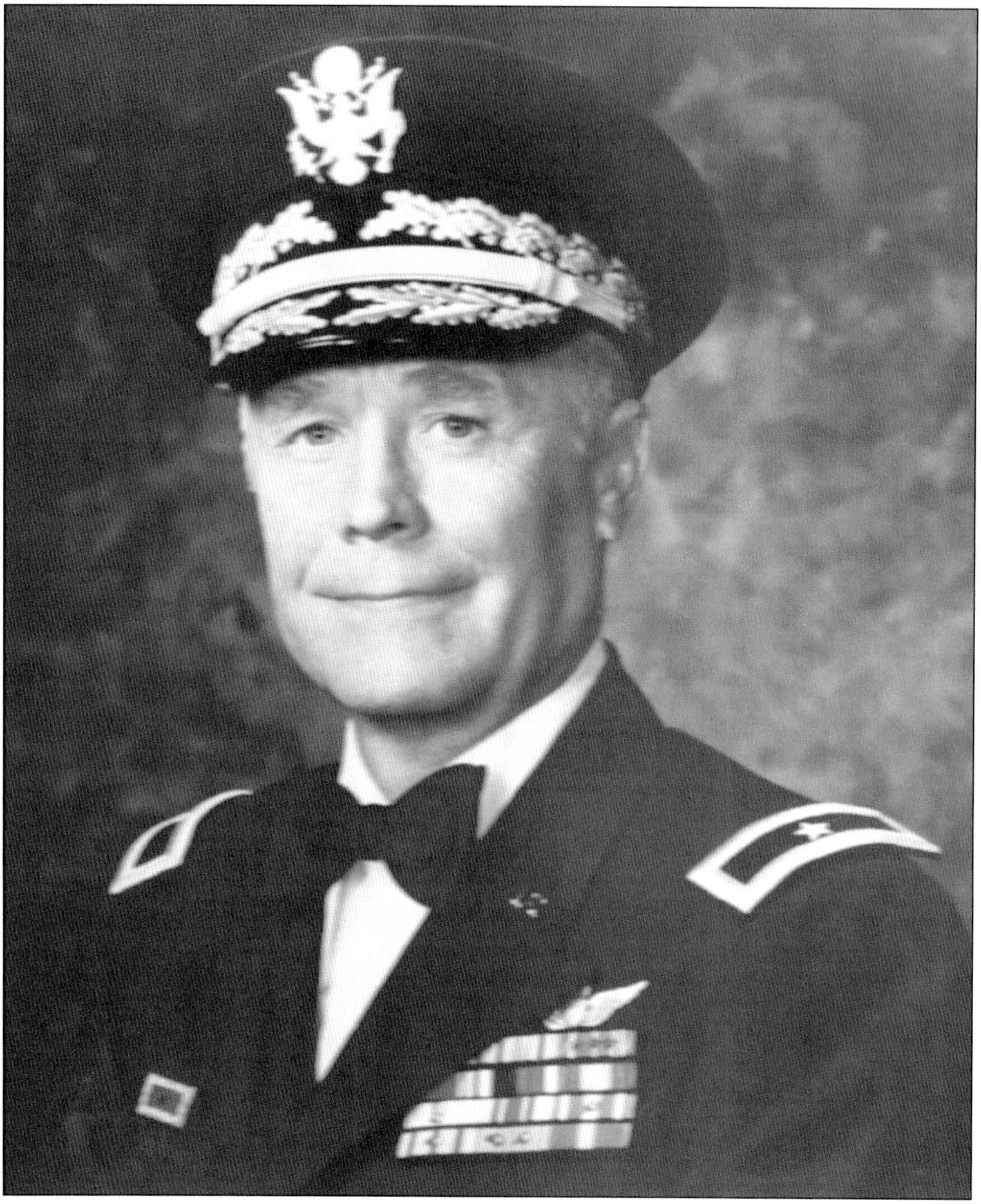

Brig. Gen. Charles Willis. With nearly 40 years of military service, Willis was qualified to operate more than 25 types of aircraft, including helicopters, fighter jets, and troop carriers. Born in Canton in 1923, Willis graduated from Canton High School in 1940. He flew missions in World War II as a bomber and an escort. After the war, he attended the Nuremberg war crimes trials. Returning to the Unites States, he worked as an air traffic controller before joining the Florida National Guard as its first full-time aviator, responsible for developing flight and maintenance programs. Willis rose to deputy commander of the Florida National Guard and was promoted to brigadier general, responsible for assisting in the readiness of more than 10,000 soldiers. He served as an aviation consultant for the Pentagon and the National Guard. After retiring in 1983 in St. Augustine, Florida, he continued to serve his community as a county commissioner and the leader of various government boards and committees. (Courtesy of the Canton Historical Museum.)

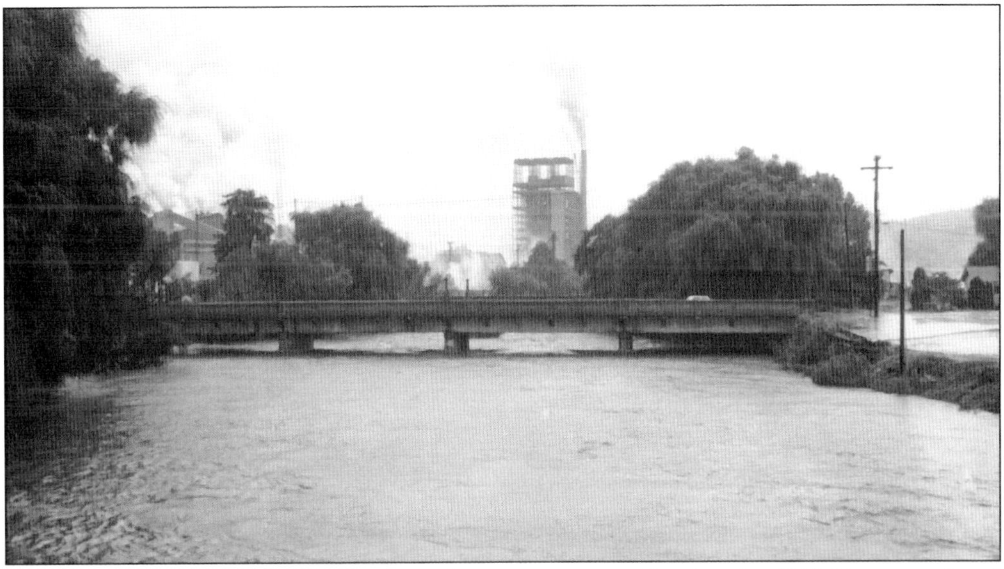

1940 Floods. Being situated near a river, Canton is prone to flooding. In 1940, Canton endured two of the worst floods in its history in one month, on August 12–13 and then again on August 29–30. In the first flood, a tropical storm dumped a foot of rain on the town, flooding dozens of homes, businesses, farms, and roads. When the next major storm brought nearly a foot of rain two weeks later, the Pigeon River crested to almost 21 feet, nearly three feet higher than it had been after the first flood. A minister and his wife died after being swept away from their home near Lake Logan. Nearly 100 Canton homes flooded during the second storm, and the Champion mill temporarily shut down after machinery flooded, offices were damaged (below), more than 1,500 cords of wood were lost, and large amounts of finished paper and cartons were ruined. In order to save its train trestles during major floods, Champion workers loaded coal cars on the bridges to keep them from washing away. (Both, courtesy of the Canton Historical Museum.)

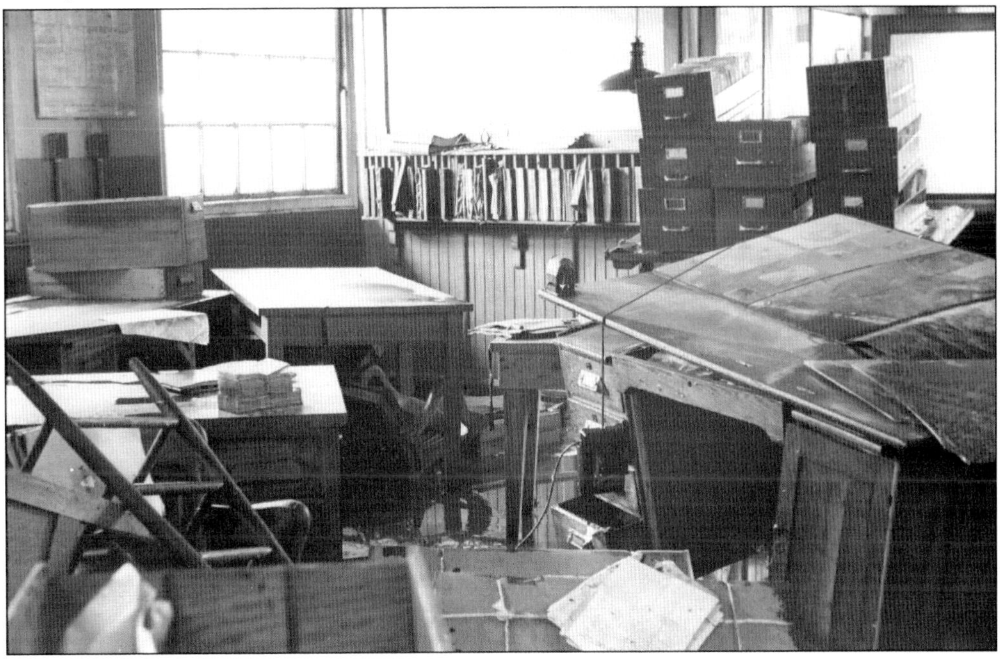

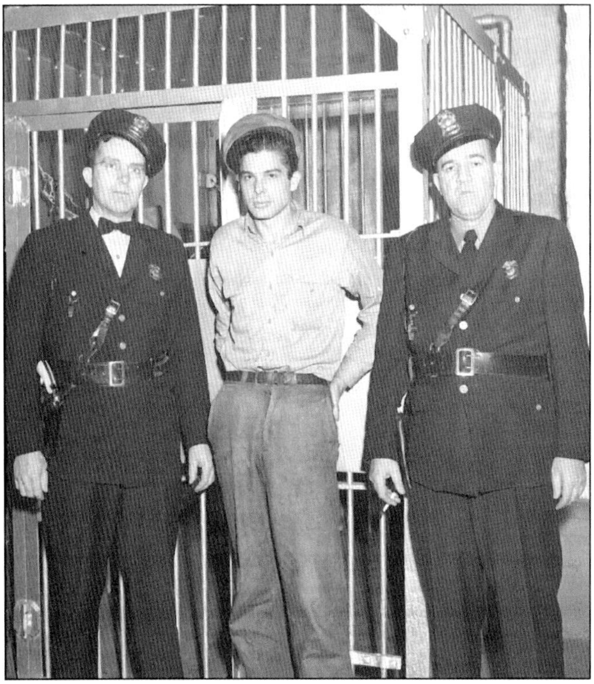

Canton Jail. The town's jail, municipal offices, and courthouse were once located in a building that is now part of the waterwheel park on the west side of the downtown district. In 1972, the current town hall and fire department buildings were erected along Park Street, on the former site of a softball field. (Courtesy of the Canton Historical Museum.)

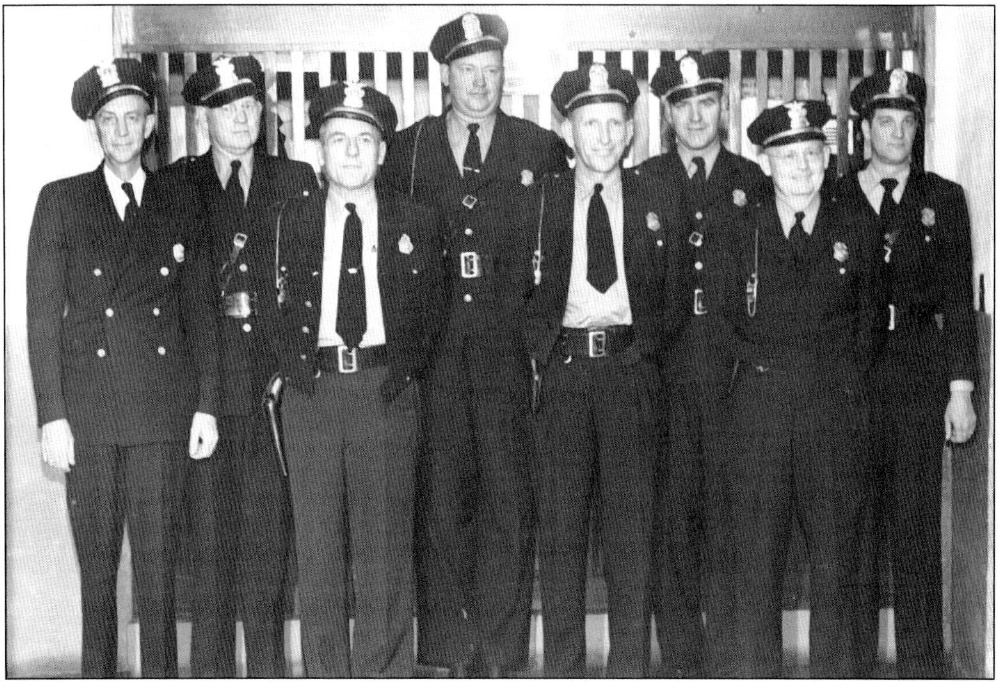

Canton Police. Bill Stroupe (far left) was Canton's longest-serving police chief, leading the department from 1939 to 1968. Pictured, from left to right, are Stroupe, "Red" Anderson, Bud Thompson, Paul Rogers, George Rogers, Albert Fouts, Everett Moore, and James Hamlett. Fouts and Hamlett went on to become Canton police chiefs. On May 21, 1974, George Rogers was shot and killed after answering a call for a domestic dispute. A recently completed bridge across the Pigeon River in Canton is named in his honor. (Courtesy of the Canton Historical Museum.)

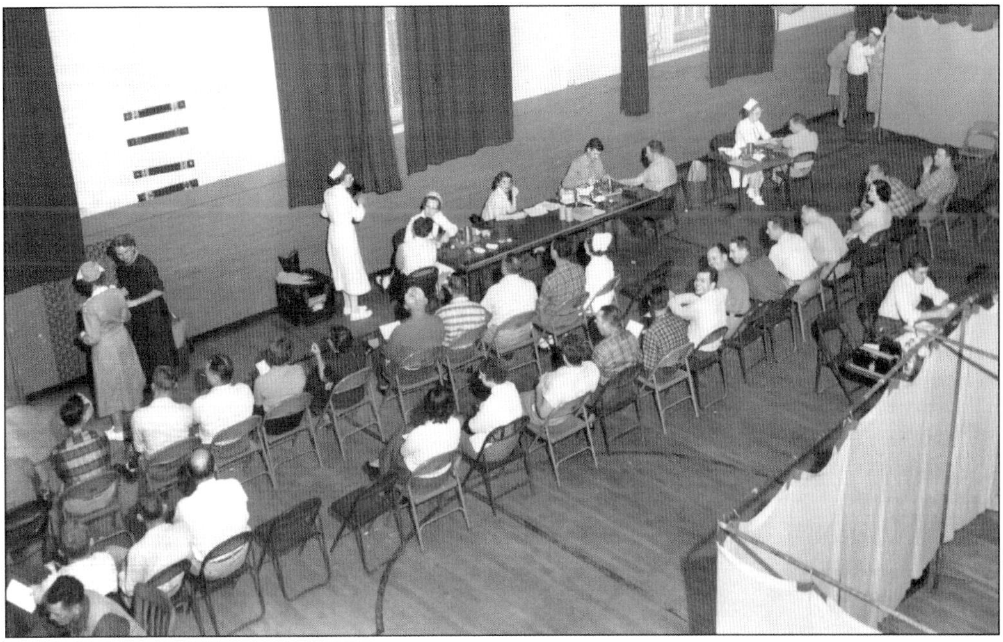

Red Cross. Nurses in Canton with the Red Cross might collect a few hundred pints of blood during blood drives like this one, held at the Champion YMCA in the 1950s. Canton's Red Cross office was especially active during World War II, with local women meeting to make bandages and first aid kits for the military. (Courtesy of the Canton Historical Museum.)

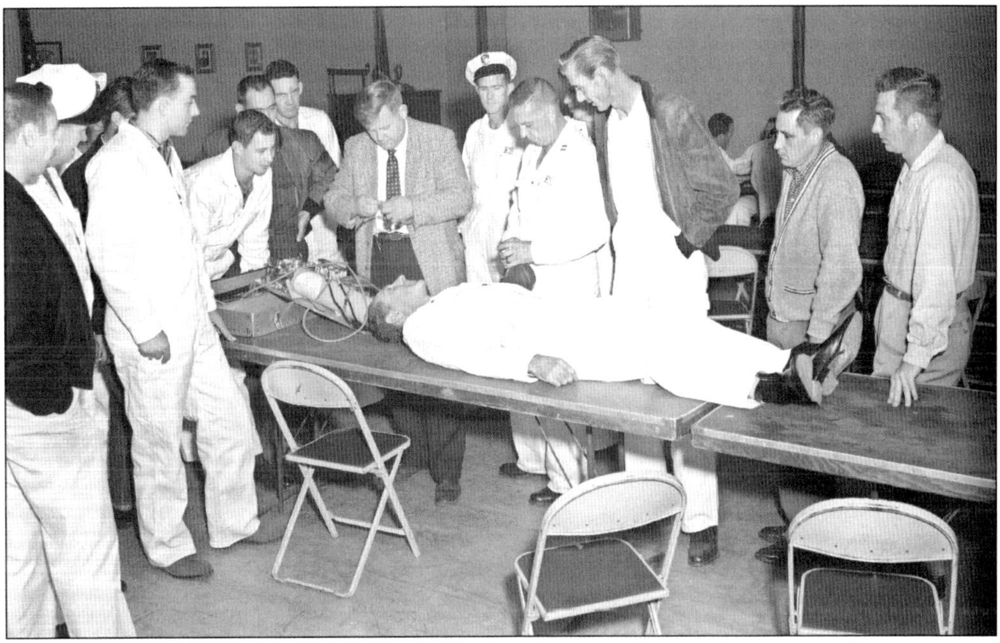

Rescue Squad. Organized in the early 1950s, the Haywood County Rescue Squad was a team of highly trained volunteers, including some from the Canton area, who were the first responders for emergencies and accidents. They were trained to administer first aid and health care and transport patients to the hospital if necessary. The name was eventually changed to Haywood County Emergency Medical Services. (Courtesy of the Canton Historical Museum.)

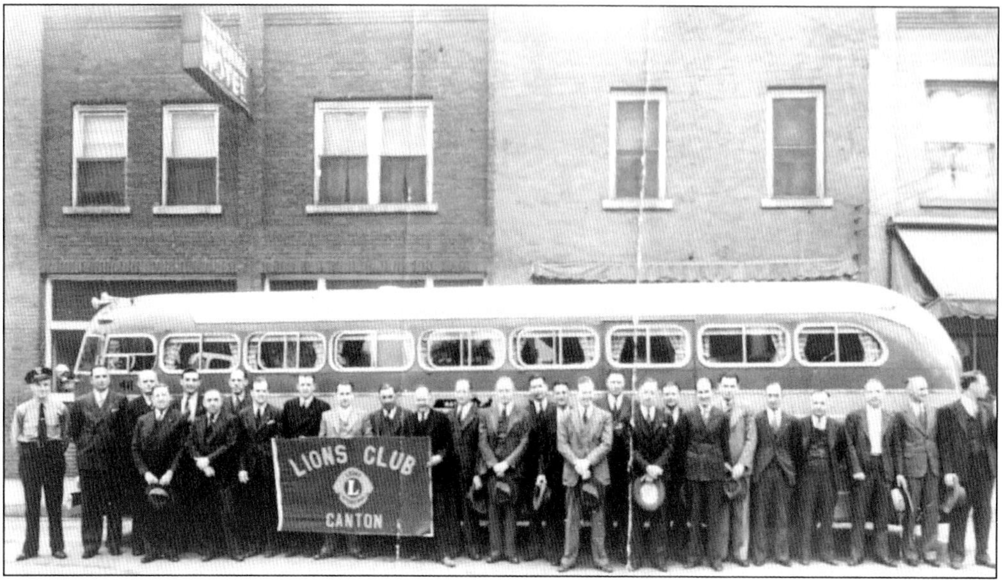

CANTON LIONS CLUB. First organized nationally in 1917 as an effort to wipe out preventable blindness, the Lions Club formed a chapter in Canton in 1938 and helped organize chapters in Clyde and Bethel. The Canton Lions continue to sponsor local events at the town's annual Labor Day Festival and provide funding for local school bands and Little League baseball teams. (Courtesy of the Canton Historical Museum.)

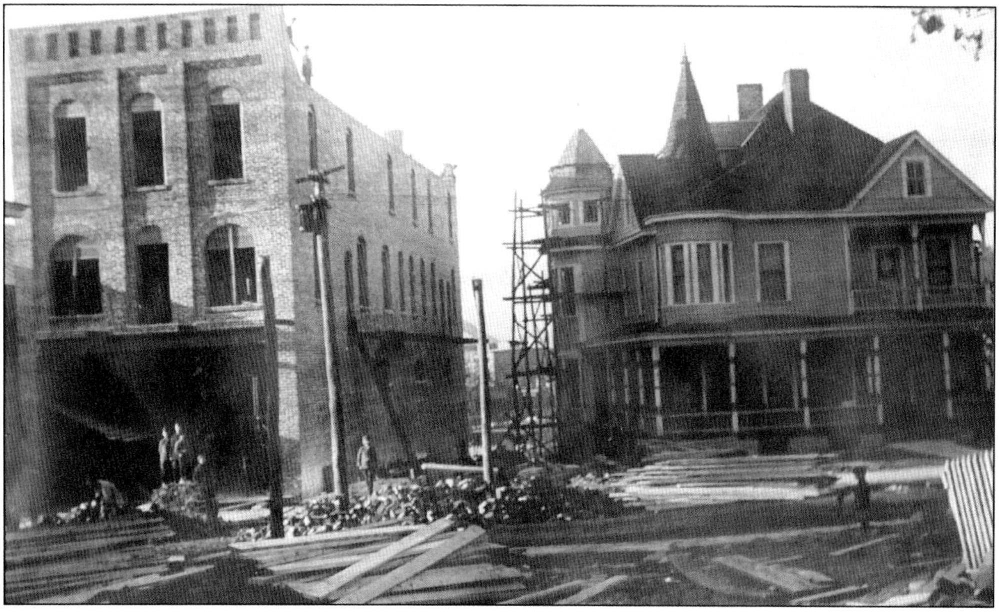

KNIGHTS OF PYTHIAS. Canton's former chapter of the Knights of Pythias met in downtown Canton at the Imperial Hotel, seen here under construction. Organized in 1904 with 15 original members, the fraternal order extolled the virtues of loyalty, honor, and friendship. The Knights took an oath to swear off gambling, drugs, and alcohol. They also rejected communism, fascism, or any organization seeking to overthrow the government or deny citizens lawful rights. By 1934, the Canton organization had swelled to more than 350 members. (Courtesy of the Canton Historical Museum.)

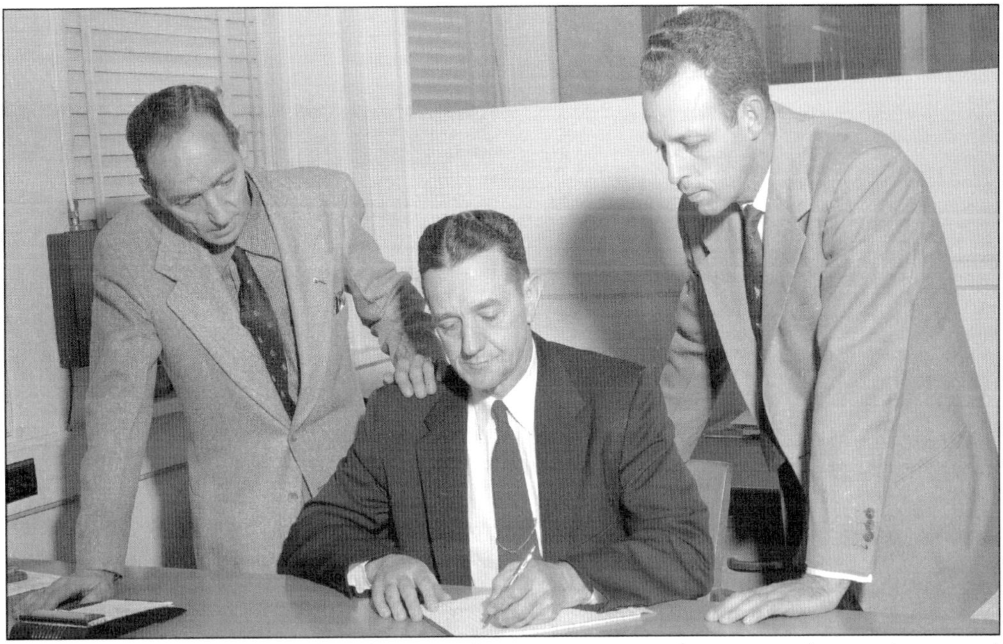

Masonic Lodge Masters. Though Masons have a reputation of secrecy in their traditions and symbols, Canton Masons operated with the simple goal of creating upstanding men with high morals and a responsibility toward community service. Canton's lodge formed in the 1890s and met at a building between the current location of Martin's Drugstore and the former post office. This photograph was taken at a meeting of Haywood County Masonic lodge masters. (Courtesy of the Canton Historical Museum.)

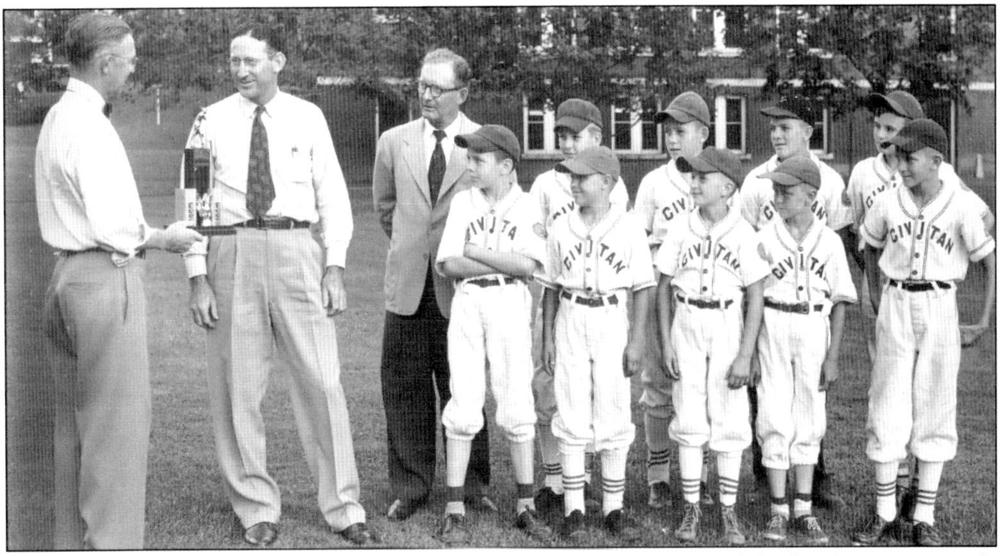

Civitans. Organized in 1917 by businessmen as a volunteer service club, the Civitans provide community service in a variety of ways, including promoting the Special Olympics and assisting people with disabilities. The Canton Civitans sponsored local youth recreation teams, like this award-winning boys' baseball team, and organized a Junior Civitans club at Canton High School. Students in local schools were recognized by the club for their outstanding citizenship. (Courtesy of the Canton Historical Museum.)

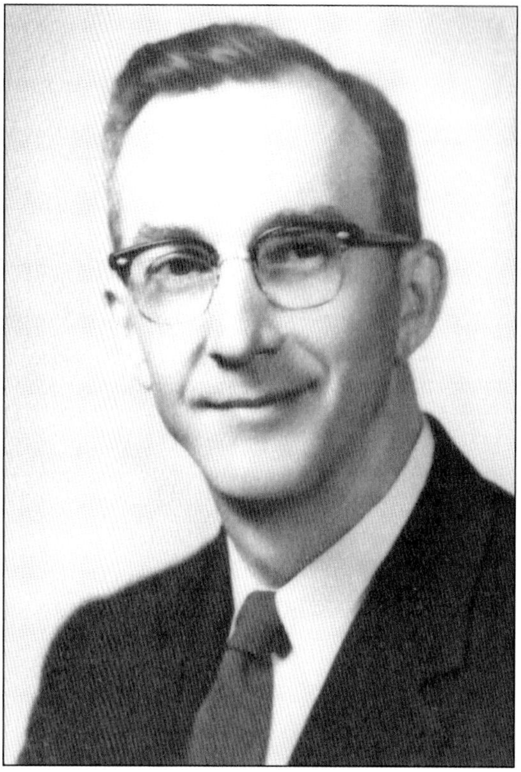

Hazel Ramsey. One of Canton's longest-serving mayors, Ramsey held the town post from 1959 to 1967 and again from 1977 to 1981. He oversaw a period of local growth that included the construction of Interstate 40, as well as periods of national turmoil, including the civil rights movement and the Vietnam War protests of the 1960s and the economic downturn and gas shortages of the late 1970s. (Courtesy of the Canton Historical Museum.)

Bob Phillips. A longtime Champion employee, Bob Phillips served as mayor of Canton from 1989 to 1997. Phillips actively promoted Appalachian culture, attending local folk festivals and performing and directing a clogging team known as the Rough Creek Cloggers. (Courtesy of the Canton Historical Museum.)

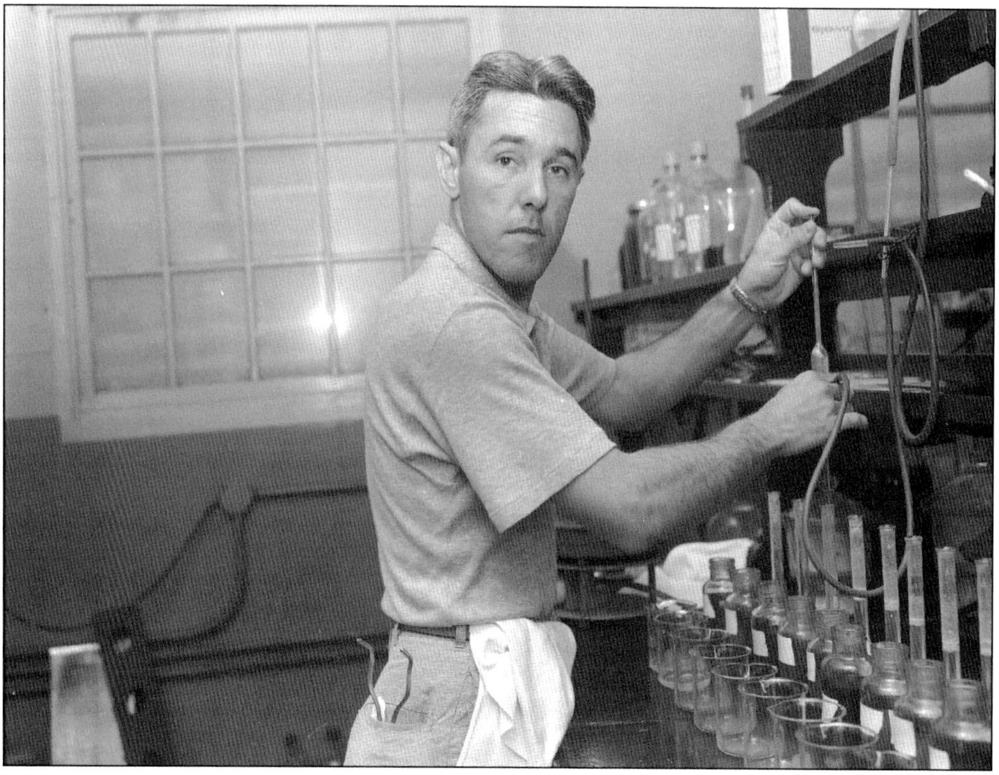

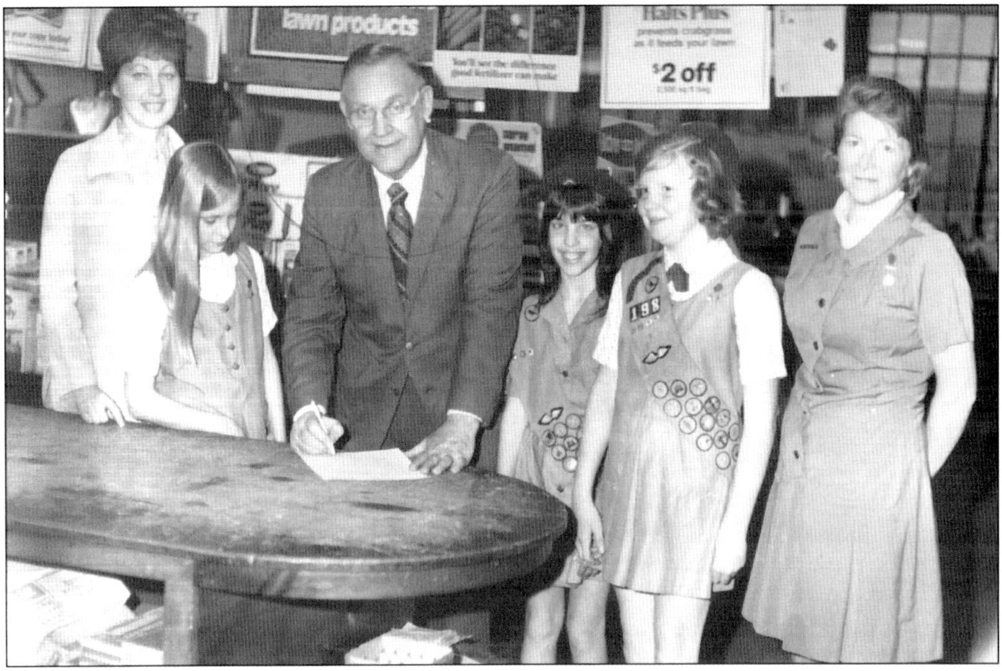

Girl Scouts. Canton has enjoyed an active Girl Scouts program over the years. In this March 1975 photograph, Canton mayor F.E. Shull meets with Girl Scouts to sign a formal proclamation for Girl Scout Week. (Courtesy of the Canton Presbyterian Church.)

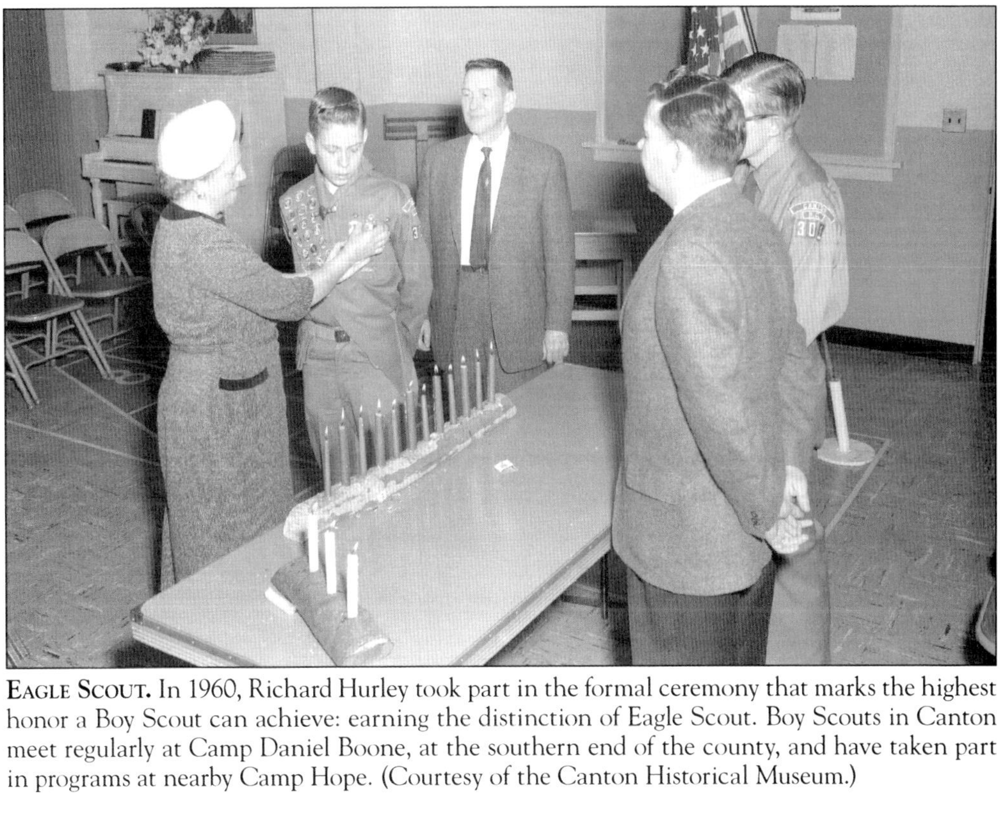

Eagle Scout. In 1960, Richard Hurley took part in the formal ceremony that marks the highest honor a Boy Scout can achieve: earning the distinction of Eagle Scout. Boy Scouts in Canton meet regularly at Camp Daniel Boone, at the southern end of the county, and have taken part in programs at nearby Camp Hope. (Courtesy of the Canton Historical Museum.)

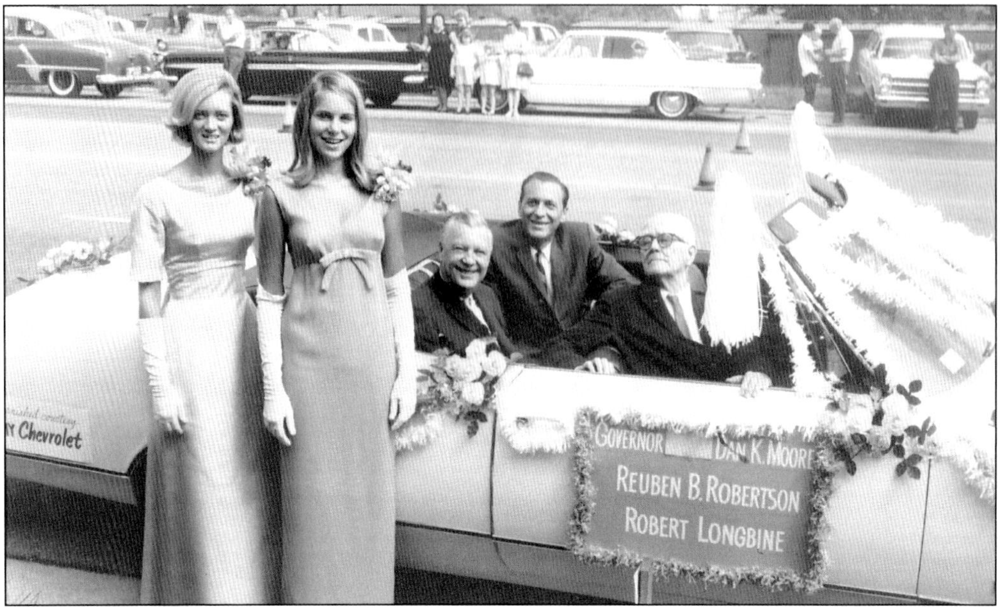

Public Servant. Dan K. Moore had an extensive career in public service as a lawyer, judge, state representative, Army veteran, North Carolina governor, and North Carolina Supreme Court justice. In 1958, he moved to Canton and worked as a legal counsel for Champion. In 1964, he was elected governor of North Carolina and enjoyed plenty of Canton support. He is seen here (backseat, left) as an honored guest in Canton's Labor Day parade along with Champion executives Robert Longbine (backseat, right) and Reuben B. Robertson (front seat). (Courtesy of the Canton Historical Museum.)

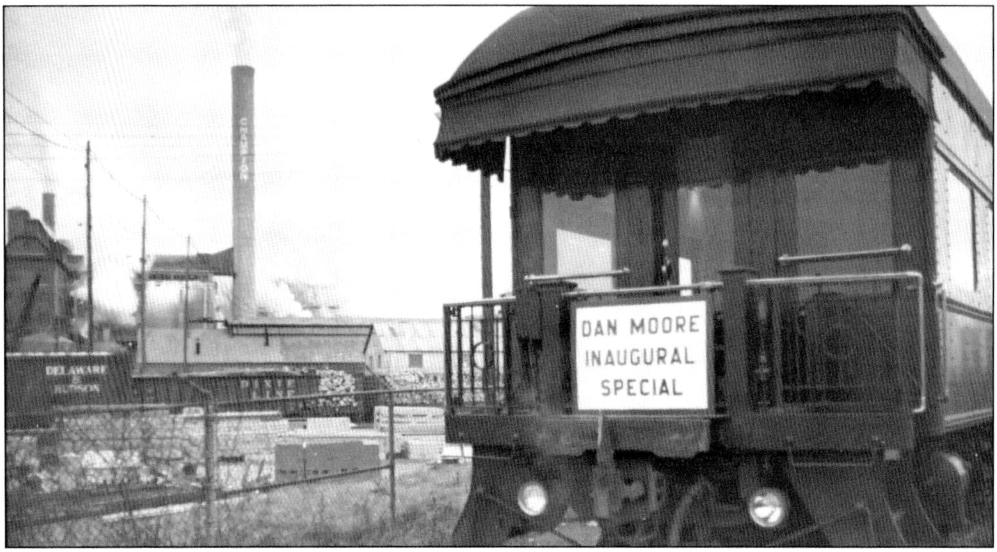

Inauguration Special. When Dan Moore was elected governor, a sizeable contingent of Canton residents boarded a train for Raleigh to join in the festivities. Moore brought a reasoned, calm approach as governor during the turbulent 1960s. Among his accomplishments were increased state employee salaries and the passage of a $300 million road-building referendum. After concluding his term as governor, he was appointed to the North Carolina Supreme Court. (Courtesy of the Pack Memorial Library, North Carolina Collection.)

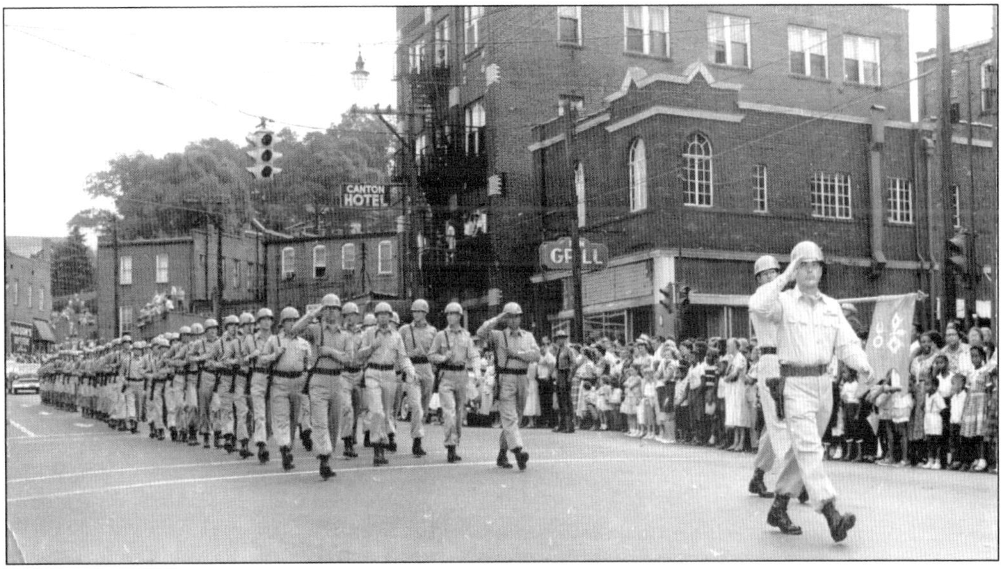

National Guard. Canton is home to the 30th Signal Company of the National Guard, which operated in the upstairs rooms of several different buildings in downtown until 1936, when a brick, two-story armory was built at 81 Penland Avenue. Because of its proximity to Canton High School and the town's recreation park, the armory became a common meeting place to host sports and recreational events, as well as dances, balls, and various special events. After the National Guard closed the site in 1979, the town remodeled the building to serve as a senior citizens' center and the headquarters for the town's recreation department. Recently renovated once again after devastating floods in 2004, the armory continues to host weddings, dances, and community events. (Both, courtesy of the Canton Historical Museum.)

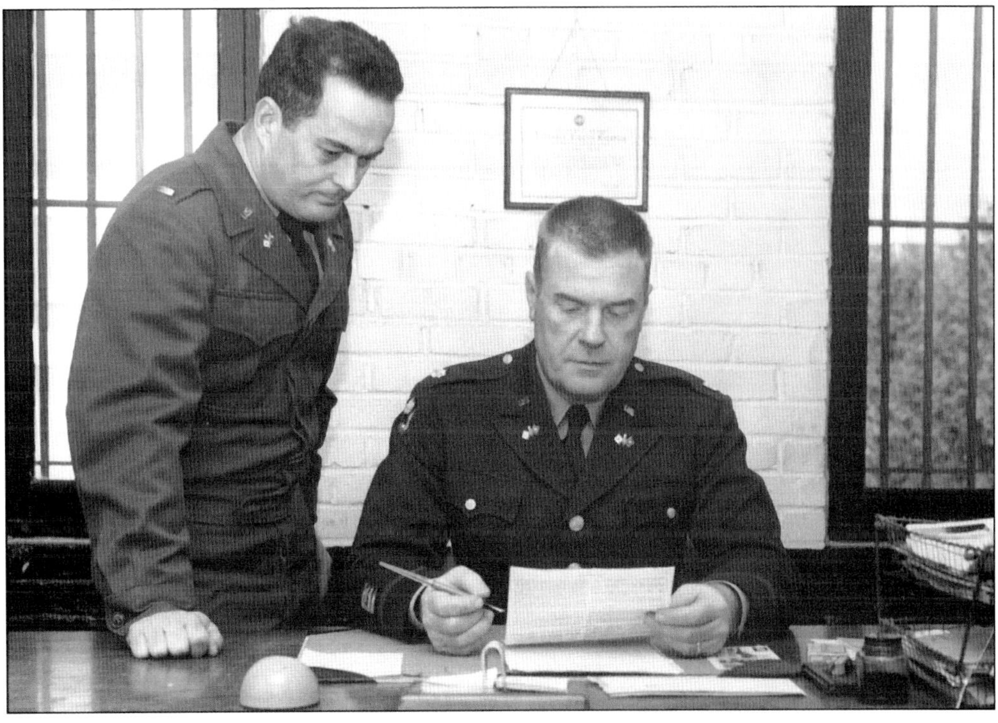

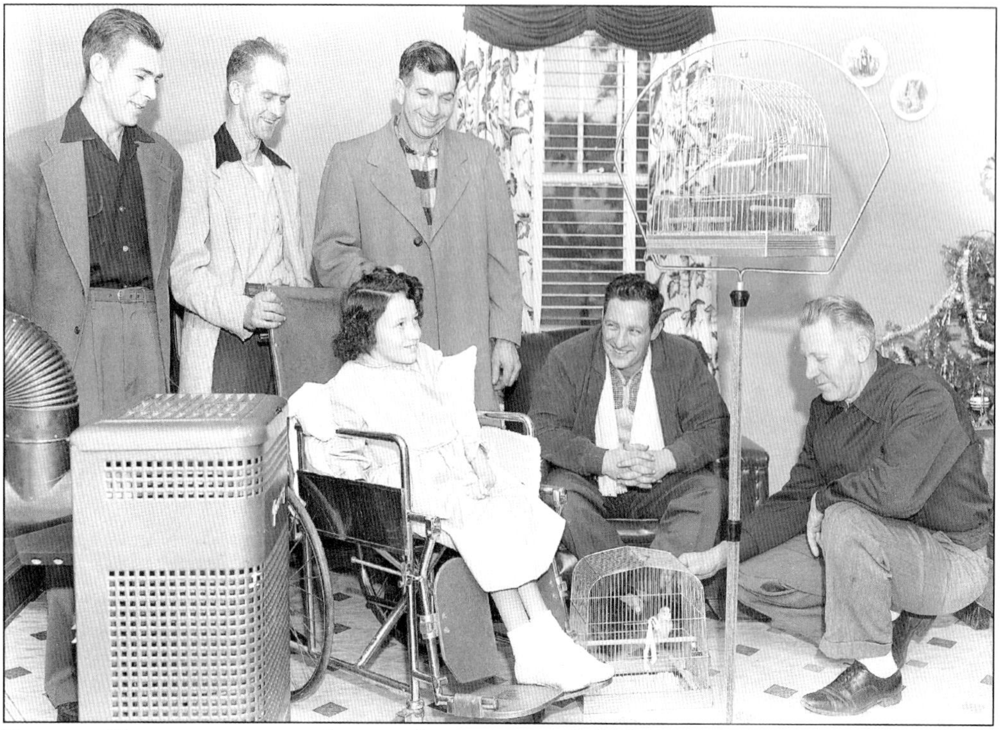

RIGGERS. These men are part of a crew that transported the heaviest equipment and machinery at the Champion mill in Canton. The very demanding work included moving digesters that towered 60 to 70 feet in the air and spanned 15 feet. Here, Champion riggers deliver a bird to a local girl. (Courtesy of the Canton Historical Museum.)

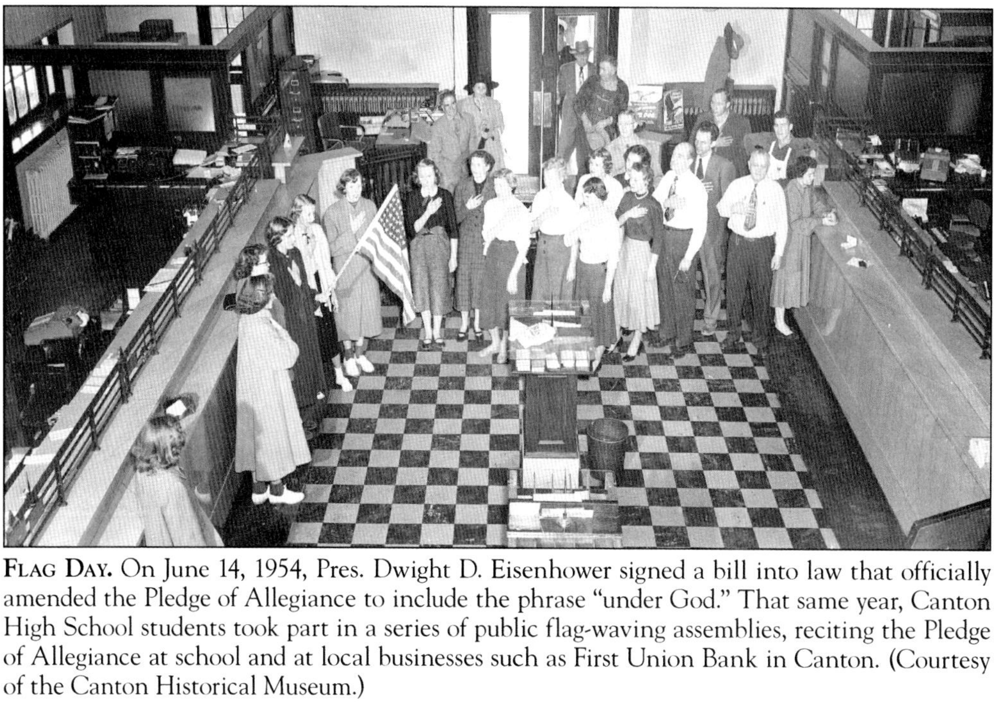

FLAG DAY. On June 14, 1954, Pres. Dwight D. Eisenhower signed a bill into law that officially amended the Pledge of Allegiance to include the phrase "under God." That same year, Canton High School students took part in a series of public flag-waving assemblies, reciting the Pledge of Allegiance at school and at local businesses such as First Union Bank in Canton. (Courtesy of the Canton Historical Museum.)

Bill Stamey. After earning fame as a high school football star, Bill Stamey (left) went on to become town manager for Canton. Over a career that spanned 39 years—the longest tenure of any town manager in North Carolina history—Stamey secured more than $29 million in grants for the town, helped develop the Beaverdam Industrial Park, and oversaw improvements to a number of town facilities. In 2003, the town hall building was renamed in his honor. A tireless community servant, Stamey worked on many community boards and legislative committees, earning numerous awards, including the prestigious Order of the Long Leaf Pine from North Carolina governor Jim Hunt (right). (Courtesy of Bonnie Stamey.)

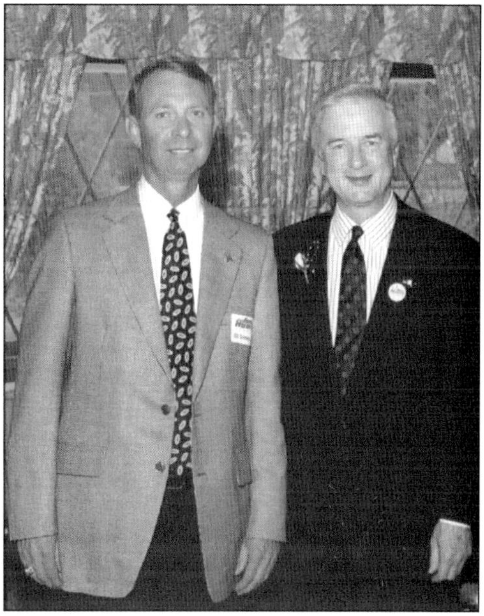

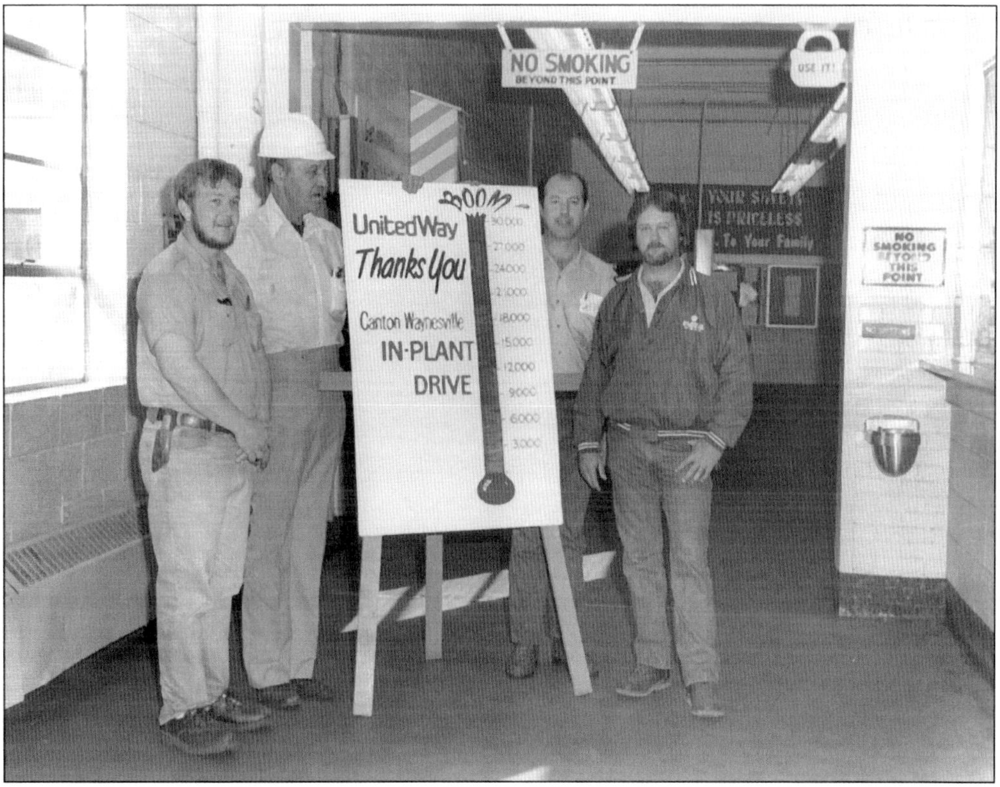

United Fund. For years, Canton residents have participated in charity programs such as the United Way fund drive. Mill employees are approached with pledge cards and asked to deduct a certain amount from their paychecks each month to help with the variety of programs the United Way supports. This countywide fundraiser includes signs to show how much is collected. (Courtesy of the Canton Historical Museum.)

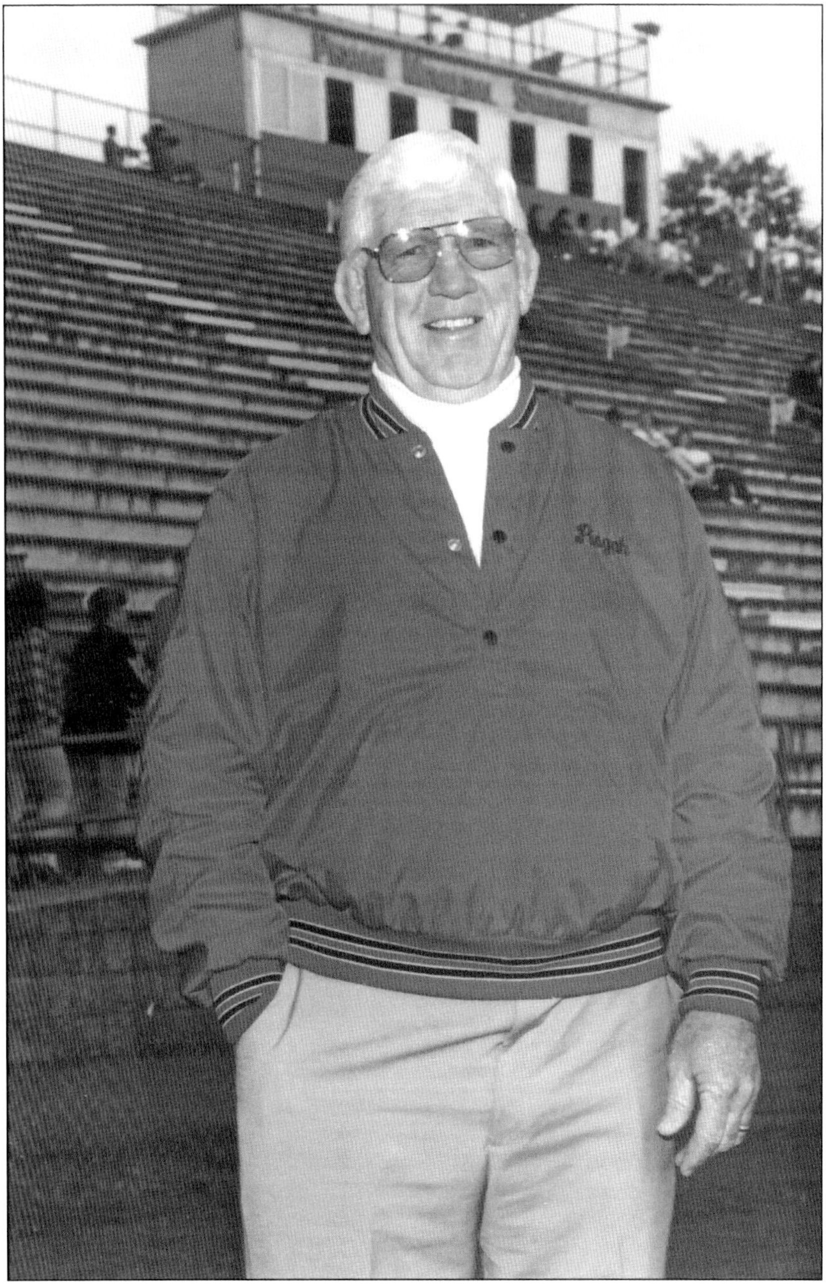

VOLUNTEER. Bill Churm symbolized the kind of unselfish dedication that makes a town like Canton a tightly knit community. He volunteered countless hours as an assistant coach for Canton and Pisgah High School football teams for more than 45 years and was part of the coaching crews on four state championship teams. He was elected into the Pisgah High School Hall of Fame in 1998, its inaugural year, and received a Lifetime Achievement Award from the Mountain Amateur Athletic Club in 2003 for his years of coaching, which included 15 years in Little League baseball. Churm was also active in Canton's First Baptist Church and in civic organizations, serving as president of the Canton Lions Club and the Jaycees. He was awarded the Man of the Year Award for both clubs. (Courtesy of Anita Churm.)

Bibliography

Farlow, Betsy, et al. *Haywood Homes and History*. Hazelwood, NC: Oliver Scriptorium, 1993.

Haywood County Genealogical Society. *Haywood County Heritage, North Carolina, Vol. 1*. Marceline, MO: Walsworth Publishing Company, 1994.

Wells, Camille. *Canton: The Architecture of Our Home Town*. Waynesville, NC: Mountaineer Graphics, 1985.

Wood, Curtis, ed. *Haywood County: Portrait of a Mountain Community*. Greenville, SC: Southern Historical Press, 2009.

Discover Thousands of Local History Books Featuring Millions of Vintage Images

Arcadia Publishing, the leading local history publisher in the United States, is committed to making history accessible and meaningful through publishing books that celebrate and preserve the heritage of America's people and places.

Find more books like this at
www.arcadiapublishing.com

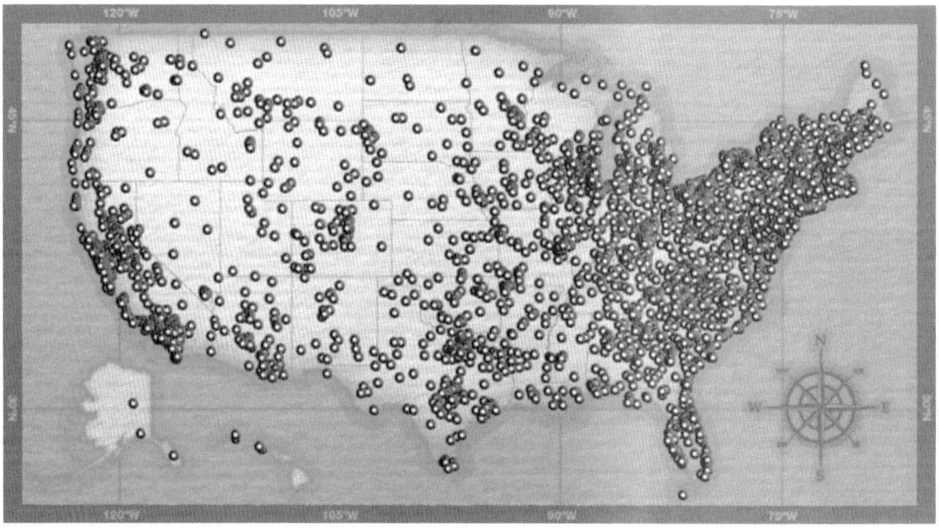

Search for your hometown history, your old stomping grounds, and even your favorite sports team.

Consistent with our mission to preserve history on a local level, this book was printed in South Carolina on American-made paper and manufactured entirely in the United States. Products carrying the accredited Forest Stewardship Council (FSC) label are printed on 100 percent FSC-certified paper.

MADE IN THE USA